ABSTRACTS from NEWSPAPERS of WILMINGTON, NORTH CAROLINA

- 1765-1775 and 1788-1797 -

(VOLUME #1)

(NEW HANOVER COUNTY)

Compiled by:
Raymond Parker Fouts

Southern Historical Press, Inc.
Greenville, South Carolina

This volume was reproduced
from a personal copy located in
the Publishers private library

Please direct all correspondence and book orders to:
SOUTHERN HISTORICAL PRESS, Inc.
PO Box 1267
Greenville, SC   29602-1267

Copyright 1984 by: Raymond Parker Fouts
Copyright Transferred 2023 to:
                Southern Historical Press, Inc.
ISBN #978-1-63914-210-1
Printed in the United States of America

PREFACE

These abstracts were made from microfilm of the original newspapers, obtained from the North Carolina State Archives at Raleigh, North Carolina.

Information concerning dates available, and location of the originals, is included at the beginning of each year. All issues located are noted, though nothing may have been abstracted from them.

Advertisements are recorded only from the first issue in which they appear in legible form. Each item has been assigned a number, within parentheses. The name index and location index refer to these numbers.

TABLE OF CONTENTS

	Pages
1765 - THE NORTH-CAROLINA GAZETTE; AND WILMINGTON WEEKLY POST-BOY	1-7
1769 - THE CAPE-FEAR MERCURY	7-22
1788 - WILMINGTON CENTINEL AND GENERAL ADVERTISER	23-53
1795 - THE WILMINGTON CHRONICLE: AND NORTH-CAROLINA WEEKLY ADVERTISER	53-72
1797 - HALL'S WILMINGTON GAZETTE	72-91
Index	93-108
Location Index	109-112

ABSTRACTS FROM NEWSPAPERS OF WILMINGTON,

NORTH CAROLINA

1765-1775 and 1788-1797

VOLUME 1

1765 - All issues missing except for the following: From the Philadelphia Public Library-July 10. Filmed from photostats, in the North Carolina Department of Archives and History, from the British Public Record Office in London, England-November 20, 27.

THE NORTH-CAROLINA GAZETTE; AND WILMINGTON WEEKLY POST-BOY.
(July 10, 1765.)

(1) Printed by Andrew STEUART; by whom Subscriptions for this Paper are taken in at 16 s. per Annum:-Advertisements of a moderate Length, inserted at 4 s first Time and 1 s for each Continuance.-Blank Instruments of all Sorts done by said STEUART.

(2) Wilmington, July 10. For Philadelphia, (And will sail in about 14 Days from this Date;) The Schooner Industry, Thomas FISHER, Master... (Wilmington, July 8th, 1765.)

(3) Once More! David BROWN, of Wilmington, Taylor, begs of those who are indebted to him, to make immediate Payment...

(4) Strayed away in the Night of the 28th of May ___ from the House of Evan ELLIS, near Bladen Court House; A white Horse..-Whoever will take up the said Horse, and bring him to me the Subscriber, at Capt. George PALMER's Plantation, on South-River, shall ___ Twenty Shillings Reward, paid by me, Daniel CLARK. July 7th, 1765.

(5) Notice is hereby given, That I have two large black stray Horses in my Custody ... Thomas ROBESON, Junior, living in Bladen-County.

(6) Stray'd away from Samuel STRUDWICK, Esq; at ___ mington; A bright bay Horse.. Whoever brings the said Horse ___ livers him to Mr. James WALKER, shall have ___ Twenty Shillings Proclamation Money. Ran away from the said STRUDWICK, a Negro ___ named BETTY-Twenty Shillings,...

(7) July 10th, 17__. To Be Sold at Publick-Vendue, at W____ under the Court-House on the first Day ___ next County-Court,..A Tract of Land lying on the North ___ Side of the Northwest River.. Likewise, To be Sold, as soon as a Dividend? ___ 1280 Acres of Land on Rock-Fish-Creek, upon ___ West-River; being a Moiety left my Father, by the ___ John Baptista ASHE, Esq. Thomas MOS___.

(8) Philadelphia, June 6. John HUGHES, Esq; in this province, and William COXE, Esq; for New Jersey, are appointed Stamp-Officers.

(9) New-York, May 27. By letters from London, we have certain accounts, that a clause is added to the mutiny and desertion bill, whereby justices of the peace are impowered to billet soldiers on the inhabitants in America, at their discretion.

(10) The Subscribers to the Church in Wilmington, who have not already paid their several Subscriptions to the former Commissioners, are desired immediately to discharge the same; otherwise they may depend on being noticed, according to Law. C. HARNET, John DU BOIS, G. WAKELEY, Commissioners. Wilmington, July 3, 1765.

(11) Wilmington, July 3, 1765. Ran away on Thursday Night last, a Negroe Fellow called BOSTON; about 40 Years of Age; middle siz'd.. Any Person who apprehends said Negroe, and brings him to the Subscriber in Wilmington, shall have Twenty Shillings Reward. George PARKER.

(12) Wilmington, July 3, 1765. The Vestry of St. James's Parish, New-Hanover, having agreed with John DU BOIS, Esquire to employ Workmen to finish the Church in Wilmington, the Gentlemen who have lately subscribed for the same, are desired to pay one Third of their several Subscriptions to Cornelius HARNET and Frederick GREGG, or either of them, on or before the 15th of this Instant...

(13) Brunswick, July 2, 1765. To Be Sold at Brunswick, by Public Vendue, on the Third Tuesday in this present Month July, the Estate of Revel MUNRO, deceased;-Viz. A House and two Lots of Land, in the Town of Brunswick; two Negroe Boys; sundry Houshold-Furniture, Stores, &c. &c. &c.... William HILL. Executor.

(14) Just Imported in the Brigantine Anna, Capt. FOSTER, from Bristol, and to be Sold cheap, By Alexander ROSS, At his Store, in Wilmington; Variety of Dry Goods...

(15) Just Imported, and to be Sold by John BURGWIN, & Co. At their Store in Wilmington, very cheap for Cash or Country Produce, A Fine Assortment of Oznabrigs; Checks; white Linens; Cambricks; Chintz and Callicoes..Shoes..Saddles; Wool and Cotton Cards ..Rum..Sugar...

(16) To Be Sold by the Subscriber, the pleasant Plantation called Providence, situate on the North-East? about 10 Miles from Wilmington; whereon is two H___ with five Rooms..a..double Store, a new House clos'd in and shingled,...a Dairy-House, Kitchen, Poultry-house, Chaise house, Stable, Mill-house, and sundry good Negroe houses, Smoakhouse &c, a good Garden, an Orchard with 200 bearing Apple-Trees, Peach-Trees, &c. a very fine Mineral Spring and other good Springs..contains near 1300 Acres... William MOUAT.

(17) Brunswick Ferry, June 25th, 1765. Whereas Elizabeth EAGEN, in order that Gentlemen, and Others, travelling to and from Brunswick, may be properly accomodated at, and speedily transported over the Ferry of Brunswick, has removed fro_ Brunswick to the Ferry-house herself...

(18) Cross-Creek, June the 30th, 1765. Whereas the partnership of HADLY and WILCOX is almost expir'd;..This is..to inform all and every of those concerned, that they must immediately pay off their respective accounts.. To Be Sold by said HADLY and WILCOX, or ___ for a number of years..the followi___ tracts, messuages, lands, &c.- Viz. A good dwelling ___ situate in the town of Cross-Creek, with a kitchen ___ acres of land belonging thereto; on the premises ___ a good merchant grist-mill, a saw-mill, store-house.. Also, ___ of land, well timber'd, lying on both sides of R___ Creek, in Bladen-County, containing 1700 acres.. For Terms, apply to the subscribers..at Cross-Creek. Thomas H___, John WILCOX.

(19) This Day is publish'd, and to be sold by the Printer ___ Price Two Shillings and Eight Pence; <u>Primitive Physick</u>, Or An Easy and Natural Method of Curing Most Diseases. By John WESTLEY.

<u>(November 20.)</u> <u>(Numb. 58.)</u>

Continuation of the North-Carolina Gazette.
Note: Pages are numbered.

(20) Wilmington, November 20. On Saturday the 16th of this Inst. William HOUSTON, Esq. Distributor of STAMPS for this Province, came to this Town; upon which three or four Hundred People immediately gathered together, with Drums beating and Colours flying, and repaired to the House the said Stamp-Officer put up at, and insisted upon knowing "Whether he intended to execute his said Office, or Not?" He told them "He should be very sorry to execute any Office disagreeable to the People of the Province." But they, not content with such a Declaration, carried him into the Court-House, where he signed a Resignation satisfactory to the Whole. (p. 2) Immediately after the appointed Stamp-Master had comply'd with their Commands, they call'd upon Mr. A. STEUART, the Printer,-(who had not printed the Gazette for some Weeks before the ACT took Place, it having pleased GOD to afflict him with a dangerous Fever) when he appeared, they ask'd him, if "He would continue his Business, as heretofore?-And Publish a News Paper?" He told them, that "As he had no Stampt Paper, and as a late ACT of Parliament FORBID the Printing on any other, He Could Not.-He was then positively told, that "If He Did Not, he might expect the same Treatment of the STAMP-MEN," and demanded a positive Answer:-Mr. STEUART then answer'd, "That rather than run the Hazard of Life, being maimed, or have his Printing-Office destroy'd, that he would comply with their Request," but took the WHOLE for Witness, That he was compell'd thereto.

(21) We hear from Newbern, that the Inhabitants of that Place, try'd, condemn'd, hang'd, and burn'd Doctor William HOUSTON, in Effigy, during the Sitting of their Superior Court.-Mr. HOUSTON, however, thinks that there was too much of the Star-Chamber Conduct made Use of, in condemning him unheard; especially as he had never sollicited the Office: Nor had he then heard that he was appointed Stamp-Officer.-At Cross-Creek, 'tis said, they hang'd his Effigy and M'CARTER's together, (he who murder'd his Wife:) nor have they spar'd him even in Duplin, the County where he lives.

(22) From New-York we learn, that the most of the Gentlemen there, have resolved not to buy any European Manufactures, till their Trade is more opened, the STAMP ACT repealed, and the Sugar Act altered.

(23) And, From Detroit, That PONDIAC, and the other Indian Chiefs, having made Peace with Us, went away seemingly contented; but, that two Days after the Councils were over, one of the Chiefs frankly declared, That they had talked friendly to the English only from their Teeth out, but hated them in their Hearts.

(24) (p. 3) We hear from South Carolina, that the Stamped Paper for that Province, was arrived at Charlestown, in the Ship Planter's Adventure, Miles LOWLEY, Master, and lodged in Fort Johnson; and that George SAXBY, Esq; Inspector, and Caleb LLOYD, Esq; Distributor of Stamps for the said Province, had resigned their respective Offices.

(25) Philadelphia, Oct. 10. On Saturday the 5th inst. the ship Royal-Charlotte, Capt. HOLLAND, came up to this city, attended by his Majesty's ship Sardine, James

(25) (Cont.) HAWKER, Esq; commander, Capt. HOLLAND having brought from London the Stamp'd Papers for Maryland, New-Jersey, and this province, remained some time at New-castle on Delaware, under the protection of the man of war. On the first appearance of those ships round Glo'ster Point, all the vessels in the harbour hoisted their colours half mast high, the bells begun to ring, being first muffled, and continued so until the evening, and every countenance added to the appearance of sincere mourning for the approaching loss of Liberty. At 4 o'clock in the afternoon several thousand citizens met at the State House, to consider the proper Ways and Means for preventing that unconstitutional Act of Parliament, (the STAMP-ACT) being carried into execution.---The first measure, was to send 7 of their number to Mr. HUGHES, Stamp-Distributor for this province, to request he would resign that office. He assured them that no act of his should tend to carry that Law into Execution here, until it was generally complied with in the other colonies; but refused to sign any resignation at that time.. Whereas, about six o'clock on Saturday evening last, a paper was sent to me, expressing, That a great number of the citizens of Philadelphia, assembled at the State House, do demand of Mr. John HUGHES, distributor of Stamps for Pennsylvania, that he will give them assurance, under his hand, that he will not execute that office; and expect that he will give them a fair, candid, and direct answer by Monday next, ten o'clock, when he will be waited on for that purpose. Saturday, October 5, 1765. I Do Therefore return for answer..that I have not hitherto taken any step to put the late Act of Parliament into execution in this province; and that I will not..until the said Act shall be put into execution generally in the neighbouring colonies.. (p. 4) And whereas my commission includes the three counties of Newcastle, Kent, and Sussex, upon Delaware, I do..inform the good people of those counties, that no act of mine shall..involve them into any difficulties, with respect to the said Stamp Act... John HUGHES.

(26) New-York, September 10. On Tuesday Evening arrived the Ship Edward, Capt. William DAVIS, in nine Weeks from London..with whom Maj. CARY, of the Royal-Americans, and his Lady; Mr. WEBB, another gentleman of the Army, Mr. KINDRICK, Merchant, and Mr. B OWNJOHN, of this City; Mrs. NICOLLS, of Amboy, and others, came Passengers; by some of whom we learn, That Sir Harry MOORE, Governor of this province, was on board the Minerva, Capt. TILLET, lying at Portsmouth..may be daily expected here.

(27) New-York, October 14. On Monday last the Commissioners from the several colonies, appointed for holding the general congress, being all arrived, assembled and entered upon business, the most important that ever came under consideration in America. The following is a list of the gentlemen assembled. Massachusetts-Bay. James OTIS, Oliver PARTRIDGE, and Timothy RUGGLES, Esquires. Rhode Island. Metcalf BOWLER and Henry WARD, Esquires. Connecticut. Eliphalet DYAR, Samuel William JOHNSON, and David ROWLAND, Esquires. New-York. John CRUGER, Robert R. LIVINGSTON, Philip LIVINGSTON, William BAYARD, and Leonard LISPENARD, Esquires. New Jersey. Robert OGDEN, Hendrick FISHER, and Joseph BORDEN, Esquires. Pennsylvania. John DICKINSON, John MORTON, and George BRYAN, Esquires. Government of the Counties of Newcastle, Kent, and Sussex, on Delaware. Jacob KOLLOCK, Caesar RODNEY, and Thomas M'KEAN, Esquires. Maryland. William MURDOCK, Edward TILMAN, and Thomas RINGOLD, Esquires. South Carolina. Thomas LYNCH, Christopher GADSDEN, and ___ RUTLIDGE, Esquires.

(28) (p. 6) New York Oct. 24. Upon the Convention of the Commissioners from the several Governments, in this Place, they made Choice of the Honourable Timothy RUGGLES, Esq; for their President, and Mr. John COTTON, for their Secretary.

(Extract.) (November 27.) (Numb. 59.)

Continuation of the North-Carolina Gazette.

(29) (The following is taken from the South-Carolina Gazette, of October 31st; being the last Paper intended to be printed in that Province, till an alteration of Affairs in America.) Charles-Town, October 30. Friday the 18th instant, late in the evening arrived, and came to an anchor under the cannon of Fort Johnson, the ship Planter's Adventure, Capt. Miles LOWLEY, from London. It having been some time before reported, that a Distributor of Stamps for this province was coming over in this ship.. Early on Saturday morning, (October 19th) in the middle of Broad street and Church street, near Mr. DILLON's (being the most central and public part of town) appeared suspended on a gallows twenty feet high, an effigy, designed to represent a distributor of stampt paper.. In the evening the figures were taken down, received in a cart or wagon..commenced down Broad street to the Bay, attended at least by 2000 Souls,..thence to the exchange, and up Tradd-street, halting at the door of a house belonging to George SAXBY, Esq. (the then supposed distributor of stamps) occupied by Captain William COATS. (p. 2) .. Upon the doors being..opened, and no such (stamped) papers being found, the cart..proceeded to the Green, back of the brick barracks, were the effigies were committed to the flames...

(30) Friday evening, Oct. 25th, arrived the Carolina Packet, Capt. DOBSON, from London..Mr. SAXBY had taken his passage, and was on board the Heart-of-Oak, Capt. GUNN. Saturday evening, Oct. 26th, the Heart-of-Oak also arrived. Mr. SAXBY..went ashore at Fort Johnson; and it being then certainly known, that Mr. Caleb LLOYD was actually to be Distributor of the stamps for this province, numbers of people again assembled and seemed very uneasy; but Mr. SAXBY..made a voluntary offer to suspend the execution of his office..till the determination of the King and Parliament.. should be known, upon a united application to be made from his Majesty's Colonies, for a repeal of an act that had created so much confusion: Mr. LLOYD..made a like voluntary declaration in regard to his office...

(31) (p. 6) Monday last died, and Yesterday was very decently interred, Mr. George WEAKELY, formerly an eminent Merchant here.

(32) The following is a genuine Copy of the Letter to Doctor William HOUSTON, appointing him Stamp-Distributor for this Province. Stamp-Office, London, July 11th, 1765. ... John BRETTELL, Secretary.

1766 - All issues missing except for the following: February 12, 26. Note: Filmed from photostats, in the North Carolina Department of Archives and History, from the British Public Record Office in London, England.

THE NORTH-CAROLINA GAZETTE

(February 12, 1766.) (Numb. 70.)

(33) Wilmington, February 5th, 1766. For Kingston, in Jamaica, The Schooner Charming Molly, Joseph ENGLISH, Master.. Any letters for the above Port, may be left a M . ROGERS's Tavern...

(34) Just imported in the Snow Mary, Captain CORRIE, from Leith; and the Ship Caesar, Captain HUME, from Glasgow; and To Be Sold By William WATKINS At his Store in Wilmington Very good oznabrigs at 1 s. & 6 d per yard a compleat assortment of checks, striped linens..lawns..gause..tick..sattin hats cloaks and bonnets..linseys Scotch plaid..men's neat shoes and pumps, coarse shoes..saddles, saddle cloths.. paper hangings, one set of maps..teas..cordage..jack screws, iron pots, frying pans ..ribbons..Rum, sugar, salt, molasses...

(35) To be sold for ready Money, or 6 Month's Credit: A valuable Set of Black-Smith's and Gun Smith's Tools: They are now set up in a good Shop, and convenient Place for Custom, on the Rich-Lands of New-River.. The Terms may be known by applying to Lewis WILLIAMS, Esq; or Joseph FIGURS, Black-Smith in Onslow-County. (Jan. 19, 1766.)

(36) Wilmington, January 15th, 1766. To Be Sold, or Let, The House and Lot now occupied by Robert WALES, a little below Mr. PURVIENCE's Tar-House: The House is new and well built, 36 Feet by 24, not quite finished on the inside, fronting Front street running down to the water..enquire of said WALES...

(37) Stolen; or taken out of the House of John ROGERS by mistake; A blue Drabb Cloth Cloak, with a double Cape, a Button on the Neck, and a Tape Loop for the same; with six blind Holes on each Side of the Fant behind..if stolen, Three Pounds Reward..for securing the Cloak and Thief; or 40 s. for the Cloak only. John ROGERS. (Jan. 23d. 1766.)

(February 26, 1766.) (Numb. 72.)

(38) Wilmington, Feb. 26. Notwithstanding what passed, relative to the Attorney-General's Opinion on the Seizure of the Sloops, by Captain LOBB for want of Stamped Clearances..In consequence of which Opinion, the People from several of the Counties round, assembled at Wilmington, on Tuesday the 18th of this Instant, appointed Officers to take the Command, compelled them to act, and entered into the following Association, which was signed by all the principal Gentlemen, Freeholders, and other Inhabitants of several Counties; viz. North-Carolina. We the Subscribers, free and natural-born Subjects of George the Third, true and lawful King of Great-Britain.. whose sacred Person, Crown and Dignity, we are ready and willing, at the Expence of our Lives and Fortunes to defend, being fully convinced of the oppressive and arbitrary Tendency of a late Act of Parliament, imposing Stamp Duties on the Inhabitants of this Province..detesting Rebellion, yet preferring Death to Slavery, Do..hereby mutually and solemnly plight our Faith and Honour, that we will at any Risque whatever, and whenever called upon, unite, and truely and faithfully assist each other, to the best of our Power, in preventing entirely the Operation of the Stamp Act. Witness our Hands, this 18th Day of February, 1766.

On Wednesday the 19th, they proceeded to Brunswick, where their Numbers were soon..upwards of a Thousand.. On their Arrival..in order to remove all Apprehensions on the Part of his Excellency the Governor, the following Letter was delivered him.. To His Excellency Col. William TRYON, Governor and Commander in Chief of North-Carolina...

(39) Wilmington, February 26th, 1766. For Bristol, The Brig Nancy, William FULLER, Master:..will sail in Ten Days..enquire of Alexander DUNCAN, Esq; or of said Master, on board..at DUNCAN's Wharf.

(40) February 26th, 1766. To Be Sold by the Subscriber, or Mr. Anthony WARD, at Wilmington; The best White-Cedar Shingles... Samuel WATTERS.

(41) A Gold Ring was found a few Days ago in the Shop of ROUKES and CHALDWELL, Peruke makers, in Wilmington...

(42) Wilmington, Feb. 26th, 1766. Wanted, About Fifty Cords of Oak Bark... John LYON. Said LYON continues to buy Hides, Skins, &c.

(43) London, November 16. .. Lord Charles MONTAGUE is appointed Governor of South-Carolina.

1769 - All issues missing except for the following from American Antiquarian Society -November 24. The Department of Archives and History-December 8.

THE CAPE-FEAR MERCURY.

(Friday, November 24, 1769.)

(44) His Excellency's speech to dissolve the Assembly.. After which The late representatives of the people..judging it necessary, that some measures should be taken in their distressed situation, for preserving the true and essential interests of the province, resolved upon a meeting for that..purpose, and..repaired to the courthouse in this town, where..it was first proposed..that a moderator should be appointed, and John HARVEY, Esq; late Speaker of the House of Assembly, was unanimously elected. The true state of the province being then opened and fully explained, and it being proposed that a regular Association should be formed, a committee was appointed to prepare the..regulations for that purpose, and they were ordered to make their report to the general meeting the next day at 9 o'clock.

(45) Advertisements. October 30, 1769. To be Sold, at Public Vendue, at the next Superior Court in Wilmington; Sundry Plantation Tools & Furniture, together with Five Negroes and some cattle, belonging to the Estate of William WIMBLE, deceased. Richard QUINCE, Administ.

(46) Onslow, Oct. 13, 1769. Taken up and committed to Jail Four likely Negro Men.. The Owner may have them by applying to the Jail-Keeper at New-River, on paying Fees and Charges. Lewis WILLIAMS, Sheriff.

(47) Wilmington, Nov. 4, 1769. Lost or Stolen A Man's hunting Saddle, with Silver Furniture and a short cross-barr'd Saddle-Cloth... John JAMES.

(48) Wilmington, October 28, 1769. The Subscriber returns Thanks to his Friends and Customers for all past Favors, and acquaints them that he is under an absolute Necessity of closing his Affairs; he therefore will be obliged to those indebted to him, to discharge the same as soon as possible... James EMMET. N. B. As it may be inconvenient (thro' the great Scarcity of Cash) for many to discharge their Accompts; the Subscriber will take Bees-Wax, Tallow, Deer-skins, &c. for payment, at Cash Price. J. E.

(49) Brunswick, October 30, 1769. For ready Money Will be Sold, at the next Superior Court at Wilmington, Six likely Country-born Slaves, taken upon Execution by Christopher CAINE, Sheriff.

(50) Cash Will be given for a Quantity of good ___ Turpentine; enquire of Adam BOYD.

(51) November 2, 1769. Run away, on the 11th of September last, from the Subscriber living in Bladen, a Negro Fellow named WILLIAM, aged about 25 Years, and about 5 Feet 8 Inches high..Country born..a good Cooper and very handy at Carpenters Work .. Five Pounds Reward, paid by John LUCAS.

(52) Wilmington, Nov. 8, 1769. Run away, about 6 Weeks ago, a Negro Man named RICHMOND, about 3_ Years of Age, and about 5 Feet 5 Inches high.. He belonged for-

(52) (Cont.) ...merly to Mr. BARNHILL of Philadelphia.. Whoever secures the above Negro in any of his Majesty's Jails shall have a Reward of Forty Shillings Proclamation Money, and if delivered to the Subscribers in Wilmington the same Reward, and all reasonable Charges. ANCRUM & SCHAW.

(53) To be Sold, At Public Vendue, under the Court-House in Wilmington, on the 29th of November next, sundry Household Goods and Cooper's Tools, belonging to the Estate of Jeremiah KEENAN deceased. James WHITE Administ.

(54) BOYD's Printing Office in Wilmington Cape-Fear, where this Paper may be had every Friday at the Rate of 16 s. a Year, one half to be Paid at the Time of Subscribing, or at 8 s. every Six Months. Subscriptions for this Paper are taken in by Gentlemen in most of the adjacent Counties and by A. BOYD who has for Sale sundry Pamphlets and Blanks; Also, Epsom & Glauber Salts by the lb. or larger quantity. N. B. Advertisements of a moderate Length will be inserted at 4 s. Entrance, and 1 s. a Week Continuance; Those of an immoderate Length to pay in Proportion.

(Friday, December 8, 1769.)

Note: Much of the following seven items is missing because part of the right side and the bottom of the sheet are torn away.

(55) Decem. 9, 1769. ___en James BELL's ___ ___ d Town-Creek ___

(56) ___ Pocket-Book, con ___ Bonds and Notes to ___ unt, with many other ___ Letter of Conse ___ ohn WALKER, and a ___ roclamation Money. Brunswick or to the ___ ilmington, shall receive ___ rd, all the Money that ___ and no Questions ask'd, ___ John MC DOUGAL.

(57) ___gton, Dec. 7, 1769. ___ indebted to the Estate ___ EAGLES, Esq; deceased, ... ___ GIBBS, ___ d ___ SCHAW, Executors.

(58) ___ be hired ___ good Negro Coopers, ___ Adam BOYD.

(59) December 1, 1769. ___ ns who have demands ___ ROSS of Wilmington, Tay___ ___ bring in their Bills; ___ to him to settle their ___ e has left off business, ___ ing the place as soon ___ settled. David ROSS.

(60) November 26, 1769. ___ t Bladen Court-house ___ Negro Man, named ___ ... Dennis LENNON.

(61) ___ovember 26, 1769, ___ the Subscriber, a ___ age, a Negro Fellow called JERRY; is well built, near six Feet high, and about forty Years of Age;.speaks French and English pretty well, and was imported from Jamaica about five Years ago. Also, about two Years ago, a Negro Man named FRANK,..well Sett, about five Feet six Inches high, and near Thirty-five Years of Age... Richard QUINCE.

(62) Lewis BARGE, Hatter in Cross-Creek, purposes to carry on the Hatter's Business with great Care...

(63) Wilmington, December 5. Taken up, near HARRISON's Creek, a small Canoe. Inquire of John DU BOIS.

(64) Wilmington, December 8, 1769. We hear Captain HALL of the Prosper, who sailed from this about the beginning of August last, is arrived at Bristol. The honourable

(64) (Cont.) Benjamin HERON? Esquire, his lady, and two daughters; the Honourable Samuel STRUDWICK Esquire, and his lady went passengers in the Prosper.

(65) Died a few days ago, much lamented, James HASELL Esquire, only son of the Honourable James HASELL Esquire president of this province.

(66) Mr. COLLET's proposals for a Ma_ were omitted, thro' mistake and will be in the next.

1770 - All issues missing except for the following from Massachusetts Historical Society-March 9-Supplement. From the University of North Carolina Library-October 13-Supplements 48, 50, 51, 52. (Note: Some supplements are not dated.)

Supplement to the Cape-Fear Mercury.
Friday, March 9, 1770. No. 22.

(67) Mr. BOYD, There have been many attempts made towards a clear ascertainment of the longitude at sea, but I have not heard of any so much to be depended on, as that of observing it, by measuring the distance of the moon from the sun, or a fixed zodiacal star.. Agreeable to your request---I here give you an example of an observation calculated by the tables of the astronimical ephemeris, as it was observed a little without the bar at my arrival here on the 22d of December last. I am, &c. John WALKER. On board the Achilles,-March 2, 1770.

Supplement to the Cape-Fear Mercury,
Wilmington, October 13th, 1770.

Supplement to the Cape-Fear Mercury, No. 48.

(68) North-Carolina, ss. By his Excellency, William TRYON, Esquire, His Majesty's Captain-General, Governor, and Commander in Chief, in and over the said Province. A Proclamation. Whereas I have received information that a great Number of outrageous and disorderly Persons did tumultuously assemble themselves together in Town of Hillsborough, on the 25th of last Month,..to oppose the Just Measures of Government..and..attacking His Majesty's Associate Justice in the Execution of his Office .. To the End..that the Persons concerned..may be brought to Justice, I do..issue this my Proclamation..requiring..all Justices..to make diligent Inquiry into the above recited Crimes, and to receive the Deposition of such..as shall appear before them to make Information..concerning the same which Depositions are to be transmitted to me, in Order to be laid before the General Assembly, at Newbern, on the 30th Day of November.. Given under my Hand, and the Great Seal of the Province, at Newbern, the 18th Day of October, in the 10th Year of his Majesty's Reign, Anno Dom. 1770. William TRYON. By his Excellency's command, John LONDON, Sec. God save the King.

Supplement to the Cape-Fear Mercury No. 50.

Supplement to the Cape-Fear Mercury No. 51.

(69) John MC DONNELL takes this method to acquaint his friends and the public, that he has just opened an assortment of goods suitable for the present and approaching season... Wilmington Nov. 1770.

(70) To be Sold, by the subscriber..Rum, sugar, oznabrigs, checks, salt, linnens, broad-cloth, blue and white negro cloth, &c &c.-Also, will be exposed for sale on

(70) (Cont.) the 30th instant, eight or ten negroes... Richard BRADLEY. Wilmington, Nov. 15.

Supplement to the Cape-Fear Mercury No. 52.

(71) Wilmington, (Cape-Fear) printed for Adam BOYD, who will be obliged to such of his Subscribers as are in arrears for this Paper, if they will observe that the first Year is expired.

1771 - 1772 - No issues located.

1773 - All issues missing except for the following from Department of Archives and History-January 13. From the University of North Carolina Library-September 22. Note: December 29 filmed from photostats in the Department of Archives and History, from British Public Records Office, London, England.

THE CAPE-FEAR MERCURY
Wednesday, January 13, 1773. No. 156.

(72) Three Hundred Pounds Reward. St. Stephen's Parish, (in South-Carolina) September 15, 1772. Run-Away from the Subscriber about Fifteen Months since, Two Negro Fellows and a Wench, WILL, GEORGE, and SYLVIA. WILL, is about Twenty-five Years of Age, Five Feet Eight Inches high, of a yellowish Complexion, slim made..his Teeth filed, and his Country marks in his Face; a Cooper & Rough Carpenter: GEORGE is about Twenty Years of Age Five Feet Five Inches high, of a dark Complexion, is very artful.. SYLVIA, is a likely young Wench, about Five Feet Five Inches high, of a yellowish Complexion, her Teeth filed; she has attended in a House. A Reward of 150 Pounds, Currency..on Delivery of the above Negroes to the Warden of the Work-House, or at his Plantation in St. Stephen's Parish, near MURRAY's Ferry.

Thomas WEST, An Overseer, about twenty five years of age, five feet seven inches high, very slim of a swarthy Complection, who lived at the Subscriber's Plantation about three years, and just about the time the said three Negroes Run-away, he left him: It is generally thought the said Thomas WEST has carried the Negroes into North-Carolina, Virginia or Maryland, and may offer them for sale... John GAILLARD.

(73) On Monday the 14th of December 1772. Came to the Plantation of the Subscriber within two miles of Wilmington, a Black natural pacing Mare... Daniel AUSTIN.

(74) Absented himself from the Subscriber an Indented Servant, named George THOMAS, a native of Wales, about 19 years of age of a swarthy complection, black hair about 5 foot high..deliver him to his Master in Wilmington..receive 20 shillings reward... Herrall BLACKMORE.

(75) Just Imported from London and Bristol a general Assortment of Goods suitable for the season, which are now selling off by John BURGWIN at a trifle above the first cost and charges for Cash or Produce only. N. B. He requests all those Indebted to John BURGWIN, & Co. to make immediate payment.

(76) Just Imported in the Brig Expedition from Bristol, and to be sold by Robert KENNEDY, (at Capt. BLACKMORE's)..Oznabrigs, Womens shoes, Slops of different sorts.. Hats..Blankets, white and colored Negro Cloth, Delt and Queen's Ware, small Cordage, Pipes, &c. &c.

(77) Run away from the subscriber sometime in November last, a tall negro fellow

(77) (Cont.) called JAMEY;..deliver him either to the subscriber at Fishing-Creek, to Travis DORAM at Long-Creek, or to the Sheriff of New Hanover county, at Wilmington, shall be paid the sum of three pounds proc. by James MOORE. N. B. The said slave is outlawed.

(78) Five Pounds Reward, Run away from the subscriber a negro fellow named VALENTINE belonging to Mr. George ___ER..was hired some time ago to Mr. Francis LUCAS... Thomas ALLON.

(79) To be sold cheap, a Plantation in Bladen County on the ___ side of Cape-Fear. It has a large Front upon the River..well timbered, and well waterd by excellent Springs... James STUART.

(80) Forty Dollars Reward. Ran away from his Bail, a certain Man, named John DAY, a Pedlar, supposed to be gone to Carolina; he is about five Feet eight Inches high, looks to be about 35 Years of Age, a very talkative Fellow, addicted to Drinking, and pretends to understand Latin. Whoever takes up the said DAY, and secures him in any of his Majesty's Jails, in the Province of Pennsylvania, shall be entitled to the above Reward, and reasonable Charges, paid by the Subscribers in the Jerseys, or WILLING and TAYLOR, in Philadelphia. Roger FLAHAVEN, Daniel CAHALT. N. B. Whoever secures the said John DAY in any District Jail, in North-Carolina shall receive the above Reward,..on applying to Mr. John ROBESON in Wilmington, Cape-Fear. R. F. D. C.

Wednesday, September 22, 1773. Numb. 190.

(81) The Confession of Spencer DEW, lately Executed at Duplin, taken by Felix KENAN, Esq. Sheriff of the said County, and signed by the said Spencer DEW, at the Gallows, in presence of a large concourse of people.. I Am about 38 years of age, I was born in Northampton County in this Province, of honest Parents. I was first induced to Steal Cattle and Horses by George DUKES and Constantine NEWTON, in which we had great success. I then joined in partnership with Isom and Michael ROGERS, and we Stole six Horses, and Passed to the amount of One Thousand Pounds Counterfeit Money, but the greatest part thereof was Virginia Currency, which the said Isom and Michael made themselves.

In the Year 1771, I joined..with Ephraim and George LANE; and George LANE and myself Stole two Horses and a Mare.. Then Ephraim LANE and myself Stole eight head of fat Hogs..the property of John TURNER. After this, Thomas HUNTER and myself broke open a House of Joseph PRICE on Roanoak river, and took a small Trunk with some money in it, and a large shot Gun. In the Year 1772, I joined with William and Pearson LANE, and we Stole six Horses and two Mares; we also unlatched the Door of Sarah HUNTER, went into the House, and lighted a candle, took a Key out of a Boy's pocket, unlocked the Store door..took about Four Pounds in Proclamation Money, and about 50 Pounds in Goods. I was also..with Thomas ORMOND, and we Stole three Horses and a Mare and about 17 or 18 Pounds Virginia Money from John HILL in Craven County, in South-Carolina. Then with Ludowick OUTLAW we passed about 400 Pounds Counterfeit Proclamation Money that one Captain JOHNSTON made; (he lives on THOMSONs Creek in South-Carolina) afterwards ORMOND, Joseph CLARK, William JOHNSTON and myself, broke open the Store of Thomas COLLINS on Broad-River, and Stole about 150 Pounds Virginia Money and 20 Pair of Blankets. Then with Drury GOODWIN, and Samuel LANE, we passed about 300 Pounds Counterfeit Gold, Silver, and Virginia Money. John Nicholas SMITH and myself Stole from John M'INTOSH, a Horse & a Mare, and about 40 Shillings Cash; and from William WHITE in South Carolina about 13 Pounds Virginia Money. About the first of March last, we were all apprehended in Hillsborough, and Samuel LANE made

(81) (Cont.) his escape..hid our Counterfeit Money..when..searched, finding none about us, we were Discharged. I was in combination with J__s D V S, P__t r in N__b__n, and received from him 300 Pounds Proc, which I saw him make to Pass, and I was to give him one half of what I got for it: and in 1773, he also gave me 800 Pounds more of his own make on the same terms, which I left in the possession of William MARSAULT. I have seen Ja__s C__R receive from said D V S to the full amount of 2000 Pounds Counterfeit to Pass and I verily do believe that John & George KENNEDY, are in Confederacy with said DAVIS.

William MARSAULT and myself Stole from Joseph HOLT, nine barrels of Pitch; three barrels of Tar from Mr. CORNELL, and two barrels from Mrs. SMITH. In January or February, 1772, Robert M'LEAN and myself Stole from Mr. CORNELL, two Barrels of Pork.. About a Month ago William STRINGER got from J__s D V S 150 Pounds Counterfeit to Pass on the same terms that I had mine. Since I broke custody after my Condemnation, I broke open Thomas SMITH's House, on Neuse River in Dobbs County.. William MARSAULT and myself Stole from Samuel PARSONS, 38 pounds of Bacon; and from Samuel CORNELL, two barrels of Corn: We made an attempt to break open John GREEN's Store, but were prevented by Fierce dogs. It has been maliciously reported..that Felix KENAN, Esq. high Sheriff of Duplin County received a Bribe from me when I was last in his Custody, to favour my Escape. I now Declare..that neither he..nor any other Person, ever received any Bribe or Reward from me..nor was..Felix KENAN privy to the means by which I made my Escape. (Signed) Spencer his X mark DEW. Spencer DEW was Condemned last June, and Executed the 2d. of August following.

(82) Taken up by the subscriber in New-Hanover county on the North-East of Cape-Fear river in North-Carolina, a new-negro man, calls himself ABRAHAM, he is about 5 feet 7 inches high, between 25 and 30 years of age, with his upper teeth fil'd... John BUFORD. September 1, 1773.

(83) Just Imported in the ship Spencer, Captain MC LEOD from London; A Large and compleat assortment of European and East-India goods suitable for the season..sold.. by SUTHERLAND and CRUDEN in Wilmington and John CRUDEN and Company at Cross-Creek. September 21, 1773.

(84) The Partnership of COBHAM and TUCKER will be dissolved the first Day of October next... September 22.

(85) Any person having a plantation to dispose of from 500 to 1000 acres of land fit for rice, indico or wheat may hear of a purchaser by sending a particular description and the price that will be asked therefor to Adam BOYD.

(86) North-Carolina, ss. By his Excellency Josiah MARTIN, Esq. Captain-General, Governor, and Commander in Chief, in and over the said Province. A Proclamation. Whereas the General Assembly of this Province stands prorogued to Monday the Fourth Day of October next: I have thought..to issue this Proclamation, hereby further proroguing the said General-Assembly to Monday the Twenty Ninth Day of November..to meet at Newbern.. Given..at Newbern, this 11th Day of September, Anno Dom. 1773... Jo. MARTIN. By his Excellency's Command, J. PARRATT, D. Sec'ry.

(87) Notice is hereby given, that a Court of Chancery will be held at Newbern on Thursday the Fourteenth Day of October next. By Order, J. BIGGLESTON, R. C. C. September 15th, 1773.

(88) Whereas Mr. James ERWIN has by an advertisement of the 10th current, forbid any person from purchasing a tract of land upon the Sound, lately advertised for

(88) (Cont.) sale by the subscriber, upon a pretence of his having a right thereto; and whereas the subscriber is fully satisfied of the validity of his right to them,.. he will warrant the titles to be good... Jo. MURRAY.

(89) To Be Sold, A quantity of..negro cloth, ruggs, blankets, and a variety of other articles... J. BURGWIN.

(90) Taken Up by the Subscriber, a bay Mare...apply to John BELL.

(91) As several Persons in this Town make a practice to purchase from my Negroes whatever they pillage from my House in town or Plantation below, and I have certain information of rum having been sold them and am no stranger to those who are concerned; I give this notice that I will for the future prosecute any person so offending against the Laws of the Province with the utmost rigour. William HOOPER.

(92) Four Pounds Reward. Ran Away, from the Subscriber, an Irish Servant Man, named Patrick MURPHEY, of the Age of 24 Years, about five Feet, ten Inches High..dark Hair inclining to curl... James BLYTH. N. B. Said Patrick MURPHY is a Sawyer by trade. Wilmington, August 3, 1773.

(93) To be Sold and entered upon immediately That..lot and tar-house at the lower end of Wilmington formerly called PURVIANCE's wharf and tar-house, but now the property of John EDWARDS esq. of South-Carolina..terms by applying to John BURGWIN.

(94) Three Pounds Reward. Run away from the subscriber September 8th 1773, an Indented Servant Girl named Mary KELLY lately from Ireland, but says she has lived 14 years in London; is about 18 or 20 years of age, five feet six or eight inches high, stoops in her walking, fair complection and redish hair... George BARNES, at the sign of the Harp & Crown in Wilmington. September 13, 1773.

(95) The Subscribers to this Paper and to the Salsbury Rider, are requested to Pay their Subscriptions; in Anson County to Mr. KERSHAW or his Agent;-at the Court-House in Mecklenburg to Mr. William PATTERSON, or Mr. Jeremiah M'CAFFERTY;-in Charlotte to Mr. John M'Khit ALEXANDER;-in Rowan to Mr. Maxwell CHAMBERS, or Mr. William STEEL in Salisbury;-in Surry to Mr. LANIER, or Col. ARMSTRONG;-in the upper part of Guilford, to Maj. John CAMPBELL, or the Revd David CALDWELL;-in the lower part of Guilford to Col. John M'GEE.

(96) This Is To Give Notice, That Thomas BROWN Copper-Smith from Philadelphia, has set up his business in Wilmington, where he makes..Stills, brew-kettles, wash-kettles and tea kettles, also all other kinds of copper work...

(97) To be Sold at Public Sale, On Monday the 6th of December next, at the Plantation of the late Mr. Henry HYRNE deceased, About 18 Negroes..cattle..work-horses and oxen, a good waggon, carts, plows..sheep..hogs, also good beds, beding, chairs, tables and ..other..household furniture..on giving judgment bonds..to Frederick JONES executor.. The house (which is large..having four good rooms on a floor, with four dry cellars) and plantation, are to be rented.. There is also another plantation joining the above to be rented... Frederick JONES, Executor. September 8, 1773.

(98) Whereas my office of sheriff for New-Hanover county will expire next month, and there is an immediate necessity for collecting the different taxes..before the sitting of the General Assembly, and it being inconvenient for me at present to attend for that purpose: This is to give notice that Mr. John JAMES of the WELCH Tract is properly authorized to collect such taxes as are due to me. And I give this further notice

(98) (Cont.) that all persons who are indebted to me for taxes during my former shrievalty for the years 1763, 1764 and 1765, will be called upon after the 10th day of September next... Arthur BENNING. Wilmington, August 25.

(99) To The Publick. Doctor WARD makes his warmest acknowledgments of thanks to the province in general, for the great encouragement it has given to one of his medicines, namely the ___ purging cake ___ at Mr. WAID's Store in Wilmington may be had of Mr. Robert DICKSON, Esq. in Duplin, Mr. ___ in Brunswick, Mr. DEBBING of Cross-Creek, also of Mr. MING? tavern keeper near New-River.. N. B. Doctor WARD..had two boys in this province which he has also cut and cured of hair-lips, Robert DIXON of Duplin, (one of his Majesty's magistrates) and Andrew FULLARD of the Sound can certify as to the two boys.

(100) This is to let all persons know that I fully intend to sell all my possessions of lands..in North-Carolina, which is 1050 acres in Onslow county, all in one body.. and also 900 acres in Anson county..the whole will be sold, and that for no other reason than I want to make a division amongst my children, whilst I live, if God will permit.. Also a number of household furniture..hogs..oxen..cattle..horses..negroes &c &c. The sale to begin, if my life should re___, on the first day of March. 1774... John WILKINS. Onslow, Dec. 25, 1773.

(101) One Hundred Pounds Reward. Supposed to be stolen or inveighed, about July 1771, on the road leading from my river to my seashore plantation on Waccamaw neck nearly opposite to George-Town, a sensible old negro man, named HECTOR, about six feet high..and his son CARLOS, a very likely mustee boy about seven years old.. A reward of 100 l. currency will be paid on conviction of the offenders, and delivery of the slaves to John ANCRUM Esq. in Wilmington Cape-Fear, or to me... Robert HERIOT. George-Town S. Carolina, Dec. 10.

(102) For Newry The Brigantine William, Bartholamew MC'CANN Master. Two thirds of her Cargo already engaged and will sail by the first of February.-For Freight of Flaxseed and Flour or Passage apply to the Master or John BURGWIN.

(103) Broke Jail, on the night of the 6th instant, a Mustee fellow, calls himself PETER,..says he belongs to Nathaniel JONES of Chowan County, near Edenton,..is about 5 feet 8 inches high..forty shillings reward. Felix KENAN. Duplin County, Dec. 7.

(104) For Bristol The brigantine Adamant, Josias WALKER commander.. For freight or passage apply at Mr. BURGWIN's wharf, to Josias WALKER.

(105) My Wife Mary CONNER having eloped from my Bed and Board and otherways treated me ill, this is to give Notice that I will not pay any Debts of her contracting after the Date hereof. Morris CONNER. Brunswick, Dec. 11.

(106) To Be Sold, A valuable Tract of Land in Duplin county, containing by patent 260 acres, well known by the name of Golden Grove, joning the plantation of Captain MC INTIRE..apply to James MC INTIRE at Rockey Point. December 14, 1773.

(107) Five Dollars reward will be given by Solomon TOWNSEND to any person who can give information of a Box of Boots that was in the possession of the late Samuel TOWNSEND deceased, which cannot be found. And as Solomon TOWNSEND intends leaving this place in a few days, the above reward will be given by Mr. John FORSTER in Wilmington, if not found before... Solomon TOWNSEND, Administrator. Wilmington, December 22, 1773.

(108) I Burrell LANIER acknowledge that what I have reported in Respect to John HILL's Character is entirely False and Groundless and without Foundation, and I am heartily sorry for it, and humbly ask his Pardon, as that what I said was through Passion. Burrel LANIER. Acknowledged before us this 30th Nov. 1773. Andrew THOMPSON, Isaac HILL, Richard CLINTON, James KENAN, Richard BROCAS, Michael KENAN.

(109) To be Sold at private Sale. The well known valuable Lands of Rockey Point, belonging to the Subscriber, containing by Patent, 1920 Acres. As also a Tract of Land upon the Sound, containing 320 Acres, and another lying upon the Side of the River between Wilmington and Mr. HARNETT's, containing 168 Acres.. For further particulars enquire of the proprietor, or..Mess. ANCRUM and SCHAW, or Mr. CLAYTON, merchants in Wilmington. John MURRAY.

(110) Strayed or stolen from Fort Johnston, a Dun horse... Richard WILSON.

(111) To be Rented or Leased for a Term of Years, That pleasant plantation lately the seat of General WADDELL, deceased,..on Prince George's Creek, 8 miles from Wilmington..terms by applying to Mrs. WADDELL, in Bladen county or in Wilmington to John BURGWIN.

(112) Just imported in the ship Grenada Packet, captain BROWNETT, from Grenada, Twenty seasoned slaves, which will be sold..by Mr. Robert THRELSAL at Mr. DEKEYSER's Tavern. Wilmington, Dec. 7, 1773.

(113) Just imported in the brig William, Capt. MC CAIN? from Bristol, and to be sold..by Jonathan DUNBIBIN at his ready money store near the Market-House, an assortment of goods... Wilmington, December 15.

(114) Just imported from Jamaica and to be sold by Dugald THOMPSON, a parcel of choice negroes; best proof rum and excellent coffee. Inquire of Messrs. ANCRUM FORSTER and BRICE. Wilmington, December 14.

(115) The subscribers having purchased of Messrs. John MURGATTOYD and Richard RUNDLE their proportion of stock in the distillery company under the firm of HARNET, WILKINSON and company, All persons indebted to the said company..are desired to make immediate payment..to Mr. John LOUDON..impowered by us to receive payment... Cornelius HARNETT, William WILKINSON.

(116) For London, The ship Good Intent, Henry DICKSON, Master..for Freight..apply to HOGG & CAMPBELL. Decem. 14, 1773.

(117) To be Sold at Public Vendue at the Plantation of the late Mr. John Swan PORTER, deceased, on Rockey Point, on the 3d day of January next..household furniture, plantation tools,..Corn, black ey'd and clay Pease, &c. Horses, Hogs, Cattle and Sheep..all persons that have any accounts against said Estate, will send them to me, or..to Samuel ASHE, Esquire... John Baptist ASHE, Administrator. December 6th, 1773.

(118) To Be Sold, By virtue of a letter of attorney from Joseph MORRIS Esq. of the city of Philadelphia, a valuable sawmill and lands near Cross-Creek in Cumberland county, a house and lot and two stores in Cross-Creek, divers parcels of lands contiguous thereto..three negro slaves, some household furniture and other things, all late the property of John WILCOX, and purchased from the sheriff of Cumberland..by the said Joseph MORRIS and George Anthony MORRIS deceased.. For terms apply to Robert COCHRAN, Esq. in Cross-Creek, or in Wilmington to A. MACLAINE, or John ROBE__.

(119) To be Sold A valuable tract of land in Brunswick county,.. A house and lot in Wilmington known by the name of the Lodge..500 acres of land joining the lands of John MOORE on Rockey Point-500 acres on the N. West branch of Cape-Fear river, joining the upper line of Robert SCHAW Esq... George MOORE, Sen.

(120) George and Thomas HOOPER South side of Market street, a few doors above the sign of the Harp and Crown. Have just received from London per the Good-Intent Capt. DIXON, A..assortment of English and India goods...

(121) Wanted a few wild Turkies for which a good price will be given. Apply to A. BOYD.

(122) Seven Pounds Reward. Run Away from the brig Roger seven indented servants, one Thomas MOORE of London by trade a white-smith, with a mole on his right cheek, long black hair, about 5 feet 6 inches high, dark complexion, 27 years old.. William MILLER a Scotchman, a taylor by trade, about 5 feet 1 inch high..24 years old.. William RICHARDSON, fair complexion, born in Yorkshire, a taylor by trade, 23 years old ..about 5 feet 8 inches high. Samuel SIMPSON, a farmer, about 22 years old; William BODDINGTON Cabinet-maker __, 23 years old; Robert WILLIAMSON, a Brick Layer, 31? years old; George WOODWARD, a White Smith, 29 years old. Whoever will deliver said servants or any of them to William CAMPBELL Esq. in Wilmington, shall receive 20 shillings for each of them.

(123) To be sold for Cash or Lumber four likely young Negro Men and one young Negro Wench.. Inquire on Board the sloop Dolphin at Market-Street wharf. J___ SIMSON. Wilmington, December 28, 1773.

(124) Died in Town last Friday Mrs. Sarah NEWTON, and yesterday at his Plantation Mr. Thomas GRAINGE.

1774 - All issues missing except for the following from Dept. of Archives and History -May 11, 18.

Wednesday, May 11, 1774. Numb. 223.

(125) The copartnership of SUTHERLAND and CRUDEN at Wilmington and that of John CRUDEN and co. at Cross-Creek being this day dissolved by mutual consent: It is requested that all those indebted to them, would speedily make payment of their respective balances to John CRUDEN Senr. as he alone is impowered, to collect..until the return of John CRUDEN Jun. from Britain.. The business will henceforth be carried on, both here and at Cross-Creek, under the firm of John CRUDEN and co. who have just imported in the Ajax, captain CUNNINGHAM from Glasgow an assortment of goods..suitable to the season... John CRUDEN & Co. April 29, 1774.

(126) Wanted a few Pair of Summer Ducks that are well grown and will feed in a Coop, for which a good Price will be given. Apply to A. BOYD.

(127) Boston. In the House of Representatives, March 1, 1774. Whereas this House did on the 12th day of February last, address his Excellency the Governor and Council, on the removal of Peter OLIVER, Esq; Chief Justice of his Majesty's Superior Court of Judicature, Court of Assize, and General Goal Delivery over this whole Province, for certain reasons..set forth..praying that he would further consider..the removal of the said Chief Justice..did utterly refuse.. And whereas this House did also on the 24th day of February proceed to impeach..Peter OLIVER, Esq. of certain high crimes and misdemeanors..his Excellency hath..declared..to be unconstitutional..we exhibit

(127) (Cont.) the same article of charge and complaint.. "Province of Massachusetts Bay, To his Excellency, Thomas HUTCHINSON, Esq...Peter OLIVER..did..take and receive ..a grant or salary for his services __ Chief Justice of the said Superior Court.. cannot but have the effect of a continual bribe..."

(128) To the Honorable the House of Representatives, General Court convened February, 1774. "May it please your Honours.. With respect to my not taking any future grant from his Majesty; permit me to say, that without his Majesty's leave I dare not refuse it.. And as the tenor of the grant is during my residence in the province as Chief Justice I receive it as during good behavior, which in my opinion preserves me from any undue bias in the execution of my office. I am with the most profound respect... Peter OLIVER."

(129) Wilmington. At the late Election of Representatives the following Gentlemen were chosen. For New-Hanover, Col. John ASHE and William HOOPER Esqr. For Wilmington, Cornelius HARNETT Esq. For Onslow, Col. William CRAY and Henry ROADS Esqrs. For Craven, Messrs. Lemuel HATCH and James COOR. For Newbern, Isaac EDWARDS Esq. For Dobbs, Col. Richard CASWELL and Capt. MC KINNIS?. For Duplin, Thomas GRAY Esq. and Mr. Thomas HICKS. For Chatham, Doctor PYLES, and Mr. GREAVES. For Cumberland, Farquahard CAMPBELL and Thomas RUTHERFURD Esqrs. For Campbellton, Robert ROWAN Esq. For Bladen, Messrs. William SOLTER and James WHITE. Col. Robert HOWE, and John ROWAN Esq. for the County, and Parker QUINCE Esq. for the town of Brunswick.

(130) We hear George MONTAGU Esq. is made Post-Captain and is appointed to command the Fowey?, Vice Capt. WARDEN?, who resigned; Capt. JAMES succeeds Mr. MONTAGUE in the King's Fisher; and Capt. THORNBOROUGH succeeds Mr. JAMES in the Tamer.

(131) To be sold at Cross-Creek on Wednesday the 25th day of May instant, at the house of Mr. BARGE, sundry dry goods, hard ware, beding wearing apparel, a silver watch, buckles, &c. being the personal estate of Mitchell CORRELL, deceased. A. MACLAINE, Admr. May 3, 1774.

(132) To be Hired, An excellent House Wench-inquire of A. BOYD.

(133) London, January 31. The fate of America, and, in that, of Great-Britain, depend upon the advice or rather report, which the Privy Council shall make to the King upon this occasion. The situation of affairs in America is become more truly alarming than ever. The union throughout that continent to reject the Tea, while it is subject to a duty to be paid there shews that the Ministers, or rather that miserable Cabinet-Junto in whom only the King thinks proper to confide, are as cordially despised in America as they are detested..in England.. The throwing the tea into the sea at Boston irritates the court extremely, and while it shews the indignity with which the legislative authority of this country is treated in America, gives room to apprehend, that if force is attempted, it will be opposed.

(134) Having sold off all my stock of dry goods with an intention of settling my affairs and leaving the province for this summer, I must request..all those who have accounts open to call and settle... John BURGWIN. April 24, 1774.

(May 18, 1774) Numb. 224.

(135) Charlestown, April 29. Deaths. At Dorchester, on Saturday last, April 23d, Archibald MACNEILL, Esq. Physician. In the course of 17 years, during which he practiced physick in that parish; he merited, acquired and preserved the esteem of every one...

(136) North Carolina, ss. By his Excellency Josiah MARTIN, Esq. Captain General, Governor, and Commander in Chief in and over the said Province. A Proclamation. Whereas it hath been represented to me by John STEWART, Esq; his Majesty's Superintendant of Indian Affairs, that sundry Persons, supposed to be Emigrants from this Province, had settled on the Cherokee Lands, in Violation of the most solemn Treaties, which had given just Umbrage to the said Indians, and may be attended with the most fatal consequences; I..therefore..issue this proclamation hereby strictly enjoining and requiring the said Settlers immediately to retire from the Indian territories, otherwise they are to expect no Protection from his Majesty's Government. Given at Newbern..the 25th Day of April, 1774.. Jo. MARTIN. By his Excellency's Command, J. PARRAT, D. Sec'ry.

(137) This is to give notice to all persons, that the subscriber has purchased John DUNN's deed for 320 acres of Land at the mouth of DUNN's Creek on Cape-Fear in Bladen county, known by WOODROW's place... Joseph COOPER. Bladen, April 11, 1774.

(138) William ROWAND, Sadler from Glasgow, takes this opportunity to inform the Public, that he has taken a Shop, in Wilmington, near the Court-House, where he intends to carry on that branch of business... May 15, 1774.

(139) Eighteen prime Negroes just imported from Jamaica and to be sold cheap for Cash or Produce. Alexander HOSTLER & Co. May 13, 1774.

1775 - All issues missing except for the following-July 28; August 7, 11, 25; September 1. Note: Filmed from photostats in the Department of Archives & History, from British Public Records Office, London, England.

Friday, July 28, 1775. (No. 266.

(140) A Circular Letter To the Committees of South-Carolina. Charlestown, June 30, 1775. Fellow-Citizens, This year will be a grand epocha in the history of mankind. In this conspicuous and ever-memorable year, America has been abused, and Britain has disgraced herself, in an unexampled manner.. We lay before you the case as Stated by general GAGE.. The general sent a detachment of about 800 soldiers into the country, to seize and destroy the property of the people of the Massachusetts Bay. This detachment, in their way to Concord, at Lexington, saw "about 200 men drawn up on a green, and when the troops came within 100 yards of them..they began to file off." The soldiers upon "observing this," "ran after them, to surround and disarm them. Some of them, who had jumped over a well, then fired four or five shot at the troops," and, "upon this," the soldiers "began a scattered fire, and killed several of the country people." ..

However, the voice of America thus describes the commencement of this unnatural war: about eight or nine hundred soldiers came in sight, just before sunrise of about 100 men, training themselves to arms, as usual; and the troops running within a few rods, of them, the commanding officer called out to the militia, "disperse you rebels, damn you, throw down your arms and disperse." Upon which the troops huzz'd- immediately one or two officers discharged their pistols, and then there seemed to be a general discharge from the whole body. Eight Americans were killed upon the spot, and nine were wounded.. Another party of militia, about 150 men, alarmed at such violences, had assembled near a bridge at Concord. The soldiers fired upon them and killed two men.. They now returned the fire-beat the King's troops out of town.. to retreat to Lexington..in this battle of Lexington, the Americans had 39 men killed and 19 wounded. The King's troops lost 266 men killed, wounded and missing.. Let it be delivered down to posterity, that the American civil war broke out on the 19th day of April, 1775.

(141) Wilmington. At a Monthly Meeting of the Committee for the Town of Wilmington, and County of New-Hanover,...July 20th, 1775. .. Whereas it appeared, upon incontestible evidence, that John COLLETT, commander of Fort Johnston was preparing the said fort (under the auspices of Governor MARTIN) for the reception of a promised reinforcement, which was to be employed in reducing the good people of this province to a slavish submission to the will of a wicked and tyrannic minister..detained vessels, had threatened vengeance against magistrates, whose Official opinion he chose to disapprove-had set at defiance the high sheriff of the county-had..detained and embezzled..goods..wrecked near the fort... Copied from the minutes. Thomas CRAIKE, Sec. .. In Committee. In consequence of a letter from Samuel JOHNSTON, Esq; appointing the 20th of August next for the meeting of the provincial convention at Hillsborough, and recommending that five delegates, at least, should be sent by each county; Resolved, that Tuesday the 8th day of August be appointed for an election of additional delegates..freeholders do attend at the court-house in Wilmington... By order of the committee, Cornelius HARNETT, Chairman. The Freeholders of the respective Counties and Towns in this Province are requested to choose and elect Delegates, to meet in Provincial Convention, at Hillsborough, on the Twentieth Day of August next. Sam. JOHNSTON. July 10, 1775.

Monday, August 7, 1775. (No. 267.

(142) By a letter from a gentleman in Charlestown to his friend here, we are informed, that the honourable John STEWART superintendant of Indian affairs for the southern district, has actually been tampering with the southern Indians to take up the hatchet against us. This has been proved on him, for which he fled to Georgia...

(143) Wilmington. "On Thursday the 20th instant (July) a court of Oyer and Terminer was held here, when a bill was preferred against Patrick TRAVERS, for the murder of Mitchell CARROL, which the grand jury returned ignoramus.. On the 26th instant, at the close of the court, Mr. TRAVERS was discharged by proclamation."

(144) The following Proclamation is published at ___ of our Governor. By his Excellency the Honourable Thomas GAGE, Esq; Governor, and Commander in Chief, in and over his Majesty's Province of Massachusetts-Bay, and Vice Admiral of the ___. A Proclamation. Whereas the infatuated multitudes have long suffered the misives? to be con___ by certain well-known incendiaries and traitors, in a fatal progression of crimes, against the constitutional authority of the state, have, at length, proceeded to a vowed rebellion; and the good effects which were expected to arise from the lenity and patience of the King's government, have been often frustrated..offer, and I do hereby in his majesty's name; offer and promise his most gracious pardon to all persons who shall forthwith lay down their arms..excepting only, from the benefit of such pardon, Samuel ADAMS and John HANCOCK, whose offences are of too flagitious a nature to admit of any other consideration than that of condign punishment.. Given at Boston this 12th day of June..1775. Tho. GAGE.

(145) Run away from the subscriber about 10 days ago an old Negro man, named CUFFEE?, a carpenter; he formerly belonged to the estate of Job HOWE, senior, deceased... Cornelius HARNETT. Wilmington, August 4, 1775.

Friday, August 11, 1775. (No. 268.

(146) August 10, 1775. An account from Watertown says, one PORTER, (a Salem attorney) has been detected in conveying a letter from general GAGE to governor CARLETON of Quebec. In this letter Mr. GAGE "requires his good friends the catholics may be sent to assist him in cutting the throats of all heretics". In attempting to make

(146) (Cont.) his escape, he was shot, and instantly expired.

(147) In Committee, July 10th, 1775. Whereas..it is manifest, that Governor MARTIN hath used his utmost endeavors to erect the king's standard in this province, and to procure experienced officers to lead the disaffected persons therein..the committee of Craven county have forbid all persons whatsoever from communicating personally or by letter, with the said governor... Copied from the minutes, Thomas CRAIKE, Sec.

(148) At an election of delegates on the 8th instant for the town of Wilmington and county of New-Hanover, on the recommendation of Samuel JOHNSTON Esq; moderator, Archibald MACLAINE Esq; for the town, William HOOPER, James MOORE, and Alexander LILLINGTON, Esqrs. for the county, were chosen additional delegates to represent this town any county in general convention to be held at Hillsborough on the 20th instant, with Cornelius HARNETT, Esq; for the town, and George MOORE, John ASHE, and Samuel ASHE, Esqrs. chosen at a former election for the county.

(149) The reverend Mr. REED of Newbern refused to preach on the general fast day.. which so offended his parishoners, that we hear, they have dismissed him from his parochial charge there.

(150) Exchange of Guns by Mistake. Taken out of Robert BANNERMAN's in Wilmington, a small shot gun, with a double bridle lock and silver sight. The butt end of the rammer is broke half off, and is fastened with a piece of wire. Left in its stead much such another gun, with the same sort of lock and sight, but is bushed with gold, and has a crack in the breech. Whoever has the first mentioned gun may have the other one by applying to Joseph SPEIGHT. Bladen, July 24, 1776.

(151) In Provincial Congress, New-York, June 2, 1775. Friends and Countrymen,.. The great question between Britain and her colonies, is, whether they are subjects, or whether they are slaves..in the defence of those rights, some persons have taken certain forts in this colony, which are near your frontiers..our only intention is to prevent any hostile incursions upon us by the troops in your province.. Your brethren and friends, P. V. B. LIVINGSTON, President. To the inhabitants of the province of Quebec.

(152) Philadelphia, July 4. The following is the Staff lately appointed by the continental congress: ___ral and Commander in Chief of all the American Forces, George WASHINGTON, Esq; of Virginia. Major Generals, Artemus WARD, Esq; of Massachusetts-Bay. Charles LEE, Esq; Philip SCHUYLER, Esq; of Albany, in New-York Province. Israel PUTNAM, Esq; of Massachusetts-Bay. Adjutant General, Horatio GATES, Esq;

(153) In Congress, July 4. Resolved, that the two acts passed in the first session of the present parliament.."an act to restrain the trade and commerce of the province of Massachusetts-Bay and New-Hampshire, and colonies of Connecticut and Rhode Island and Providence plantations in North-America, to Great-Britain, Ireland and the British islands in the West-Indies.." and "an act to restrain the trade and commerce of the colonies of New-Jersey, Pennsylvania, Maryland, Virginia, and South-Carolina.. under certain conditions and limitations" are unconstitutional, oppressive and cruel ... A true copy from the minutes, Charles THOMSON, Sec.

(154) Duplin County, July 17, 1775. Mr. BOYD, Looking over your Mercury of the 7th of this month, I observed a piece signed by the chairman, in behalf of the committee of this county, reflecting on my conduct, as Illegal, Unwarrantable, Arbitrary, and Oppressive..I received an instrument of writing, mandate, warrant or whatever they may please to call it, from his excellency, directing me, at my peril, to issue my

(154) (Cont.) warrants to the several constables, to act agreeable to the scheme he sent.. But I do solemnly declare and protest, that I neither did myself, or give orders to the constables..to use any language, either to persuade the people into the measure proposed... Felix KENAN.

We, the Subscribers, constables for the county of Duplin, do hereby certify.. that we did not..receive any instructions..to use threatening language to any person, touching the execution of a certain warrant, directed by Felix KENAN, Esq; high sheriff of the said county, commanding us to take an exact list of all persons in said county. Witness our hands this 20th of July, 1775. William FREDERICK, Michael KING, James BUTLER, Daniel WARD, Jacob BROWN, William SOUTHERLAND, John HOUSMAN, William CIG, John CROOK, William ME____, Jonathan FRYIC?.

Friday, August 25, 1775. (No. 2__

(155) An Address To the Ministers and Presbyterian Congregations in North-Carolina. Reverend and Respected Friends and Brethren,... Signed at Philadelphia, the 12th? day of July, Francis ALISON, James SPROUT, George DUFFIELD, Robert DAVIDSON.

(156) The Twelve United Colonies, by their Delegates in Congress, to the Inhabitants of Great-Britain... By order of the Congress, John HANCOCK, President. Attested by Charles THOMSON, Secretary. Philadelphia, July 8, 1775.

(157) Cambridge, July 6. The following addresses have been presented to his Excellency General WASHINGTON and the Honourable Major-General LEE... To the Honourable Charles LEE, Esquire, Major-General of the Continental Army...

(158) On Friday last..arrived from Bladen, where they had been stopped by the ___ committee, lieutenant colonel James CO___? and Messrs. Samuel and Jacob WILLIAMS, it appeared after repeated examinations before the committee of this town, that they had been ____ on ____ the Cruizer, with governor MARTIN..all requested to sigr the association, and voluntarily took an oath, to obey the regulations of the continental congress, and provincial convention; to which they are now gone under the escort of Messrs. EWANS and BLYTH.

Friday, September 1, 1775. (No. 270.

(159) Savannah (Georgia) August 2. The schooner Harriot, Peter BACHOP, master, arrived here last Friday from St. Augustine, with provisions on board, but was ordered by the committee to leave this port.

(160) Newbern August 14. Committee Chamber. Whereas all those who have not subscribed the articles of the association, have sufficiently testified to the public, that they are enemies to the liberties of America..it is Ordered, that the Captains of the several companies..require of all such suspected persons, as well their fire arms, as swords, cutlasses, &c. and all gunpowder, lead, and other military stores.. and give receipts for all such guns, &c. and deliver them out to such persons of his or their company, not having arms &c. as may be willing to serve in the American cause. By Order, R. COGDELL, Chairman. A true copy from the minutes, J. SITGREAVES, Secretary.

(161) To be Sold Six hundred and forty acres of Land in Dupplin county, at the head of Richard WILLIAM's branch near the head of ROADS swamp..enquire of John ANCRUM. Wilmington, September 1, 1775.

(162) Note: A letter dated 9 January 1924, from Massachusetts Historical Society, to Mr. R. B. HOUSE of the North Carolina Historical Commission stated, concerning the following issue, that "it is supposed forgery by Millington MILLER." It has been included here in numerical order by issue number, instead of chronological order.

(Friday, June 3rd 1775.) No. 294.

(163) In conformity to an order issued by the Colonel of Mecklenburg County, in North Carolina, a Convention vested with unlimited powers, met at Charlotte..on the Nineteenth day of May, 1775, when Abraham ALEXANDER was chosen Chairman, and John Mc'Knitt ALEXANDER, Secretary..resolved. I. That whosoever..abetted..the..invasion of our rights, as claimed by Great Britain, is an enemy to this country.. II. Resolved, that we, the citizens of Mecklenburg County, do hereby dissolve the political bands which have connected us to the mother country.. III. Resolved, that we do hereby declare ourselves a free and independent people, to the maintenance of which independence we solemnly pledge to each other, our mutual cooperation, our lives, our fortunes, and our most sacred honor. J. M. ALEXANDER, Secretary, Abraham ALEXANDER, Chairman. Adam ALEXANDER. Hez. ALEXANDER. Ezra ALEXANDER. Chas. ALEXANDER. Waitstill AVERY. Eph. BREVARD. Hez. J. BALCH. Richard BARRY. John DAVIDSON. Wm. DAVIDSON. Henry DOWNS. John FLENNIKEN. John FORD. Wm. GRAHAM. James HARRIS. Robert IRWIN. Wm. KENNON. Matt. MC'CLURE. Neill MORRISON. Samuel MARTIN. D. OCHLETREE. John PHIFER. Thomas POLK. Ezekiel POLK. Benj. PATTON. John QUEARY. David REESE. Zach. WILLSON. Wm. WILLSON.

(164) Salem, April 25. The following is a list of the Provincials who were killed and wounded in the late action. Killed. Messrs. *Robert MUNROE, *Jonas PARKER, *Samuel HADLEY, *Jonathan HARRINGTON, *Caleb HARRINGTON, *Isaac MUZZY, *John BROWN, John RAYMOND, Nathaniel WYMAN, and Jedediah MUNROE, of Lexington.-Messrs. Jason RUSSELL, Jabez WYMAN, and Jason WINSHIP, of Menotomy. Deacon HAYNES, and Mr. LEAD?, of Studbury. Captain James MILES of Concord.-Captain Jonathan WILLSON of edford.-Captain DAVIS, Mr. ___ HOF_ER, and Mr. James HOWARD, of Acton.-Mr. Azael PORTER, and Mr. Daniel THOMPSON, of Woburn.-Mr. James MILLER, and Captain William BARBER's Son, aged 14, of Charlestown.-Isaac GARDNER, Esq, of Brookline.-Mr. John HICKS, of Cambridge.-Mr. Henry PUTMAN, of Medford.-Messrs. Abednego RAMSDELL, Daniel TOWNSEND, William FLINT, and Thomas HADLEY, of Lynn.-Messieurs Henry JACOBS, Samuel COOK, Ebenezer GOLDTHWAIT, George SOUTHWICK, Benjamin DALAND, jun., Jotham WEBB, and Perley PUTNAM, of Danvers.-Mr. Benjamin PEIRCE, of Salem.

Wounded. Messrs. John ROBBINS, John TIAD, Solomon PEIRCE, Thomas WINSHIP, Nathaniel FARMER, Joseph COMEE, Ebenezer MUNROE, Francis BROWN, and Prince EASTERBROOKS (a Negro man) of Lexington.-Mr. ___ HEMMENWAY, of Framingham.-Mr. John LANE, of Bedford.-Mr. George REED, and Mr. Jacob BACON, of Woburn.-Mr. William POLLY, of Medford. -Mr. Joshua FELT, and Mr. Timothy MUNROE, of Lynn. Mr. Nathaniel PUTNAM, and Mr. Dennis WALLIS, of Danvers.-Mr. Nathaniel CLEAVES, of Beverly. Missing. Mr. Samuel FROST, and Mr. Seth RUSSELL, of Menotomy. 39 Killed. 20 Wounded. 2 Missing. Those distinguished with this mark (*) were killed by the first fire of the enemy.

(165) Philadelphia, May 5. The worthy Dr. Benjamin FRANKLIN, agent for this province and Massachusetts-Bay, arrived here from London, and was by the Assembly, then sitting, appointed a Delegate in Congress.

1788 - Wilmington Centinel and General Advertiser. Filmed from originals in the University of North Carolina Library-June 11, 18, 25; July 2, 9, 16, 23, 30; August 6, 13, 20; September 3, 10, 17, 24; October 15, 26; November 5, 12, 19, 26; December 3, 10, 18, 25. From American Antiquarian Society--June 18.

(Vol. I.) WILMI_____ AND GE_____ (Issue of June 11, 1788.)

(166) Miscellany. Genuine copy of a letter from Capt. John SULLIVAN, to his Excellency Thomas PINCKNEY, Esq. governor of the state of South-Carolina. State of Georgia, Flint River, Frontier of the Spanish Dominions, December 27, 1787. May it please your Excellency,...

(167) Wilmington, June 1. William HOLT, a noted offender, who was indicted before the Superior Court when sitting in this place in December last, for the ___rid crime of murder..made his escape...

(168) The Concern formerly carried on in Wilmington by the subscriber, being dissolved on the first day of January last..stock of Dry Goods... Peter MAXWELL. Wilmington, June 11, 1788.

(169) _____ Any person desirous of purchasing a plantation on the Sound,..may be accomodated on easy terms, by the proprietor of the above... John BURGWIN. Wilmington, May 7, 1788.

(170) State of North-Carolina. Hillsborough district. In the court of equity, in April term, 1788. In the suit there depending, wherein John WILCOX is complainant, and Archibald MACLAINE and MORRIS, defendants. It is ordered, that James MORRIS, the heir, and the executors of Joseph and George Anthony MORRIS, put in their answer to the complainant's bill, on or before..the first day of October next.. A commission to issue to Philadelphia to take the answer. Published by order of the court, W. WATTERS, Clerk and Master in the afore___ Court and District.

(171) The Administrators of Robert SCHAW, Esq. Deceased, Request all persons indebted to the said Robert SCHAW, Alexander DUNCAN, deceased, DUNCAN, ANCRUM, and SCHAW and ANCRUM and SCHAW, to settle and make payment, or renew their obligations with Mr. John BRADLEY, who is fully empowered for that purpose... Wilmington, May 21, 1788.

(172) To Be Sold, On the 12th day of June next..Public Sale, That well known Plantation near Brunswick..belonging to the Estate of the late Gen. HOWE, containing 440 acres... Robert HOWE, Administrator.

Wilmington: (North-Carolina) Printed and Published by BOWEN and HOWARD, at their Printing-Office, opposite the Naval-Office; where Subscriptions for this Paper (at Forty Shillings, per Annum) Essays and Articles of Intelligence will be gratefully received.-Advertisements inserted on reasonable Terms.

(Vol. I.) Wednesday, June 18, 1788. (Numb. 16.)

(173) To the Public. The advantages which the commerce of this river would derive from deepening the channel over the flats are..obvious.. The subscriber..would undertake to clear the channel... A. MACLAINE and John H__KE, Esquires, Col. READ, Messrs. William CAMPBELL, Henry TOOMER, and George HOOPER of Wilmington, Colonels BROWN and OWEN of Bladen, Doctor INGRUM and William B. GROVE, Esq. of Fayette-Ville, will receive subscriptions... A. JOCELIN. Wilmington, June 15, 1788.

(174) Run Away from Mount Pleasant estate, on the North-West, a Negro fellow named TONY, late the property of Miss COBHAM, well known in..Wilmington, as he was one of the fiddlers to the assemblies. He is tall, well made, and thin vissaged, between black and yellow.. He has a wife at Mr. Frederic JONES's, on the Sound, named BELLY,

(174) (Cont.) (his cook).. A reward of 10 Pounds..and any moderate expence to deliver him to Mr. Sheriff WRIGHT, or by giving information by letter to Goodin ELLETSON, At Mount Pleasant, on North-West of Cape Fear. Bladen, May 17, 1788.

(175) Wanted, By the Commissioners of the Navigation, 100,000 Bricks. Apply to William NUTT, Clerk. Wilmington, June 11, 1788.

(176) New Publications. Just received from New-York, and for sale by the Printers hereof; The genuine information, delivered to the legislature of the state of Maryland, relative to the..general convention.. at Philadelphia; by Luther MARTIN, Esquire, Attorney General of Maryland,..together with a letter to the hon. Thomas C. DYE, Speaker of the house of Delegates... Price Six Shillings.

(177) For Sale, A Valuable Plantation, Pleasantly situated, on Top-sail sound, about a mile and a half to the northward of George MERRICK's, Esq; consisting of 540 acres ..a commodious, well built, framed house, 40 by 20, with suitable out houses..enquire of John BURGWIN. Wilmington, May 7, 1788.

(178) Wilmington. On Sunday last arrived in this port, the Schooner General Washington, Capt. William MEADS, after a passage of 9 days from New-York...

(179) New-York, May 23. On Wednesday last arrived here the British Packet Thyne, WOLF, from Falmouth, in 6 weeks and 4 days. Col. SMITH, secretary and son-in-law to his Excellency John ADAMS, Esq. with his lady, arrived in the Thyne.

(180) Charleston, June 12. Yesterday were executed for the murder of Mr. Nicholas John WHITEMAN, pursuant to their sentence on Saturday last, the following persons. Robert STACEY, Josiah JORDAN, John GEORGE, Thomas SMITH, Ann CONNOLLY, and Edward HATCHER. Tuesday the court having adjourned till yesterday..they passed sentence of death on ROGERS, MASTERS, and PENDERGRAS, for the murder of Mr. NATHAN; also upon CAIN and WILLIAMS, for the murder of Capt. WEBB and Mr. M'CLODE. They are to be executed on Monday next...

(181) Wilmington, June 18. Last Saturday, a man by the name of HOOPER, was detected in feloniously taking from Mr. M'CULLOCH of this town, a sum of money to the amount of nine pounds.-It appears from HOOPER's confession, that himself and one other person, had, a few days since, robbed John CAINE, Esq. Sheriff of Brunswick County...

(182) The following gentlemen are chosen to represent the City and County of New-York, in their state Convention, which were to meet at Poughkeepsie yesterday. John JAY, Richard MORRIS, John Sloss HOBART, Alexander HAMILTON, Robert R. LIVINGSTON, Isaac ROOSEVELT, James DUANE, Richard HARRISON and Nicholas LOW, Esquires. His excellency John HANCOCK, is re-elected governor of the commonwealth of Massachusetts. His excellency Samuel HUNTINGTON, is re-elected governor of the state of Connecticut.. His excellency John COLLINS, is re-elected governor of Rhode-Island.

(183) Some evil minded persons having thought fit to take up letters directed to me, coming by way of New-York and Charleston, three different times, I must hereby forewarn them of the danger attending such proceedings... Severin ERICHSON. Wilmington, June 18.

(184) For New-York & Boston, The Schooner Success, Abner LOVELL, Master, Will sail in 15 Days. For Freight or Passage, apply to the Captain on bord, or Philip SPAULDING, At Capt. CALLENDER's. June 18, 1788.

(185) A Few Quarter Casks of Madeira Wine, For Sale, By Edward JONES. May 21.

(186) Run-Away, or Kidnapped, From the subscriber, on Friday the 13th instant, a mulatto fellow named CHARLES.. The subscriber has great reason to believe that CHARLES has got on board of Capt. STEWART's vessel, bound to Jamaica, in which went passenger, a Mr. BARNES, merchant, who has resided in this town for some considerable time past. Any person that will give such information as will enable me to prosecute the captain or his securities to effect, shall receive a reward of Twenty Pounds. James GEEKIE. June 16, 1788.

(Vol. I.) Wednesday, June 25, 1788. (Numb. 17.)

(187) New-York, June 12. Last Sunday sailed for Havre de Grace, his Most Christian Majesty's packet La Fortune. Joel BARLOW, Esq. of Connecticut, and a son of the late Gen. GREEN, are passengers...

(188) Yesterday morning departed this life, in the 46th year of her age, to the great regret of all her acquaintance, Mrs. Lydia LOUDON, wife of Mr. Samuel LOUDON, state printer, and sister to his excellency Matthew GRISWOLD, Esq. late governor of Connecticut.

(189) Wilmington, June 25. We hear that the honorable Edmund PENDLETON, esq. is elected President of the Convention of the commonwealth of Virginia.

(190) The inhabitants of Wilmington, and districts Middle and Head of the Sound, are desired to call on Mr. Isaac BERNARD, who is empowered by me to receive their respective taxes, on or before the First Day of July next, as no further indulgence can be given. John ERWIN. Wilmington, June 25.

(191) To Be Rented, The House where the late Mrs. LYON resided. Inquire of A. MACLAINE. June 25.

(192) For Sale, The Sloop Sally.. For terms apply to James STEPHENS, Shipwright. Wilmington, June 25.

(193) To the Public. Whereas Mr. John ASHE in the year ____ (blank), consigned to the late Arthur HARPER, of Wilmington, a parcel of Negroes for sale. Hearing of their arrival, I wrote to Mr. Donald BAIN, requesting him to choose from among them a boy for me; and..that that letter should bind me to any terms he should agree on.. Mr. BAIN made choice of a boy for me, at the price of 90 pounds.. Mr. BAIN..left his own note as security.. The first payment was punctually made to Mr. Arthur HARPER, by Mr. James WALKER, at my request, in turpentine. And before the second payment became due, having advanced for Mr. ASHE, to whom the negro had belonged, in cash, to more than that amount, I informed Mr. Arthur HARPER, that I should adjust the balance with Mr. ASHE, to which he acquiesced. Upon the death of Mr. Arthur HARPER..soon after, Mr. James HARPER, as his administrator, became possessed of Mr. BAINS's note, and requested payment..he evades..the giving up said note..to Mr. BAIN's prejudice..the note has been justly..discharged. Samuel ASHE. June 25, 1788.

(Vol. I.) Wednesday, July 2, 1788. (Numb. 18.)

(194) Miscellany. From THOMAS's Massachusetts Spy. Mr. THOMAS, You are requested to give a place in your paper, to the following brief account of Kentucky, extracted from a letter of Isaac MONISON, Esq. to the Rev. Jordan DODGE, at Sturbridge, in

(194) (Cont.) this county, it is dated Nelson county, Kentucky, January 11, 1788...

(195) Providence, May 3. Monday last being the anniversary election of officers to command the united company of artillery in this town, the day was ushered in by a discharge of six cannon, in honour of the six states which have adopted the federal constitution. In the forenoon the company paraded in complete uniform.. At half past one, they partook of an entertainment at Mr. James GREEN's...

(196) Charleston, June 19. On Monday last were executed pursuant to sentence of the Court of Admiralty Sessions, for piracy on the American Seas, Capt. William ROGERS, of New-London, in Connecticut-John MASTERS, of Cheshire, in England and William PENDERGRASS, of Derbyshire, in England, charged and found guilty of the murder of Mr. Abraham NATHAN, of the Jewish nation, joint owner with ROGERS, and passenger on board the sloop Betsy, in October last.-Also, Richard WILLIAMS and William CAIN, both of England, for the murder of Capt. Nathaniel C. WEBB, and Mr. CLEOD or M'CLEOD, on the 19th or 20th of May last, on board the schooner Two-Friends. The unhappy..ROGERS.. the contemplation of leaving an aged father and mother-an affectionate, respectable wife and five young children, seemed to distress him beyond expression...

(197) Newbern, June 19. Last Friday night, between the hours of 11 and 12, the sloop Fanny, Capt. Joshua PLUMMER, of Bedford, bound to Wilmington,..being about 40 miles south of Cape Hatteras, laden with iron ware, bar iron and West-India produce, was struck with lightning and sunk in less than 10 minutes. The crew and one passenger (Mr. Samuel FOSDICK, of New-York, bound to Fayette-Ville) happily saved themselves ...

(198) Wilmington, July 2. In the night of the 26th ult. a very daring robbery was committed..upon the warehouse or cellar under the dwelling-house of Thomas MACLAINE, Esq....

(199) The statement of votes for members of the convention of the state of New-York, which we published in our last..ought to have stood thus: Columbia County. Anti-Federal ticket. Peter VAN NESS, 1848; Matthew ADGATE, 1850; John BAY, 1863. Federal ticket. Peter VAN SCHAICK, 1483; Henry LIVINGSTON, 1498; Jacob FORD, 1482. Montgomery County. Anti-Federal ticket. William HARPER, 1206; John FREY, 1301; John WINNE, 1202; Volkert VEEDER, 1199; Henry STRAING, 1105; Christopher P. YATES, 1209. Federal ticket. Abraham VAN HORNE, 756; James LIVINGSTON, 811; Abraham ARENOT?, 796; Peter SCHUYLER, 803; Josiah CRANE, 806; A. VAN VECHTEN, 806. Albany County. Anti-Federal ticket. Robert YATES, 4670; John LANSING, 4681; Henry OOTHOUDT, 4678; Peter VROOMAN, 4671; Abraham TEN EYCK, 4657; Dirck SWART, 4673; Israel THOMSON, 4666. Federal ticket. Abraham TEN BROECK, 2627; Jacob CUYLER, 2620; Francis NICOLL, 2617; P. GANSEVOORT, jun., 2621; Jerom HOAGLAND, 2613; James GORDON, 2617; John W. SCHEMERHORN, 2610. Dutchess County. Anti-Federal. Zephaniah PLATT, Melancton SMITH, Jacobus SWARTWOUT, John DE WITT, Gilbert LIVINGSTON, Ezra THOMSON, Jonathan AKINS. Ulster County. Anti-Federal. His Excellency Governor CLINTON, 1372; John CANTINE, 1339; Cornelius C. SCHOONMAKER, 1045; Ebenezer CLARK, 1356; James CLINTON, 905; Dirck WYNKOOP, 1055. Federal, unsuccessful. Johannes BRUYN, 68; Jacobus S. BRUYN, 35; Cornelius T. JENSEN, 29. Orange County. Anti-Federal. Jesse WOODHULL, Henry WISNER, sen. John HARING, John WOOD. Queen's County. Anti-Federal. Samuel JONES, John SCHENCK, Nathaniel LAWRENCE, Stephen CARMAN. Suffolk County. Anti-Federal. Thomas TREADWELL, Jonathan N. HAVENS, John SMITH, David HEDG , Henry SCU R. For the City and County of New-York. Federal ticket. John JAY, 2735; Richard MORRIS, 2716; John Sloss HOBART, 2713; Alexander HAMILTON, 2713; Robert R. LIVINGSTON, 2713; Isaac ROOSEVELT, 2701; James DUANE, 2680; Richard HARRISON, 2677; Nicholas LOW, 2651. West-Chester County. Federal. Lewis MORRIS, Philip R. LIVINGSTON, L. W. SARLS, Richard HATFIELD,

(199) (Cont.) Thaddeus CRANE, Philip V. CORTLANDT. Richmond County. Sentiments unknown. Abraham BANCKE, Cozen RYERSS. King's County. Federal. Peter LEFFERTS, Peter VANDEVOORT. The above is extracted from the New-York Daily Patriotic Register, printed the 5th ult. by Mr. Thomas GREENLEAF.

(200) To be Sold cheap,..the following valuable Lands, Lying between 10 and 20 miles from Wilmington. Smithfield, situate on both sides of the North-West, between Blue Banks and Drury ALLEN's, containing 2200 acres of land.. Blue Banks, situate on both sides of the river, below Smithfield, containing 2331 acres.. There is a Dwelling-House containing a hall, parlour, four chambers and three closets, a kitchen, stable, and large brick barn.. Bellefont, situate on both sides of the North-West, joining and below Blue Banks..about 3000 acres.. There are on the premises a Brick House, containing four rooms, a kitchen, barn, and other necessary out-buildings. One thousand acres of land on the waters of Livingston creek... A small piece of land lying on Rattle-Snake Branch, near the North-West road..200 acres. A piece of land on the North-East side of Black River, in the neighbourhood of MAULTSLY's point..200 acres. A tract joining and below the last-mentioned, formerly patented to James COLSON..about 1000 acres. Appleby, adjoining the above, containing in the whole 866 acres.. An island of tide swamp..276 acres. A piece of land on the North-East side of the North-West, just below the mouth of Black River..200 acres. A piece adjoining..320 acres. Another piece called the Cat Fish lands.. about 200 acres.. Approved old bonds, especially of the late Mr. DRY's or Capt. ROWAN's and any debts of the subscriber will be allowed in part payment.. Benjamin SMITH. Belvidere, July 2, 1788. To Be Let. The Brick House, Tavern, and Ferries, opposite Wilmington.

(201) To the Public. The advantages which all commercial places derive from a regular communication by post, from one town to another, are too many and too obvious to require any demonstration..the subscribers..will engage provided sufficient encouragement is given; that a Post shall go once in every week from this town to Fayette-Ville, one week by the way of the North-West, and return through the Counties of Sampson and Duplin-the next week go to Fayette-Ville, by the way of Duplin and Sampson, and return by the North-West.. BOWEN & HOWARD. Wilmington, July 2, 1788. Subscriptions for the above purpose, are received by A. MACLAINE, Esq. John HUSKE, Esq., Mr. George HOOPER, Mr. A. MACNAUGHTON, Mr. E. JONES, Mr. John CAMPBELL, and at the Printing-Office, Wilmington-by Dr. INGRAHAM, James BLOODWORTH, Esq. and Col. PORTERFIELD, Fayette-Ville.

(202) For Sale, At Public Vendue, On Friday the Fourth instant, The Sloop Sally,... Henry TOOMER, Auctioneer.. June 2, 1788.

(203) Whereas Margaret M'KAY, the spouse of Neil M'GEACHY, late of Cumberland County, has in the absence of her husband, made her elopement, and went off with a certain Martin DYE, to the interior ___ of Georgia, with whom she has lived several years past, and has children by him. This is to forwarn all persons not to credit the said Margaret M'KAY on account of the said Neil M'GEACHY, as he has taken the proper steps for a divorce, and will never pay any debts she may contract. Neil M'GEACHY. Wilmington, July 2.

(204) For Charter, To Charleston, or a Northern Port, A Stout Sloop.. Apply to Edward JONES. July 2, 1788.

(205) Notice. Whereas, by a decree of the honourable the Court of Equity, in the suit therein depending, wherein Severin ERICHSON is complainant and Samuel VANCE, defendant.-It is ordered by and with the consent of the parties that the Master in

(205) (Cont.) said Court do forthwith collect and recover the debts due to Samuel VANCE or Samuel VANCE and Co.... Thomas DAVIS, C. & M. E. Wilmington, July 2, 1788.

(206) Wilmington district, ss. Gabriel DUBRUTZ, complainant, vs. Aaron PIMENTAL, defendant. In Equity, June Term, 1788. Ordered, That the defendant do appear to complainant's bill, on or before..the sixth of December next in default whereof the complainant's bill shall be taken pro confesso... Thomas DAVIS, C. & M. E.

(207) Wilmington district, ss. John Ablen CAMPBELL, complainant vs. John GRANT, defendant. In Equity, June term, 1788. Ordered, That the defendant do appear to complainant's bill, on or before..the sixth of December next in default whereof the complainant's bill shall be taken pro confesso... Thomas DAVIS, C. & M. E.

(Vol. I.) Wednesday, July 9, 1788. (Numb. 19.)

(208) Savannah, May 29. We are informed that six negro men, the property of James SPALDING, Esq; of the island of St. Simon, runaway lately to St. Augustine. Mr. SPALDING followed them, and requested the Spanish governor to permit him to take his negroes, but he was refused...

(209) Wilmington, July 9. On Saturday the 5th instant..the commonwealth of Virginia ..convention of Delegates appointed to take into consideration the proposed confederated Constitution, had unequivocally adopted the same...

(210) Died-On Monday evening last, Mr. John COLEMAN, of this town.

(211) For New-Providence, The Brig John, John HOWELL, Master, Will sail the 15th instant. For passage only, apply to the Master on board, or to Dennis REARDAN & Co. Wilmington, July 9, 1788.

(Vol. I.) Wednesday, July 16, 1788. (Numb. 20.)

(212) The following curious advertisement is taken from a late Exeter paper... John HOPKINSON. Exeter, April 18.

(213) Baltimore, June 14. Copy of a letter from the illustrious George WASHINGTON, to the Gentlemen Proprietors of the Ship Federalist. "Mount Vernon, June 8, 1788. Gentlemen, Captain BARNEY has just arrived here in the miniature ship called the Federalist, and has done me the honour to offer that beautiful curiousity as a present to me, on your part... George WASHINGTON.". To William SMITH, Esq. and the other gentlemen proprietors of the ship Federalist.

(214) Wilmington, July 16. Tenth Pillar Raised! Extract of a letter from Concord, (New-Hampshire) dated June 21, 1788. "I have the great pleasure of informing you, that the Convention of this state have this day adopted the Federal Constitution..."

(215) Died-On Sunday evening last, Mr. Clement ORNSBY, aged 83? years.

(216) To Be Sold, At Auction, On Tuesday the Fifth Day of August next, A Negro Wench, Belonging to the estate of John LYON, Esq. deceased.. By order of the Executor, Thomas WRIGHT, sheriff. Wilmington, July 16.

(217) To Be Let, A Convenient Dwelling-House, with a Wash-House, Yard, and Garden. For terms apply to William HOOPER, jun. Wilmington, July 16.

(218) The Journals of the last Assembly are now ready to be delivered at the Superior Court Office. John HUSKE, Clerk. Wilmington, July 16.

(219) The Administrators of the late Mr. SWANN, request those who are indebted to the Store in Wilmington, kept by Mr. James MILLS, to call upon Mr. Isaac BERNARD, who is authorised to settle..debts. Wilmington, July 16.

(220) The subscriber forwarns all persons from purchasing a note of hand given by him to Mr. John LONDON, merchant, of Wilmington..about the 11th of June, 1785, for a sum of money between 14 and 20 pounds. Mr. Nathaniel TWINING paid Henry CUMMING for the said note, which was taken up by him, and yet the said CUMMING refuses to give up the note to the subscriber..although..he has paid Mr. TWINING for the said note near two years since, and has CUMMING's receipt for the same. James FOY. July 16, 1788.

(Vol. I.) Wednesday, July 23, 1788. (Numb. 21.)

(221) To Be Sold Cheap. For Cash or Produce, Two valuable Plantations at the White Marsh, Bladen County, containing 900 acres, the property of the late Robert ROWAN, Esq. deceased. For further particulars apply to H. J. RICHARDS, or Archibald MACLAINE. Wilmington, July 16, 1788.

(222) Wilmington, July 23. Married-Last Thursday evening, Mr. Charles CROPTON, to Mrs. Jane SMITH.

(223) The Public are respectfully informed, that a Post will ride once in every week from this town to Fayette-Ville.. All commands from Fayette-Ville, must be left with Mr. John ECCLES, at that place.

(224) Wanted, An Apprentice to the Cabinet Making and Riding Chair business. Apply to John NUTT. Wilmington, July 23.

(225) For Falmouth or Plymouth, in England, The Brigantine Fame, John HANDS, Master, Will sail..in 14 Days. For light freight or passage, enquire of the Captain on board..or of John BURGWIN. Wilmington, July 23.

(226) To be Sold, The following tracts or parcels of Land, Being part of the estate of the late General WADDELL, viz. 200 acres of land in Anson County, on JONES's Creek, adjoining the upper line of J. MEADOWS, on the North side of said Creek. 500 acres..in Anson County, on the S. W. side of Pedee River, the North fork of Wild Cat, on the East side of Waxhaw Path. 640 acres..in Anson County, on the S. W. side of Pedee River, on the S. E. side of RICHARDSON's Creek. 640 acres..on the S. W. side of Pedee River, on Wild Cat, in the upper line of James M'MANUS's land on said Creek. 500 acres..on the S. W. side of Pedee River, South side of a Fork of LYNCHE's Creek, about half a mile above STROUD's, the upper settlement. 600 acres..on the S. W. side of Pedde River, on the N. side of THOMPSON's Creek. 300 acres..on the waters of Dutch Buffalo, adjoining the lines of John BRANDON's and Henry SWISSER's lands. 490 acres..on LEAN's Creek, below the Catabaw Path. 500 acres..on the S. W. side of Pedee River, on the Waxhaw Path, where it crosses the North Fork of Wild Cat. 320 acres..on the S. W. side of Pedee River, on the N. side of the North Fork of Cat Creek. N. B. The above-mentioned tracts were all patented in Anson.. 140 acres patented in Cumberland County, but now in Chatham, upon the East side of Bear Creek. 720 acres in Rowan County, situate on both sides of Crane Creek adjoining Salisbury town line. Also, a lot in the town of Salisbury, known by No. 13, in the North-East square, joining John DUNN, Esquire's lot. For

(226) (Cont.) further particulars, enquire at Wilmington, of Hugh WADDELL or John B. WADDELL. Wilmington, July 23, 1788.

(227) The Subscribers request all persons having any demands against the estate of the late John GRANGE, sen. Esq. deceased, to render in their accounts to them as speedily as possible... Thomas NEALE, jun., John HALL, Administrators. July 15, 1788.

(228) Messrs. BOWEN and HOWARD, The last General Assembly having ordered the Comptroller of Accounts to commence suits against several persons who were held up to public view as delinquents in the payment of arrears due..I think proper to request you to publish the underwritten certificate of my final settlement... Peter MALLETT. Wilmington, July 16.

Copy. State of North-Carolina, ss. No. 532. This certifies, that Peter MALLETT, Esq. former Commissary General, exhibited into the Comptroller's office his account upon oath, wherein he charges the public for cash credited in his account settled in the Comptroller's Office, in December 1782, and for cash and a warrant paid into the hands of Thomas AMIS, Assistant Commissary.. And he credits the public for cash received for sundry warrants on the treasury, and for 10 barrels of flour received of John BRADLEY for Joseph GREEN... Given at Hillsborough, this 18th day of May, anno domini 1788. Francis CHILD, Comptroller.

(Vol. I.) Wednesday, July 30, 1788. (Numb. 22.)

(229) Wilmington, July 30. Extract of a letter from Kentucky, Danville, June 4, 1788. "The news from this country is exceedingly unfavourable; the Indians have done us more mischief this year, than for at least four years past.. They lately took a boat, in which was a Capt. ASHBY with his family; a son of Capt. ASHBY's having been very spirited in opposition, the savages immediately put him to death..the father who has since made his escape from them and come in.. Five Indians had penetrated into the country within a few miles of Capt. Benjamin LOGAN's, but two of them forfeited their lives for their temerity..."

(230) From the Virginia Independent Chronicle. Previous to the adjournment of the late Convention, a proposition was made by Mr. MASON, that the minority should meet at the public buildings and prepare an address to reconcile..their constituents to the new plan of government. Accordingly a very full meeting was had, when..an address was offered for their signatures, tending to irritate, rather than to quiet the public mind. A number..immediately withdrew; others..either remained in silence, or,..recommended temper and moderation,-till at length, Benjamin HARRISON, Esq. of Charles City rose..opposed not only the address..but..recommended an adjournment.. The opinion was supported by the Honorable John TYLER and Gen. LAWSON...

(231) For Greenock, The Brigantine Queen, William MORRISON, Master, Will sail in all next month. For passage, apply to James FLEEMING. Wilmington, July 30.

(232) For Barbadoes, The Brigantine Jenny, William THOMPSON, Master, Will sail in Eight Days. For passage, apply to James FLEEMING. Wilmington, July 28.

(233) Catharine MARTIN, Lately from Germany, Who has attained a liberal Education in all kinds of needlework, purposes opening A School, for the Instruction of young ladies.. She at present resides at Mr. M'CULLOCH's...

(Vol. I.) Wednesday, August 6, 1788. (Numb. 23.)

(234) Messrs. BOWEN & HOWARD, I Observed a piece in your paper of the 16th July, under the signature of A. MACLAINE, addressed to the electors of the town of Wilmington... William TATHAM.

(235) Wilmington, August 6. Extract of a letter from Hillsborough, July 28. "The state of Franklin is come to an end, and Governor SEVIER gone off with about forty adherents, with whom he has made an attack on an Indian town, killed a Chief called the GREAT TASSEL, his son, and 25 more..."

(236) Married-At Fayette-Ville, on Thursday the 24th ult. Mr. Daniel M'MURPHEY, to Miss Agatha DUDLEY.

(237) To the Public.. My character having been arraigned by sedition! my life having been sought after by conspiracy, in my own house, I am obliged in this public manner to vindicate myself by the following observations and I call upon any to deny my remarks. Has not the cold hand of poverty ever shared of my bounty? Has not my table (when keeping house) been ever spread to the stranger? Has lenity and compassion been strangers to the unfortunate prisoners whose fate led them within the compass of my power? Has not my life, for eight years, been devoted to honorable pursuits, of which testimonies can be given in this place, by the officers and soldiers who have fought with me? When was I ever backward at an attack? When was I wanting to be foremost in danger, when the calls of my country demanded me? Did not I, when captured, endure the rigid treatment of an enemy without murmur? .. In my domestic apartment, I wish to be considered by the public, as rashly faulty; though even this matter would have been easily accomodated, had not uncommon pains been taken to perpetuate and revive the breach by the base and designing artifices of contempt. Peter BACOT. Wilmington, August 6, 1788.

(238) To Be Let, And entered immediately. A Large and commodious Dwelling-House, with a convenient yard and garden..apply to Wm. GREEN. Wilmington, August 6, 1788.

(Vol. I.) Wednesday, August 13, 1788. (Numb. 24.)

(239) In Congress, July 3, 1788.. Resolved, That a copy of the proceedings of Congress, relative to the independency of the district of Kentucky, be transmitted to the Legislature and the inhabitants of the district aforesaid, be informed, that as the constitution of the United States is now ratified, Congress think it unadvisable to adopt any further measures for admitting the district of Kentucky into the Federal Union..but recommend it to the said Legislature and the inhabitants..to alter their acts and resolutions relative to the premises, as to render them conformable to the provisions made in the said Constitution... Charles THOMPSON, Secretary. (A copy) Attest. Samuel COLEMAN, A. C. C.

(240) Friends and Fellow-Citizens, In the Wilmington Centinel, of the 30th July, an apology appeared from the Printers for not publishing two essays in answer to a letter signed Archibald MACLAINE, addressed to the electors of Wilmington-viz. that "as the charges they contained were pointed, they (the printers) conceived it necessary that the names of the authors should be communicated to them, previous to their publication." On the 6th instant, a copy of one of the said essays appeared in the Centinel, signed William TATHAM, a signature I conceived to be disingenuously borrowed by the real author, because William TATHAM had left this state to return to England, his native country, in pursuit of some family possessions, prior to the Printers apology, and also as Mr. TATHAM is a professional man-a lawyer, it would be an insult to suppose him the author... Edward JONES.

(241) Wilmington, August 13. On Thursday the 7th inst. was executed in this town, pursuant to sentence, PETER, commonly known by the description of burnt mouth PETER, a Negro belonging to Mr. _____ LUCAS. It appeared..on the trial of the Negro, that upon the night of the 6th instant, he had broke open an out-house of Mr. KENON..of this town, and carried off a number of poultry-that the suceeding morning Mr. KENON had tracked him to Mr. HOSTLER's plantation, and there discovered the stolen property in his possession-that upon Mr. KENON's attempting to take him, he presented a loaded musket at Mr. KENON's breast, with which he threatened to shoot him..seized the musket and wrested it out of the fellow's hands..afterwards he seized first a bludgeon, then a hatchet..in struggling for the hatchet, Mr. KENON had fallen under him..might have been fatal..if his apprentice had not come to his assistance, and enabled him to overcome and secure the villain. Those attrocious circumstances.. added to the notoriety of the infamous character of PETER, and that he had been a runaway for nine months..and of late associated with the gang of which QUA has been principal, who have had the audacity to carry fire-arms..and..committing depredations upon the property of the inhabitants, induced the jury that sat upon his trial, to sentence him to death.

(242) Died-On Wednesday last, Mrs. Ann WALKER.-On Sunday, Mrs. _____ CLARK.

(243) List of Letters Remaining in the Post-Office, Wilmington. The Hon. Samuel ASHE, Stephen ABBOT, Messrs. John ARMSTRONG and David CANNON, Samuel ASHE, jun. B. John BELL, Robert BOWLAND, Joseph BEALE, Peggy BALCOUR, 3, Caesar BELOAT, 2, Jonathan BOARDMAN. C. John COLLINS, John CURRIE, Joseph CARR, Sylvester CHILD, Nuton CONNELY, Matthew CLENDENNING, Clerk of the Superior Court, John COTTERELL, Hugh CARRAGAN. D. Lawrence DORSEY, Jonathan DIXON. E. Duncan EACHRAN. F. David FLOWERS, 2, Samuel FOS?DICK. G. John GUERARD, Alexander GIFFARD, Alexander GEDDES, Robert GEFFORD, James GELLESPIE, Gilbert GEER. H. Robert HUNTER, Captain George HAZARD, Henry HALSEY, 2, James HOWARD, Arthur HOWE, Solomon HAMMER, 2, William HENDRY, Jean HENDRE, Mrs. Abby HODGESON. J. Thomas JONES, 2, Thomas JENNINGS, Rowland JONES, Capt. Thomas JENNETT. K. Archibald KENNEDY, William KEDDIE, Col. Henry E. LUTTERLOW, 2, John LEVISTON, Wayne. M. The hon. Alfred MOORE, Colin MORRISON, Andrew MC KENZIE, Samuel MALLETT, William MABSON, George MOORE, Mr. MC COMMACK, tavern keeper, Wilmington, Hugh M'CORMICK, Robert MC FARLAND, Fingal MC KINNAN, Donald MC KAY, William MC VERRICK, John MC FARLANE, James MC MURPHEY, Donald MC NEAL. P. Alexander PATRICK, Aaron PIERCE, James PRENTICE, Capt. David PORTER. R. John ROSS, Samuel RUSSEL, John ROWAN, John RUTHERFORD, James ROW, J. RHODES. S. John SUTHERLAND, Dougal STEWART, George STARK, Robert SMITH, Edward SIMONT, Thomas SEWALL, 3, Isaac STARK, William SHARPE, John SELLERS, Edward SHARPE, Samuel SMITH, J. MILLER, Tavern-keeper, Samuel STRODEVICK, 3. T. William THURSTON, Charles TINNING. V. Capt. John VANCE. W. William WATSON, Jacob WILLIAMS, Doctor Lewis F. WILSON, Mr. Benjamin WILLIAMS, John WALKER, 2. The above letters, if not taken up in three months, will be sent to the General Post-Office at Philadelphia. John BRADLEY, P. M. August 8, 1788.

(Vol. I.) Wednesday, August 20, 1788. (Numb. 25.)

(244) In Convention Of the State of North-Carolina, Hillsborough, August 1, 1788. The order of the day for taking up the report of the committee of the whole convention, on the proposed constitution for the government of the United States of America, was called for, and read.. Saturday, August 2. The report of the Committee of the whole Convention..was..read..as on yesterday, when it was moved by Mr. T. PEARSON, and seconded by Mr. MACON, that the Convention do concur therewith, which was objected to by Mr. A. MACLAINE..carried in the affirmative. Whereupon Mr. DAVIE, called for the yeas and nays, and was seconded by Mr. CABARRUS, which are as follow. YEAS. Messrs. Willie JONES, Samuel SPENCER, Lewis LANIER, Thomas WADE, Daniel GOULD, James BONNER, A.

(244) (Cont.) M. FORSTER, Lewis DUPREE, Thomas BROWN, James GREENLEE, Joseph M'DOWAL, Robert MILLER, Benjamin WILLIAMS, Richard NIXON, Thomas ARMSTRONG, Alexander M'ALLISTER, Robert DICKINS, George ROBERTS, John WOMACK, Ambrose RAMSEY, James ANDERSON, Joseph STEWART, William VESTAL, Thomas EVANS, Thomas HARDIMAN, Robert WEAKLEY, William DONELSON, William DOBINS, R. DIGS, Bithel BELL, Elisha BATTLE, William FORT, Etheld. GRAY, William LANCASTER, Thomas SHERROD, John NORWOOD, Sterling DUPREE, Robert WILLIAMS, Richard MOYE, Arthur FORBES, David CALDWELL, William GOUDY, Daniel GILLESPIE, John ANDERSON, John HAMILTON, Thomas PERSON, Joseph TAYLOR, Thornton YANCEY, Howell LEWIS, Jun., Elijah MITCHELL, George MOORE, George LEDBETTER, William PORTER, Zebedee WOOD, Edmund WADDELL, James GALLOWAY, John REGAN, Joseph WHISTON, James GAINS, Charles M'ANNELLY, Absalom BOSTWICK, John SCOTT, John DUNKIN, David DODD, Curtis IVEY, Lewis HOLMES, Richard CLINTON, Hardy HOLMES, Robert ALLISON, James STEWART, John TIPTON, John MACON, Thomas CHRISTMAS, Henry MONTFORT, William TAYLOR, James HANLY, Britain SAUNDERS, William LENOIR, Richard ALLEN, John BROWN, Joseph HERNDON, James FLETCHER, A. TATOM, L. BURKIT, W. LITTLE, Thomas KING, N. BRYAN, J. H. BRYAN, E. WHITTY, R. ALEXANDER, James JOHNSTON, J. COX, John CARREL, Corn. DOUD, Thomas TYSON, William MARTIN, Thomas HUNTER, M. Joseph GRAHAM, W. LOFTIN, William KINDAL, Thomas USSERY, Thomas BUTLER, John BENFORD, James VAUGHN, Robert PEEBLES, James VINSON, William S. MARNS, H. ALLEN, Red. BUNN, John BONDS, David PRIDGEN, Daniel YATES, Thomas JOHNSTON, John SPICER, Alexander MEBANE, Wm. MEBANE, William M'CAULEY, William SHEPPERD, Orange, Jonathan LINLEY, Wyatt HAWKINS, James PAYNE, John GRAVES, John BLAIR, Joseph TIPTON, William BETHELL, Abraham PHILLIPS, John MAY, Charles GALLOWAY, James BOSWELL, John M'ALLISTER, David LOONEY, John SHARPE, Joseph GAUTIER, John A. CAMPBELL, John Pugh WILLIAMS, William MARSHAL, Charles WARD, William RANDAL, Frederick HARGET, Richard M'KENNIE, John CAIN, Jacob LEONARD, Thomas CARSON, Richard SINGLETON, James WHITESIDE, Caleb PHIFER, Zachias WILSON, Joseph DOUGLAS, Thomas DOUGAN, James KENAN, John JONES, Egbert HAYWOOD, William WOOTTEN, John BRANCH, Henry HILL, Andrew BAST, Joseph BOON, William FARMER, John BRYAN, Edward WILLIAMS, Francis OLIVER, Mathew BROOKS, Griffith RUTHERFORD, George H. BARRINGER, Timothy BLOODWORTH, Evert PIERCE, Asahel RAWLINGS, James WILSON, James RODDY, Samuel CAIN, Benjamin COVINGTON, Joseph M'DOWAL, jun., Durham HALL, James BLOODWORTH, Joel LANE, James HINTON, Thomas DEVANE, James BRANDON, William DIXON, Burwell LOCK, and Stokely DONELSON.

NAYS. His Excellency Samuel JOHNSON, Esq. President, Messrs. James IREDEL, Archibald MACLAINE, Nathan KEAIS, John G. BLOUNT, Thomas ALDERSON, John JOHNSON, Andrew OLIVER, Goodin ELLISSON?, Charles M'DOWAL, Richard D. SPAIGHT, William J. DAWSON, James PORTERFIELD, William Barry GROVE, George ELLIOT, Wallis STYRON, William SHEPPERD, Carteret, James PHILLIPS, John HUMPHRIES, Michael PAYNE, Charles JOHNSON, Stephen CABARRUS, Edmund BLOUNT, Cowhan, Henry ABBOT, Isaac GREGORY, Peter DAUGE, Charles GRANDY, Enoch SAWYER, George LUCAS, John WILLIS, John CADE, Elias BARNES, Neil BROWN, James WINCHESTER, William STOKES, Thomas STEWART, Josiah COLLINS, Thomas HINES, Nathaniel JONES, John STEELE, William R. DAVIE, Joseph REDDICK, James GREGORY, Thomas HUNTER, Gates, Thomas WYNES, Abraham JONES, John EBORNE, James JASPER, Caleb FOREMAN, Seth HOVEY, John SLOAN, John MOORE, William MACLAINE, Nathan MAYO, William SLADE, William MACKENZIE, Robert IRWIN, John LANE, Thomas READING, Edward EVEREGAIN, Enoch RELFE, Devotion DAVIS, William SKINNER, Joshua SKINNER, Thomas HARVEY, John SKINNER, Samuel HARREL, Joseph LEECH, William BRIDGES, William BURDEN, Edmund BLOUNT, Tyrrel, Simson SPRUIL, David TANNER, Whitm. HILL, Benjamin SMITH, John STIGREAVES, Nathaniel ALLEN, Thomas OWEN, George WYNS, David PICKENS, Joseph FEREBEE, William FEREBEE, and William BAKER. Extract from the Journal, J. HUNT, Secretary.

(245) Alexandria, July 31. On the evening of the 23rd instant, we had one of the most violent storms of wind and rain ever experienced here.. A sloop was lodged on

(245) (Cont.) Capt. CONWAY's wharf, which has since been ____ without much damage. A schooner was sunk at Col. RAMSAY's wharf, and a flat drove on shore near Queen-street.. Since the above storm arrived here under jury-masts, the ship Favourite, Capt. Silas JONES, from Boston to George-Town...

(246) Wilmington, August 20. Circular letter from the convention of the state of New-York, to the executives of the different states, to be laid before their respective legislatures.. By the unanimous order of the convention, Geo. CLINTON, President.

(247) The Hon. Timothy BLOODWORTH, Esq. is elected senator for New-Hanover County. John Pugh WILLIAMS, and Thomas DEVANE, Esqr's representatives in the House of Commons for New-Hanover County. Edward JONES, Esq. for the town of Wilmington.

(248) The Printing-Office is removed to the house at present occupied by Major KINGSBURY, nearly opposite the Market.

(249) For New-York, The Sloop Industry, Robert DUNN, Master, Will sail on Sunday next. For Freight or Passage..apply to the Master on board at the Market Wharf, or John MC LAREN. Wilmington, August 20.

(250) For Kingston, (Jamaica) The Brig Sally, John SIMPSON, Master. Will sail the First of September. For passage only, apply to the master on board, or A. MACNAUGHTON. Wilmington, August 20.

(251) William STEWART, Taylor, Begs to inform the public, that he has taken a room in the house of Mr. M'CULLOCH, where he intends carrying on his business...

(252) Baltimore, August 5. ... Capt. Robert ROSS, who arrived here on Saturday last, in the Brig Keener, from St. Bartholomews..informs that on the 29th ult. in lat. 35:30N and long 71:30W, he spoke Capt. WOODWARD..bound for Bristol.. The same day he spoke a sloop from St. Martin's, bound for Virginia, who had taken 4 men out of the wreck of a sloop, after having been six days in the greatest distress. Capt. William BUCKLEY, who commanded this sloop, and one of his seamen, were drowned. Capt. ROSS, on his passage, caught a shark 17 feet long, and 7 feet 9 inches round, from the liver of which were extracted 23 gallons of oil.

(253) Twenty Pounds Reward. On Thursday last a Negro fellow named TOM late the property of Colonel J. LEONARD, murdered Mr. John LEONARD, of Brunswick County, at the plantation of Mr. Arthur HOWE. TOM is a small black fellow, about 21 years of age..and will try to get out of the state..is supposed he was wounded in the head by a guard placed at Mr. S. DANIEL's last Friday night. The above reward will be given to any person who apprehends him, by applying to Mr. Lewis M'PHERSON, merchant, Wilmington, or the subscriber in Brunswick County. Jacob LEONARD. August 25, 1788.

(Vol. I.) Wednesday, September 3, 1788. (Numb. 27.)

(254) Petersburg, August 7. Beware of a Hypocrite! In Committee, convened in Joseph HARDING's Compting-room, on Monday the 5th of August, 1788. Members present, John EASTER, Deacon, Richard GARRETTSON, Stith PARHAM, Greffit (or Gressit) DAVIS, Joseph HARDING, Nathaniel LEE, James FAUCETT, Jones A. DEAN. Robert DOUGLASS, a member of the Methodist Episcopal Church was charged by the information of a person of this town, that Mr. Robert PAUL, of Halifax county, that he, the said DOUGLASS, was a married man, when he, the said PAUL, left Scotland, about three years ago-and that he, the said PAUL, was well acquainted with the family and persons of both the said

(254) (Cont.) Robert DOUGLASS, and his wife: And that on the said PAUL's setting off for America, she delivered him a letter for the said DOUGLASS, at New-York, supposing him to have been there-and that she was repeatedly at the said PAUL's house, in a forlorne and disconsolate situation, with a little daughter. And the said Robert DOUGLASS was further charged with making overtures of marriage to Miss R. B. daughter of Mr. F. B. of Chesterfield county, in violation of his marriage covenant, and in breach of all laws.. The said DOUGLASS being called on to answer before God and this Committee, whether or not the first of these charges, of his being married, is true or false. Upon which he gave in the following answer, in writing:-"Petersburg, August 4, 1788. My Dear Brethren, It grieves me unto the very heart to relate unto you, that the charges laid against me are just... I am your unworthy brother, Robert DOUGLASS." The question being separately put, the Committee are unanimously in opinion, that Robert DOUGLASS cannot be retained in our Church. Signed in behalf of the Committee, John EASTER.

(255) Salem, July 29. Last Friday, a female stranger died at the Bell tavern, in Danvers; and on Sunday her remains were decently interred.. She was brought to the Bell in a chaise from Watertown.. She remained at this inn until her death, in expectation of the arrival of her husband, whom she expected to come for her.. She said..that she came from Westfield, in Connecticut..her parents lived in that state-that she had been married only a few months-and, that her husband's name was Thomas WALKER, but always carefully concealed her family name. Her linen was all marked E. W. About a fortnight before her death, she was brought to bed of a lifeless child.. She was supposed to be about 35 years old. Copies of letters, of her writing, dated at Hartford, Springfield, and other places, were left among her things. This account is given by the family in which she resided; and it is hoped the publication of it will be a means of informing her friends of her fate.

(256) Wilmington, September 3. A Boston paper says, in the Cato from France, came passenger, Peter OTSIQUETTE, who we are told is a son to the king of the six nations and whom the Marquis de la FAYETTE some time since sent to France to be educated.- He speaks the French and English languages with accuracy, and is acquainted with most of the branches of polite education, music, &c. and is on his way to the Indian country.

(257) Receipt to cure the Ague and Fever. Take half an ounce of bark, 20 grains of salts of wormwood, and 30 grains of snake-root, to be mixed with Madeira wine, and taken three or four times every day, till the malady is removed.

(258) Died-On Wednesday last, Mr. John KEELY.

(259) Rum and Sugar, For Sale, On board the Brigantine Nancy, Capt. B. LEACH, from Martinico, Now lying at Mr. W. CAMPBELL's Wharf.

(260) Mar. R. WILKINGS, Has For Sale, At his Store the corner of Market and Front streets, the following Medicines... Wilmington, September 3.

(261) For New-Providence, The Sloop Charlotte, Mathew BRAMHALL, Master, Will sail on Monday next. For Passage only..apply to the Master on board at Market wharf, or D. REARDAN & Co. Wilmington, Sept. 3.

(262) All Kinds of Country Produce, Sold on Commission, by E. LEVY, Who has on hand 8000 excellent Laths.

(Vol. I.) Wednesday, September 10, 1788. (Numb. 28.)

(263) New-York, August 20. Thursday last, at 12 o'clock, the foundation stone of Trinity Church was laid by the Right Reverend Samuel PROVOOST, D. D. Bishop of the Episcopal Church of New-York. On the stone is the following inscription: To the honor of Almighty God; And the Advancement of the Christian Religion, The first Stone of this Building was laid (On the site of the old Church, destroyed by fire in 1770) On the 21st Day of August, A. D. 1788, In the 13th Year of the Independence of the United States of America. The Right Reverend Samuel PROVOOST, D. D. Bishop of New-York, being Rector, The Hon. James DUANE, Esq., The Hon. John JAY, Esq. (Church Wardens.

(264) The ship Light-Horse, Capt. Ichabod NICHOLS, has Sailed from Salem, New-England for Canton, in China.

(265) We learn from Providence, Rhode-Island, that Mr. Knight DEXTER, of that town, has patriotically offered to contribute 10 acres of good land in the town of Providence, towards establishing a Manufactory.

(266) Charleston, August 29. On the 4th inst. a duel was fought in Savannah, between Mr. Thomas GIBBONS and Mr. M'QUEEN, in which both were wounded, but not mortally. Seven shots were fired at the distance of 23 feet, and only one shot missed.

(267) Wilmington, September 10. For New-York, The Sloop Nancy & Polly, John BRANSBY, Master, For Freight or passage..apply to Severin ERICHSON. Wilmington, Sept. 10.

(268) To be Rented..That large and commodious Store, With a convenient Cellar, under the Printing-Office. For terms, apply to J. KINGSBURY. Sept. 10, 1788.

(Vol. I.) Wednesday, September 17, 1788. (Numb. 29.)

(269) New-York, August 20. That John Paul JONES, Esq. is appointed Admiral in the Russian service is confirmed by the late British papers...

(270) Governor HANDLY of Georgia, by proclamation, June 19, specially required the legislature of that state to convene on the 22d day of July ult. the Creek Indians, by their agent, having signified a pacific disposition, and a desire to treat; and there being other weighty and important matters to lay before them. Thursday last his Excellency the Governor, Ezra L'HOMMEDIEU, Egbert BENSON, William FLOYD, Richard VERICK, and Samuel JONES, Esqr's. six of the Commissioners appointed by an act of legislature at their last session, for holding treaties with the Indians, set off for Fort Schuyler, where..a treaty is to be held with the Indians about the 25th instant.

(271) New-York, August 20. Arrived the ship Hercules, Capt. RUSSEL, in 28 days from Antigua. In the Hercules came passengers, the lady of Walter THIBOU, Esq. of that island, her son, Doctor THIBOU, and two daughters.. Mrs. THIBOU..died on the passage. Her remains were preserved until their arrival, and on the next day were respectfully deposited in the family vault of Mr. Daniel LUDLOW at Trinity Church, in this city...

(272) Poughkeepsie, August 12. A recent effect of the bite of a mad dog. On or about the 7th of March last, Mr. James BARRIT of Fredericksburgh, in this county, with six of his children were bit by a small puppy belonging to Mr. BARRIT..the dog.. had bit a cat, which soon run mad-this gave them some alarm: The bites however had no apparent effect on either of them until the 27th of July last, at which time one of the children, a lad in the 11th year of his age, who was bit the worst was taken with exquisite pain in the knee and leg which had been bit..the morning of the 31st.. he expired...

(273) Wilmington, September 17. .. In the county of Lincoln,..the anti-federalists had not a single vote; Col. DICKSON Dr. M'LANE, and Mr. PERKINS were chosen. Mecklenburgh have chosen Major GRIMES, Caleb PHIFER, and ____ DOUGLASS, Esquires.. His Excellency Auther ST. CLAIR, Esq. Governor of the Western Territory arrived at Muskingum on the 11th of June last.

(274) Cash Given For Turpentine, By Mar. R. WILKINGS. Wilmington, Sept. 17.

(275) To be Sold, On reasonable Terms, By Philip SPAULDING, At the house of Capt. T. CALLENDER, The following Articles, viz. New England Rum, Ginn,..Pickled Fish, Smoaked and Pickled Salmon, Sweet Oil, in jars, Cheese, Raisins, Women's Shoes, White Pine Boards, Felling Axes. Sept. 17.

(276) For New-Providence, The Schooner Ulysses, Samuel HOVEY, Master, Will sail by the first of October. For passage only, apply to the Master on board, or to Samuel VANCE. Sept. 17.

(277) To be Let,..A Commodious Brick House, With a Store, Kitchen, Cellar, and Yard, all in complete repair, on the south side of Market-street, lately occupied by Mr. Patrick BRENAN. For terms apply to J. KINGSBURY. Sept. 17.

(Vol. I.) Wednesday, September, 24, 1788. (Numb. 30.)

(278) Philadelphia, August 27. The following is a copy of a letter from Capt. Daniel THOMSON, commander of the Crown Cutter, to Capt. Stephen MOORE, belonging to this port, date Gibraltar-Bay, May 26, 1788...

(279) Petersburg, August 14. Extract of a letter, dated Fort Chisel, July 14, 1788. "A most violent war has just broke out between the people of Holstein, and the Cherokee and Chicomageo Indians. It is said the whites at different times this Spring and summer have lost about 60 persons, and the Indians lost 90; among which are the FOOL WARRIOR, OLD TASSEL, and OLD ABRAHAM, the HANGING MAW's brother, who is principal Chief of those nations...

(280) Wilmington, September 17. .. By intelligence received from the westward, as late as August 15th, we learn, that a party of 40 men under the command of Major Thomas STEWARD, having unguardedly crossed the Tenassee at Chocta Ford, was, on reaching the further Bank, attacked by a large body of Indians.. Our loss is great, upwards of 20 are yet missing, and several wounded; among the killed are young KIRK...

(281) Died-On Sunday morning last, after a short illness, greatly lamented by all her friends and acquaintances, Miss Ann BRADLEY, in the 15th year of her age. Same day Master John GREEN, son of Mr. William GREEN, of this place. On Monday morning, Mr. George JACOBS, Bricklayer.

(282) The Public are respectfully informed, that Mr. KENNA's Company of Comedians Intend opening the Theatre, with a Tragedy, called The Countess of Salisbury... Sept. 24.

(283) Fayette-Ville Races. On Wednesday the 12th of November next will be run for at Fayette-Ville..a purse of 130 pounds... Robert ROWAN, G. DUDLEY, (Managers. Sept. 24.

(Vol. I.) Wednesday, October 15, 1788. (Numb. 31.)

(284) New-York, Sept. 27. Capt. Thomas REID in the ship Alliance bound to China, sailed from Philadelphia in the month of June 1787, and arrived at Canton the 22nd day of December in the same year, having navigated on a rout as yet unpractised by any other ship. Taking sounding off the Cape of Good Hope, he steered to the south-east-ward, encircling all the eastern and southern islands of the Indian ocean-passing the South Cape of New Holland: and on their passage to the Northward again towards Canton; between the latitude of 7 and 4 degrees south-and between the longitude of 156 and 162 degrees east-they discovered a number of islands-the inhabitants of which were black-with curled and wooly hair-.. About the latitude of eight degrees north-and in the longitude of 160 degrees East they discovered two other islands-inhabited by a brown people-with straight black hair..by the behaviour of the inhabitants-the ship's company..believe they were the first discoverers.-One of them was named Morris island-the other Alliance island. They did not land on any of them...

(285) Wilmington, October 15. The Printers hereof have been unable to publish a Paper the last two weeks, and only Half a Sheet this week, owing to the severe sickness which still continues in their Office...

(286) Died on Sunday Morning last, after a long and painful illness, Mr. Jehu DAVIS.

(287) Education. In order to render himself more extensively useful to Wilmington and its Vicinity-the Reverend Mr. STEWART proposes opening School... Wilmington, Sept. 30th, 1788.

(288) Wanted immediately, About 7000 Dollars In PIERCE's Final Settlements, for which good Indigo will be given. Apply to Lewis DUPRE, (Brunswick County,-Or Cornelius DUPRE, (Little River.- Sept. 15, 1788.

(289) Came to the Subscriber's Plantation on Sunday last, a Negro Fellow, who says his Name is HARRY.-He speaks very broken, & can give no account where he came from: He says his Master is dead:-He appears to be about 30 years of age, thick set, and 5 Feet high... Edward RUSSEL, (Living on the Sound.- Wilmington, October 13.

(Vol. I.) Wednesday, October 26, 1788. (Numb. 32.)

(290) From the London Gazette. St. James's July 12. The following address of the agents for the American Loyalists, has been presented to the King... W. PEPPEREL, for the Massachusetts loyalists. J. WENTWORTH, jun. for the New-Hampshire loyalists. George ROME, for the Rhode-Island loyalists. Ja. DELANCEY, for the New-York loyalists. David OGDEN, for the New-Jersey loyalists. Joseph GALLOWAY, for the Pennsylvania and Delaware loyalists. Robert ALEXANDER, for the Maryland loyalists. John R. GRIMES, for the Virginia loyalists. Henry Eustace M'CULLOH, for the North-Carolina loyalists. James SIMPSON, for the South-Carolina loyalists. William KNOX, for the Georgia loyalists. John GRAHAM, late lieutenant governor of Georgia, and joint agent for the Georgia loyalists.

(291) Newport, Sept. 11. We learn from Nova-Scotia, that the highest suspicion prevails there, that the infamous traitor Benedict ARNOLD, set fire to his own house, having previously effected an insurance in London upon it to a much larger amount than the real value of his property...

(292) Philadelphia, September 22. Tuesday the general assembly of this commonwealth elected the hon. William M'KAY and Robert MORRIS, Esquires, representatives for this state in the federal senate.

(293) Just Imported, In the Brig Recovery, And to be Sold by the Subscriber, at his Store, in Quince's Alley..New-England Rum, Brown Sugar and Loaf Sugar, Coarse Salt, Chocolate, Flax, Bar Iron, Maple Desks, Cheese... Christopher ELLERY. Wilmington, Oct. 26.

(294) Wax-Work. For the Entertainment of the Curious! The following Figures of Wax-Work may be seen at the House of Major KINGSBURY, nearly opposite the Market. An excellent Likeness of his Excellency General WASHINGTON, in his Military Dress.. The Reverend Dr. ROGERS of New-York,..The King of Great-Britain..King Herod's Wife.. Tickets..may be had at Mr. John CAMPBELL's Store, and at the Printing-Office. Wilmington, October 24, 1788.

(295) For Sale, By the Subscriber, Maple Desks and Dining Tables, Calf Skin and Neat's Leather Boot Legs, About 14 dozen pair Men's coarse Shoes. Thomas CALLENDER. Wilmington, Oct. 26.

(296) John BURGWIN, Has For Sale, At his Store, in Wilmington, A few Bales of Coarse Cloths.. Mr. BURGWIN, once more, (and for the last time) Requests All Person indebted to him, or to Charles JEWKES & Co. to make immediate payment.. He will sell all his Lands in Bladen and Cumberland Counties... Wilmington, October 21,1788

(297) At Public Vendue. The 8th of November, Will Be Sold,..Sundry Household Furniture Belonging to FONTAINE & MORIN. Who have for Sale, genuine Holland Gin... Wilmington, October 28.

(298) Whereas the subscriber did purchase of Aaron PLUMMER, a piece of Land, and did give the said PLUMMER the following obligations, in part of the sum agreed upon ..as the price of the same. A note of hand, signed William WATSON and James MOOREHEAD, for 31 pounds odd shillings, payable January, 1787. Another note for 125 pounds..payable in January, 1788. Another note for 125 pounds payable July, 1788, signed as the beforementioned. Now, having discovered that the said Aaron PLUMMER's title to the..land is not good and sufficient..-I do forewarn all persons that myself nor..James MOOREHEAD will not pay the same nor any part thereof. William WATSON. Bladen County, October, 1788. N. B. The first-mentioned note is supposed to be in the hands of Mr. Lewis BARGE, of Fayette-Ville, and the other two in the possession of Mr. James COUNCIL, of Bladen.

(299) BOWEN & HOWARD, Have for Sale at their Office, near the Market, Writing Paper Blank Account Books, The Chorister's Companion,..The American Singing Book..Wrapping Paper, Paste Board, for Bonnets, Sealing Wax, Ink-Powder, Ink-Stands, and Blanks of all Kinds.

(Vol. I.) Wednesday, November 5, 1788. (Numb. 33.)

(300) Boston, September 30. The city now forming on the banks of the Ohio, is named Merietta, in honour of the Queen of France. Joseph MAY?, Esq. of Boston, has presented a Bell to the Ohio Company, for the first public building to be erected in the territory of the Company;..the directors are to take measures for transporting the bell from Boston to the city of Marietta.

(301) Wilmington, November 5. Died-On Monday last, Mrs. Margaret HILL, aged 54 years.

(302) Wax-Work, As large as Life, For the Entertainment of the Curious! The following Figures of Wax-Work..will be exhibited at Fayette-Ville..this Wax-Work is the

(303) For Cork, The Ship Norval, David HARVIE, Master, Will sail in 12 Days. For passage..apply to the Captain on board, or Henry TOOMER. Wilmington, Nov. 4.

(304) Whereas the subscriber did..about..August last, give his obligation together with Mr. Patrick BRENAN, to Solomon HAMMER, pilot, for the sum of 85 pounds currency, or thereabouts, payable in January next-This is to forewarn all persons not to purchase said obligation, as the property for which said obligation was given proves not to be valid. James BRANAN. Wilmington, Nov. 4, 1788.

(Vol. I.) Wednesday, November 12, 1788. (Numb. 34.)

(305) Wilmington, November 12. Nothing particular has transpired from the honourable legislature since our last, except that the hon. Alexander MARTIN, Esq. is appointed Speaker of the honorable the Senate, and the hon. John SITGREAVES, Esq. speaker of the Commons.

(306) Died-On the 4th instant, Mrs. Elizabeth HILL, consort of William H. HILL, Esq.

(307) To be Leased, From this date until the 10th day of June, 1791, A Lot of Land, in Mr. TOOMER's Alley, 58 feet front and 54 feet deep, whereon there is a Warehouse.. a Cooper's Shop..three Stables, a Necessary House, and the Yard securely fenced. For terms apply to Henry URQUHART. Wilmington, Nov. 12.

(308) To Let, That pleasant and commodious Dwelling-House, Offices, Gardens, &c. which the subscriber now possesses. Who has also for Sale, A Wharf and Water Lot, in the town of Wilmington, situated between Mr. Peter MALLET's Wharf and Mrs. QUINCE's, formerly the property of Mr. FLOWERS. For..particulars enquire of James FLEEMING. Nov. 12. (Note: Issue of 19 November 1788 shows addition of "Or John BLEAKLY.".)

(309) The Subscriber has for Sale, Two Saw-Mills, On BLUNT's Creek, within three quarters of a mile of Fayette-Ville.. Also, About 2000 acres of well-timbered land.. For terms please apply to Mr. Joshua POTTS, Wilmington, Mr. Alexander MC IVER, at Fayette-Ville or the subscriber in Chatham County. James PATERSON. Nov. 12, 1788.

(Vol. I.) Wednesday, November 19, 1788. (Numb. 35.)

(310) Boston, October 8. A correspondent has favoured us with an account of the cargo of the ship Alliance, Capt. REID, lately arrived at Philadelphia from Canton- which is as follows: 1,725 Chests Bohea tea, 710 Chests Hyson do., 384 Chests Souchong do., 35 Chests Silks, 15 Chests Nankeens, 321 Chests China. Valued at 75,000 l. currency. The above ship and cargo..are owned entirely by Robert MORRIS, Esq. of Philadelphia..

(311) Wilmington, November 19. Tuesday the 11th inst. came on the election of Governor, Secretary, and Councillors for the ensuing year, when his Excellency Samuel JOHNSTON, Esq. was re-elected Governor, and James GLASGOW, Esq. Secretary. Councillors. The honorable John SKINNER, Whitmil HILL, John KNICHEN, Josiah COLLINS, James ARMSTRONG, Demsey CONNOR, and James IREDELL, Esquires.

(312) The subscriber forewarns all persons indebted to the house which went under the name of DUBRUTZ, in Fayette-Ville, from June, 1785, to delay payment..until the accounts between the said DUBRUTZ and the subscriber, who is the co-partner and principal proprietor..are adjusted..now depending in the Court of Equity, to be held in Fayette-Ville, on the 20th of December next. J. B. BROUARD. Fayette-Ville, Nov. 12.

(313) Just Landed, From the Ship Queen of France, William COOK, Master, From Martinico, And now For Sale..High proof West-India Rum, Molasses, Muscovada Sugar..Coffee ... Enquire of F. PEYRINNAUT. Wilmington, Nov. 19.

(314) To the Public. The subscriber proposes opening a School in this town, for the purpose of teaching Reading, Writing, Arithmetic, English Grammar, and Geography: -Also, the Latin and Greek Languages... Isaac SESSIONS. Fayette-Ville, Nov. 15, 1788.

(315) Notice is hereby given, to all persons whom it may concern, that my supposed wife, Priscilla HATCHER, by maiden name, and now goes by the name of Priscilla JOHNSON, as by a marriage name; the said unlawful woman has absented herself from her supposed husband's lawful commands-I the subscriber hereby forewarn all persons, under no pretence, to rely on me by the said above-mentioned woman... Matthew JOHNSON. Wilmington, Nov. 19.

(Vol. I.) Wednesday, November 26, 1788. (Numb.   .)

(316) Portland, (Massachusetts) Oct. 9. In the Salem paper of yesterday..respecting the Alliance Indiaman, viz. We feel a degree of pleasure in saying, that Robert MORRIS, Esq. is not the only individual in America of sufficient ability and enterprise to own an Indiaman and cargo. Elias Hasket DERBY, Esq. of this town, has been solely concerned in several voyages to the East-Indies: The ship Grand-Turk, Captain WEST..from New-England to Canton, in May 1787; The ship Three Sisters, Captain NICHOLS..from this port in December 1786..the bark Light-Horse, Captain TUCKER..the ship Grand-Turk, Captain DERBY..December 1787; ship Juno, Captain ELKINS, in January 1788, but foundered..ship Light-Horse, Captain NICHOLS, last August..ship Atlantic, Captain ELKINS, last month.

(317) New-London, October 24. The Honorable Legislature of this state have appointed the Honurable William S. JOHNSTON, and Oliver ELLSWORTH, Esquires, for their Representatives in the Senate of the United States.

(318) Middletown, October 13. Extract of a letter from a gentleman at Marietta to his friend in this city dated September 8, 1788. "An accurate survey of the ancient ruins within the limits of our city has been made..that we may be able to ascertain all the facts respecting them; in the course of this survey, we had several of the large trees on the parapet of those works cut down, and have examined their ages by the rings or grains from the heart to the surface, computing each grain to be one years growth: we found one tree to have stood 443 years another 289, situated so as to leave no room to doubt of their having began to grow since those works were abandoned. We find the perpendicular height of the walls of this covert to be at this time 20 feet, and the base 39, the width 12 rods."

(319) Charleston, October 27. Kalendar of Convictions, at the court of General Sessions, for October, 1788. Nathaniel WINTER, for murder, to be hanged on the 28th inst.-Jeremiah SMITH, for horse-stealing, to be hanged on the 28th inst.-William PARKS, larceny, to receive 29 lashes-William HANAGHAN, larceny, to receive 29 lashes.

(320) Wilmington, November 26. Last evening arrived in this port, the Sloop Industry, Capt. DUNN, with whom came passengers-Mrs. HARNETT, Captain HANDS, Captain BARNES, and Mr. H. J. RICHARDS.

(321) House of Commons, Fayette-Ville, November 10, 1788.. November 12. His Excellency Samuel JOHNSTON, Esq. was again elected Governor of this state for the en-

(321) (Cont.) suing year. The honorable John SKINNER, James IREDELL, John KINCHEN, James ARMSTRONG, Josiah COLLINS, Whitmill HILL, and Dempsey CONNER Esquires, were elected members of the council. November 15. The Commons went into a committee of the whole house, to take under consideration the propriety of calling another convention, to take under further consideration the constitution proposed for the future government of the United States-Mr. MEBANE in the Chair.. Resolved,..it is not now expedient to call a new Convention. On the question to concur with this Resolution, the yeas and nays were required by Mr. W. I. LEWIS...

(322) Fayette-Ville, Nov. 18, 1788. This day the Grand Lodge proceeded to ballot for the Grand Officers for the ensuing year, when The Most Worshipful Richard CASWELL Esq. was elected Grand Master, The Right Worshipful Michael PAYNE, Esq. Deputy Grand Master. The Right Worshipful James GLASGOW, Esq. Grand Senior Warden. The Right Worshipful S. W. ARNETT, Esq. Grand Junior Warden, The Right Worshipful Stephen CABARRUS, Esq. Grand Treasurer, The Right Worshipful W. J. DAWSON, Esq. Grand Secretary.

(Vol. I.) Wednesday, December 3, 1788. (Numb.   .)

(323) Wilmington, December 3. We hear from Bladen County, that on Wednesday last, Mr. BURGWIN's elegant Seat at Marsh-Castle, occupied by Mr. Donald BANE, took fire, by accident or neglect, and was consumed to ashes in a few hours.

(324) The honorable George READ and Richard BASSET, Esquires, are appointed to represent the state of Delaware in the Senate of the United States. The honorable Richard Henry LEE, and William GRAYSON, Esquires, are appointed to represent the commonwealth of Virginia in the Senate of the United States. Cyrus GRIFFIN, John BROWN, James MADISON, Jun., John DAWSON, and Mann PAGE, Esquires, are appointed to represent the commonwealth of Virginia in Congress, until the first Wednesday in March next.

(325) For London, The Snow Mariah, a prime Sailor, and a British bottom, Malcolm WILKIE, master, now lying at QUINCE's Wharf..will be clear to sail in all the month of January.-For freight or passage, apply to the Master on board, or to WALKER & YOUNGER.

(326) To be Let, (And entered immediately) That Commodious House, belonging to the Subscriber, situate in Market-street. L. DORSEY. December 3, 1788. (Note: The issues of 10 December and 18 December, respectively, show "La. DORSEY" and "L. A. DORSEY")

(327) To Let, That commodious Dwelling-House, Kitchen, Garden, &c. situate in Market-street, lately occupied by Mrs. Margaret HILL.. For terms, apply to John HILL, W. H. HILL. December 3, 1788.

(Vol. I.) Wednesday, December 10, 1788. (Numb. 38.)

(328) Norfolk, November 26. A..correspondent wonders..that among the many gentlemen mentioned of late in the newspapers as fit and proper persons (and candidates) for the Vice President's Chair..the hon. Charles THOMPSON has never been mentioned.

(329) Wilmington, December 10. The following gentlemen are appointed to represent this state in a continental convention, for the purpose of amending the constitution, should two-thirds of the states petition Congress therefor, viz. General LOCK, General PARSONS, Timothy BLOODWORTH, Esq., Joseph MC DOWEL, sen. Esq. and Col. LENORE.

(330) State of North-Carolina. In General Assembly, November 17, 1788. Resolved,

(330) (Cont.) That it is the opinion of this House, a new Convention be recommended for the purpose of reconsidering the new constitution... Alex. MARTIN, S. S. John SITCREAVES, S. C.

(331) Wanted, As an Overseer, A Steady, sober Man, who can be well recommended for his integrity, &c. and acquainted with corn and rice planting... J. BURGWIN. Wilmington, Dec. 9.

(332) To be Sold, By Private Contract, That well known valuable Plantation, situated on Cape-Fear River, in North-Carolina, containing 1000 acres..known..by the name of the Pleasant Oaks. Also, the whole or any part of the subscriber's land on Little-River... Francis ALLSTON, Little-River, Dec. 6, 1788.

(333) Stolen from the subscriber last week, a Silver Table Spoon, marked $G^M M$: Whoever will give information of the Spoon so that it may be recovered, shall receive Ten Shillings reward, by applying to Mary MEEK. Wilmington, Dec. 9, 1788.

(Vol. I.) Thursday, December 18, 1788. (Numb. 39.)

(334) Wilmington, December 18. On Saturday the 7th instant, the honorable Legislature of this state adjournes.. During their session, the following acts have been passed, viz..Empowering Thomas JOHNSTON, late sheriff of Onslow county, his heirs, executors, and administrators, to collect the sinking fund tax, due from that county, &c... To amend an act passed in..1783, entitled, an act to vest certain lands in fee simple, in Richard HENDERSON and others.. To quiet in the possession of William SCOTT, certain lands therein described.. For erecting a town on the lands of Thomas DOUGGAN in Randolph county.. To emancipate a certain Negro slave name PHILLIS, the property of George JACOBS.. To authorise and enable John COLSON to return into this state, and exercise the privileges therein mentioned.. To enable John MC GEE to inherit and recover the estate of his reputed brother, Jesse STEED, deceased.. To amend an act, entitled, an act to erect a town on the lands of Matthew FIGURES, in Northampton county.. To empower the county court of Cumberland to appoint inspectors for the warehouse built in Fayette-Ville, by Robertson MUMFORD and James PORTERFIELD.

(335) The Wilmington Centinel will infuture be published every Thursday, in order to give our readers the latest intelligence we may receive by the post, who arrives on Wednesday. This day's paper completes the term of nine months since the first publication of the Wilmington Centinel, &c.

(336) The Printing-Office is removed to the Store lately occupied by Mess. George HOOPER & Co. the South side of the Market.

(337) State of North-Carolina. Newbern District. In the Court of Equity, November Term, 1788. In the suit therein depending, whereon James ELLIS is complainant, and Eliphalet RIPLEY, defendant.-It is Ordered, That the defendant put in his answer..on or before..the 20th of May next..on the defendant failing in obedience to this order..bill is to be taken pro confesso.. Published by order of the Court. James ELLIS, Clerk & Master (of the aforesaid Court.

(338) The Store near the Market, Lately occupied by Messrs. George HOOPER, & Co. is now Improved by Amaziah JOCELIN, As A Commission Store.. He had now for Sale- Molasses, Sugar, Northward Rum, Salt, Souchong Tea, Shoes, Several Articles of Dry Goods, Also, Flax, Flax-Seed, Flour, Butter, &c. He would also, respectfully inform the Public, that he has it in contemplation, to open, in a few days, an Intel-

(338) (Cont.) ligence-Office;.. The objects of this office will be, 1st. To introduce buyers and sellers..Persons wanting employment.. 2dly. To give the best information to strangers who come into this port, for the purpose of trade... Wilmington, Dec. 17, 1788.

(339) State of North-Carolina. Newbern District. In the Court of Equity, November Term, 1788. In the suit therein depending, whereon Francois Xavier MARTIN is complainant, and Thomas DAVIS, defendant-It is Ordered, That the defendant put in his answer to the complainants bill, on or before..the 20th day of May next..on failing in obedience to this order, the complainant's bill is to be taken pro confesso... Published by order of the Court. James ELLIS, Clerk & Master (of the aforsaid court.

(Vol I.) Thursday, December 25, 1788. (Numb. 40.)

(340) Dublin, October 3. Mr. Thomas BARCLAY, the American consul-general in France, after concluding a treaty with the emperor of Morocco, visited others of the Barbary states...

(341) Philadelphia, November 24. Extract of a letter from a gentleman in New-York, to his friend in this city.. "The legislature of Massachusetts have elected Governor BOWDOIN and the hon. Caleb STRONG, Esq. the representatives of that truly federal commonwealth in the senate of the United States."

(342) Norfolk, December 3. On Monday night, 24th ult. a most daring Piracy was committed by two villains on the Schooner Nancy, Solomon ASHBY, Master, on her voyage to Baltimore. These men boarded said vessel late in the evening armed with musquets.. with menaces of instant death if any resistance was made. The master..made his escape.. The above schooner is American built; her frame and top timbers all of red cedar.. Her bottom is painted with a Spanish brown-her sides yellow-and her quarters and stern green-her cabin is of a lead colour, and has three good births. The names of the two lads belonging to her were Stephen FLETCHER and John COVINGTON.

(343) Wilmington, December 25. Died-On Friday last, Mr. John BERNARD.

(344) Those Brethren of the Antient and Honorable Fraternity of Free and Accepted Masons, who are desirous of reviving that friendly institution in this town, under the Grand Lodge of North-Carolina, are informed, that a Room will be prepared for their reception, at L. A. DORSEY's New Tavern and Coffee-House, on St. John's Day, the 27th instant, at Six o'Clock in the evening.

1789 - All issues missing except for the following from the University of North Carolina Library-January 8-March 5.

(Vol. I.) Thursday, January 8, 1789. (Numb. 42.)

(345) Charleston, December 29. Masonary. Last Saturday, being the festival of St. John the Evangelist, the Grand Lodge of free and accepted ancient Masons..met in their Lodge-Room at the house of brother M'CRADY..when the following brethren were installed Grand Officers for the ensuing year, viz. The Hon. and Right Worshipful William DRAYTON, Esq. Grand Master. The Hon. and Right Worshipful Brigadier General Mordecai GILL, Esq. Deputy Grand Master. The Right Worshipful T. B. BOWEN, Esq. Senior Grand Warden. The Right Worshipful John MITCHELL, Esq. Junior Grand Warden. The Right Worshipful Mr. Robert KNOX, Grand Treasurer. The Right Worshipful Mr. Alexander ALEXANDER, Grand Secretary.

(346) Augusta, (Georgia) October 25. We hear by way of General Joseph MARTIN, lately from the Western Waters, that about the 10th instant John SEVIER, late Governor of Franklin, with a party of his adherents, rode up to a store in that country, purchased and drank rum till they were very much intoxicated. The merchant..told them they should have no more. This conduct exasperated SEVIER; he immediately drew his pistol, and advanced towards the merchant,.. An unfortunate by-stander..stepped in between them, and was shot through the body by SEVIER. He..rode off with great precipitation, but was..pursued and overtaken by Col. TIPTON, who confined and conducted him to Burke gaol, in North-Carolina, where he is now in irons.

(347) Wilmington, January 8, 1789. A Lodge of Free and Ancient York Masons, (under the name of the Wilmington Saint John's) was opened in this town on the evening of the first instant.. The following Brethren were appointed..until the 24th day of June next, viz. The Right Worshipful Brother William CAMPBELL, Master. Brother James WALKER, Sen. Warden. Brother John MACKENZIE, Jun. Warden. Brother John CAMPBELL, Secretary. Brother L. A. DORSEY, Treasurer. Brother Peter MAXWELL, Brother John BRADLEY, Stewards.

(348) At the annual election held on Monday last, for Town Commissioners, the following gentlemen were chosen, viz.-Mr. Henry TOOMER, Mr. George HOOPER, Mr. Mar. R. WILKINGS, Mr. John CAMPBELL, Mr. John TELFAIR. Yesterday were appointed by the County Court, Inspectors of Exports for the present year, Mr. Thomas CALLENDER and Mr. Henry HOSKINS.

(349) Senators of the United States already chosen. Virginia-Honorable William GRAYSON and Richard Henry LEE, Esquires. Delaware-Honorable George REED and Richard BASSET, Esq'rs. Pennsylvania-Hon. Robert MORRIS and W. MACLAY, Esquires. New-Jersey-Hon. William PATTERSON and Jonathan ELMER, Esquires. New-Hampshire-Hon. John LANGDON and ____ BARTLET, Esquires. Massachusetts-Hon. Caleb STRONG and Tristram DALTON, Esquires. Connecticut-Hon. W. S. JOHNSON and O. ELLSWORTH, Esquires. Maryland-Hon. John HENRY and Charles CARROL, Esq'rs.

(350) Lawrence A. DORSEY, Requests all persons indebted to him to make immediate payment... Wilmington, Jan. 8, 1789.

(351) (Beginning of this advertisement torn off.) A Reward of Fifty Shillings will be given to any person who will apprehend and deliver either of the above-mentioned fellows to the subscriber, or Five Pounds for both... John GUERARD. January 2, 1789

(352) Was Found, About three Months since, near TOOMER's Bridge, by a Negro Man, A Small Red Morocco Pocket Book, containing a few papers only, which appear to be of little value-On the out side of the Pocket Book is written Jacob CAPEHART. The Pocket-Book is left with the Printers hereof, and may be had upon paying the expense of this advertisement. Wilmington, January 8, 1789.

(353) The Subscriber, for the Last Time, calls on those who are indebted to the estate of Parker QUINCE, Esq. deceased, for Negro Hire, &c. to settle the same before the First Day of February next... Thomas CALLENDER, Es'r. Wilmington, Jan. 8, 1789.

(Vol. I.) Thursday, January 15, 1789. (Numb. 43.)

(354) The American Cotton Manufactory, To the Board of Managers of the Pennsylvania Society for promoting Manufactures and the Useful Arts: The Report of the Committee for Manufacture... Samuel WETHERILL, Jun. Chairman pro tem... George CLYMER, Tenche

(354) (Cont.) COXE. The foregoing report being read and approved, was ordered for publication. Jos. B. M'KEAN, Secretary.

(355) Boston, December 18. We hear from the North Parish in Bridgwater, that last Saturday, an apprentice of Mr. James PERKINS, a lad about 14 years of age, named Ephraim GROVES, being under the spindle of a grindstone which was going by water, had the hair of his head caught by the spindle, wound around it, and drawn with such force, as to tear off all the skin where his hair grew and from his forehead down to his eyes, taking his eye-brows and one of his ears.. He received no other injury, and is at present so comfortable, that there is some hopes that he may recover from this very painful, afflicting, and hazardous disaster.

(Note: The right margin of the next three items has been torn away.)

(356) Wilmington, January 15, 1789. William SMITH, AEdanus BURKE, Daniel HUGER, Thoma____ and Thomas Tudor TUCKER, Esquires, are chosen repres____ the new Congress for the state of South-Carolina. Jonathan STURGES, Benjamin HUNTINGTON, Jonathan ____, Roger SHERMAN, Jeremiah WADSWORTH, Stephen M. Mit____ HILLHOUSE, Erastus WOLCOTT, Jesse ROOT, John TREADWELL, an____ ab SORONG, Esquires, are in nomination as representatives ____ ____ state of Connecticut to the new Congress of the United States.

(357) Married-In Charleston, ____ the 28th ult. Major Edward PL____ of the late American army, (Massac__setts line) to the accomplished ____ Susannah Frances BRACKSDALE, of ____ city.

(358) Died-On Friday the 12th ____ Mr. Miles HUNTER, Printer, of Pete__burg.

(359) To be Let, A Large Brick House, in Front-street, just finished, and well calculated for a tavern. Apply to Henry TOOMER. January 15, 1789.

(360) (All but the following torn away.) Flats, or at Thre__ at Wilmington. Apply to George HOOPER & Co. Jan. 15.

(361) North-Carolina, Salisbury District.sc. Rule of Court, September Session, 1788. Thomas PINKSTONE, vs. Daniel W. EASLEY, sc. No. 8, Chancery docquet. Be it known to all whom it may concern, that the plaintiffs bill shall be taken pro confesso, unless the defendant file his answer in the Master's office, or render reasons satisfactory to the honorable court within the first three days of the next term, which will commence on the 15th day of March, 1789. Published by order, John STEELE, Master in Chancery, (for the district of Salisbury. Jan. 15.

(362) Run Away From the Subscriber, A Negro Fellow named BUCK, well known in and about Wilmington. Also, A Mulatto Fellow, Named PARKER, a cooper by trade, well known in and about Elizabeth-Town.. The latter formerly belonged to Captain RAFORD, and was purchased by me of Capt. James BRADLEY of Elizabeth-Town. A Reward of 50 Shillings..to deliver either..or Five Pounds for both... John GUERARD. January 2, 1789.

(Vol. I.) Thursday, January 22, 1789. (Numb. 44.)

(363) Speech of his Excellency George CLINTON, Esq. to both Houses of the Legislature of the state of New-York, convened at Albany on the 11th ultimo...

(364) Charleston, January 19. The legislature of the state of North-Carolina..have appointed William STEELE, Esq. of that state a commissioner, in conjunction with the superintendant and commissioners of Georgia and this state, agreeable to the resolu-

(364) (Cont.) tions of Congress to treat with the Cherokees and Chuckamawgau Indians, respecting boundaries..they have also appointed Alexander DROMGOOLE, Esq. as an ambassador to negociate a cessation of hostilities with the Cherokees and Chuckamawgau Indians; to invite them to a treaty at Swannanoe..and to carry a letter from the executive of that state, directed to his Excellency Alexander M'GILVERY, Esq. chief of the Creek nation...

(365) On Saturday forenoon Major A. A. MULLER, a member of the house of representatives, was accosted at the corner of a street, by Mr. John Christian SMITH, in very scurrilous language, and, without receiving any answer, fired off a gun pointed at his breast. The ball only grazed the abdomen slightly, so that the wound is in a fair way of being soon cured. Mr. SMITH rode off, and has not since been heard of.

(366) Wilmington, January 22, 1789. The Commissioners of Pilotage, for the bar and harbour of Charleston, have given public notice, that the Light-House opposite the Ship Channel..is Now Lighted. Captain William HOWLAND, of the sloop Industry, from Newport, Rhode-Island, bound to this port, after he had been out from that place one day, off the Capes of Delaware, fell in with the brig Defiance, James TOMMINGS, master from Martha-Brae, Jamaica, bound to New-York, in great distress, having been at sea 70 days-entirely dismasted-her bowsprit gone-and three of the crew dead, without provisions of any kind. Capt. HOWLAND took her in tow..carried her into Newport...

(367) The Schooner Dispatch, Capt. Philip STEVENS, which sailed from this port the 15th of October last, for St. Croix, was lost the 10th November, on Anegada reef, in the West-Indies, and nothing saved but the lives of the crew.

(368) Married-On the 8th instant, Mr. John DAVIS, to Miss Harriet ASH, daughter of the late General ASH.

(369) Died-On Sunday evening last, Mr. Thomas HARRACKS, merchant.

(370) Run Away, A Young Negro Fellow, named JACOB, lately the property of Alfred MOORE, Esq. on whom he used to attend as a waiting man..a reward of Three Pounds... W. H. HILL, Wilmington, January 22.

(371) To be Sold, By virtue of powers from the widow and heirs of William WIMBLE, deceased, who was the son and heir at law of James WIMBLE, deceased. All the estate, right, title, and interest of which the said William WIMBLE died possessed, excepting such lots as have been disposed of on execution, consisting of about from 90 to 100 lots at least, on the lower part of the town of Wilmington, of which one is a water lot, joining Mr. CRAIKE's fence on the north side, divided by the new street, and containing about an acre and a quarter of ground-About 12 lots between front-street and second-street..together with about 160 acres of land joining the Back-street.. For further particulars, enquire of Gillam BASS, at Capt. Thomas CALLENDER's. Wilmington January 22, 1789.

(372) Salt. The cargo of the ship Union, Capt. COWARD, from St. Ubes, for sale.. at Wilmington... George HOOPER & Co.

(Vol. I.) Thursday, January 29, 1789. (Numb. 45.)

(373) Providence, December 23. On Tuesday the brig Polly, Capt. Samuel JOHNSON, arrived here from Rochelle, after a passage of 60 days.

(374) It is with singular pleasure that we discover, that the Hon. John ADAMS, Esq. is generally spoken of in the Eastern States for Vice-President of the United States.

(375) Baltimore, January 2. It appears by the late New-York News-Papers, that that city hath been..infested by a Gang of armed villains.. These daring miscreants have committed divers street-robberies and Burglaries, and a few nights since, they assaulted Dr. James COGSWELL, who was shot with a pistol, and narrowly escaped immediate death...

(376) Wilmington, January 29, 1789. The brig Neptune, Captain Zacha i h WOODBURY, from Kingston, Jamaica, to this port,..struck on the Middle Ground on the Bar, last Monday, and was entirely lost. The captain and crew are saved. It is said she had 1000 l. in cash on board..also lost with the vessel.

(377) Last Monday evening was Married, at the seat of Benjamin SMITH, Esq. Mr. Francis BRICE, Merchant, of the Island of Jamaica, to Miss Betsy JONES, of this place.

(378) Died-On the 22d instant, at Mr. James BURNSIDE's tavern, Fayette-Ville, Charles M'KENNA, a native of Scotland. He had been drinking freely with some of his companions, until he appeared a little intoxicated, and layed down on a bench in the Tavern, ..layed so still, that people..supposed him asleep.. He lately came into Wilmington from Barbadoes-had..followed the seas for a number of years-went up the river from Wilmington in one of the Fayette-Ville boats a day or two before his death. He appeared about 35 years of age, middle stature and of a strong healthy constitution.

(379) To be Let, By the Subscriber, For any term between one and seven years, That well known Plantation formerly belonging to Thomas RUTHERFORD, Esq. known by the name of Tweed Side, situated on Cape-Fear River, five miles above Fayette-Ville, containing near 600 acres.. There are likewise a large number of peach, apple, and plumb trees, with a comfortable Dwelling and other Out-Houses, and an excellent Garden well pailed in..apply to Jean SIMSON. Fayette-Ville, January 26.

(380) Amaziah JOCELIN, Has For Sale, At His Commission Store; Rum, Sugar..joiners and Masons Tools..Frying Pans, Beaver Hats... January 29, 1789.

(381) To Be Sold, By Henry DAYTON, At his Store in Market Street, By Wholesale, West India Rum..Coffee and Chocolate, Gin and Brandy, Powder and Shot... Wilmington, Jan. 29.

(382) For Sale, The following Lands, of the Estate of the late Cornelius HARNETT, Esquire, viz. Four Hundred Acres on the South side of Ehoree river, on DUNCAN's Creek, above William ROBISON's survey, patented by the said C. HARNETT, in the year 1754. Also-Three Hundred Acres on the South-West side of Pee Dee river, on the East side of Lick Crick, of JONES's Creek, in the home line of GOLD's land on the said Creek; bounding also on PLUNKET's line and RIDGES' branch, patented by William POWEL, in the year 1758. Apply to Mrs. HARNETT, or to John HUSKE. Wilmington, Jan. 27, 1789.

(383) On the Tenth Day of February next, will be Hired, on the Plantation of the late John GRANGE, Esquire, until the first of January next, A Number of Negroes, part of the property of the said deceased. Also, Will be rented for the said term, A valuable Plantation-with a large commodious Dwelling-House.. Thomas NEALE, jun., John HALL, Admr's. North-West, January, 1789.

(384) Run Away from the subscriber, living on Edisto river, in South-Carolina, in

(384) (Cont.) January, 1787, a Negro fellow named WILL (but am informed he now passes by the name of Joseph ASHLEY, as a freeman.) He is about five feet high, very black, round face, about 25 years of age..he was born in New-York, but has lived till within these three years past in Boston. He procured a pass from a sailor in Charleston, previous to my purchasing him..which..he got signed by Col. THOMPSON, Mr. STEELE, of Salisbury, Major MOORE, of Fayette-Ville, and several others.. Ten Guineas for..reward... James WILSON. December 21, 1788.

(Vol. I.) Thursday, February 5, 1789. (Numb. 46.)

(385) Albany, December 29. In our paper of Monday last, we mentioned that the hon. senate had nominated the hon. Philip SCHUYLER and hon. Robert YATES Esqs. to represent this state in the senate of the United States. Since which the hon. house of assembly have disagreed to that nomination, and rejected the bill.

(386) Wilmington, February 5, 1789. On the 3d ult. was married at Bloomingdale, near the city of New-York, the Hon. Hugh WILLIAMSON, Delegate in Congress from this state, to the lovely and accomplished Miss Maria APTHORP, daughter of Charles W. APTHORP, Esq. They were married by the Right Rev. Dr. PROVOOST, Bishop of the Episcopal Church, and one of the Chaplains of Congress.

(387) The Artillery Company is desired to attend at the Parade on Monday the 9th inst. for a private muster. John HUSKE, Capt. Artillery.

(388) Notice. At a meeting of the Commissioners for the town of Wilmington, held at DORSEY's on the 28th of January, 1789, .. Ordered, That the following places be the receptacles for all kinds of dirt or rubbish from the streets of the town-In Second-street, the hollow between the house occupied by Mr. Alexander HOSTLER and the house of Mrs. BOYD. In the same street, the hollow between the East end of the lot formerly belonging to Mr. John LYON and the West end of Mr. Archibald MACLAINE's lot. The hollow in Dock street, below the intersection of Front street.. Ordered, That Mr. John ALLAN be appointed to take charge of the Fire Engine..and that he be allowed the sum of eight pounds for the same, and for keeping said Engine in good order; and that he have two additional keys made to the lock of said Engine-House, one of which to be kept by Mr. Robert WILKINGS, one by Mr. John CAMPBELL, and..the other key..be kept by Mr. John ALLAN.. Resolved, That the Commissioners will visit every house in town, on the third Monday in February, for the purpose of inspecting the Fire Buckets and Bags, when all defaulters may expect to be fined as the ordinance in that case directs. By Order, Isaac BERNARD, T. Clerk.

(389) For Sale, The Ship Charming Polly, Lying in this River, With all her tackle and apparel as she came from sea, burthen about 240 tons... P. MANGEON & Co. Wilmington, Feb. 5.

(390) For Sale, By the Subscriber, at his Store in Market-Street, opposite the Naval-Office..Wines..Rum, Brown Sugar, Cotton Cards, Pickled Salmon. Philip SPAULDING. Wilmington, Feb. 4.

(391) Maurice CARMICHAEL, Of Fayette-Ville, in Cumberland County, Merchant, Being about to leave this state, takes this opportunity of publicly notifying to all.. that being about to close all matters of business transacted by him, either during the co-partnership of CARMICHAEL and BOGLE, or on his own account, since the decease of his late partner Mr. Robert BOGLE. He therefore requests..immediate payment... Fayette-Ville, Feb. 1.

(392) Imported, By the Subscriber, and For Sale at JEWKES's Warehouse, Jamaica Rum, Sugar and Coffee. Also, New and seasoned Negroes of both sexes. Cash, or Lumber of every species will be received in payment. F. BRICE. Wilmington, Feb. 3.

(393) For Sale, An Elegant New Fall-back Chaise, with Harness complete... Samuel LOWDER. Feb. 5, 1789.

(Vol. I.) Thursday, February 12, 1789. (Numb. 47.)

(394) New-York, Jan. 8. Last Sunday afternoon sailed for Bombay, the ship America Indiaman, Jacob SARLEY, Esquire, commander.

(395) New-York, Jan. 8. Mr. John GIBB, of PHILLIP's-Manor, Westchester county, on Thursday night last, was robbed of near 900 l. about seven miles of this city...

(396) Jan. 22. On Wednesday the 7th instant the general assembly of Connecticut appointed the following gentlemen electors of a President and Vice-President of the United States, viz. His excellency the Governor, his honor the Lieutenant Governor, hon. Richard LAW, hon. Matthew GRISWOLD, hon. Erastus WOLCOTT, Jedediah HUNTINGTON, Esq. Thadeus BURR, Esq.

(397) Proposals are published in Boston for printing a French newspaper, to be entitled "Le Courier De Boston"..and will be compiled and conducted by that celebrated literary character Mons. P. J. G. DE NANCREDE, a French gentleman well known..for his strong attachment to the liberties and government of this country, of which he has lately become a denizen, by a connubial tie with an amiable young lady, of a very respectable family in that town.

(398) Charleston, January 26.. The hon. Pierce BUTLER, and the hon. Ralph IZARD, were elected senators from this state in the senate of the United States. January 29. Monday last the hon. Charles PINCKNEY, elected governor of this state, attended in the house of representatives...

(399) Wilmington, February 12, 1789. To be Let, The Loft of the Market-House.-For terms apply to I. BERNARD, Town-Clerk. Feb. 12.

(400) At a meeting of the Commissioners for the town of Wilmington, held at DORSEY's on the 4th instant..Ordered, That Caleb THOMAS be, and he is hereby appointed Clerk of the Market, whose duty it shall be to inforce the foregoing ordinances... By Order, Isaac BERNARD, T. Clerk.

(401) To be Sold On Board the Brig Two Friends, Thomas DEAN, Master, Now Lying at MAXWELL's Wharf, New-England Rum.. Also-A few Bundles of choice Hay.

(402) State of North-Carolina. Fayette-Ville District. In the Court of Equity, December Term, 1788. Augustine STAUNTON, vs. Charles MC KERNAN. It is Ordered, That the Defendant do appear and answer the Complainant's bill, on or before..the 20th day of June next or in default..Complainant's bill be taken pro confesso against the Defendant. Published by order, R. MUMFORD, (Clerk and Master of the aforesaid Court. Fayette-Ville, Feb. 3, 1788.

(403) Ran Away, From the Subscriber's plantation 14 miles above Wilmington, Three Negro Men, Viz. CUFFE, about 35 years old, country born, six feet high..ship carpenter..SAMPSON, a well set black fellow, about 27 years old, country born, five feet eight or nine inches high..it is probable he is lurking about Town Creek, in Bruns-

(403) (Cont.) wick County. HARRY, a slim fellow of middle age, very small limbs, formerly belonged to the estate of Mr. SHUBRICK, of South Carolina.. Ten Pounds Reward..for each... John P. WILLIAMS, February 10, 1789.

(404) Wilmington District. John Ablen CAMPBELL, complainant, vs. John GRANT, defendant. In Equity, December Term, 1788. Ordered, that the defendant do appear to the complainant's bill, on or Before..the sixth of June, next..the complainant's bill shall be taken pro confesso. Published by order of the Court, Thomas DAVIS, C. & M. E. February 12, 1789.

(Vol. I.) Thursday, February 19, 1789. (Numb. 48.)

(405) New-York, Jan. 31. Among other curious natural productions presented to Mr. PEALE's American Museum, in Philadelphia, since his late arrival in Baltimore, are the following: A Fish of the South Sea, 4 feet long, and not more than 4 inches in the girth, the head and eyes disproportionately large, and the jaws set within single row of very sharp teeth-..By Captain Daniel HOWLEN.. A piece of Crystal, dug out of Mr. Christopher RABORG's cellar, whose diameters, when entire, were 4 inches by 3..By Mr. Christopher RABORG. .. A Grinder, of the non descript Animal of the Western Country, found at the Big Bone Salt Lick and weighing four pounds-By Mr. William LUX.

(406) Savannah, January 15. On Saturday the 27th December last, being the feast of St. John the Evangelist, and general Communication of Free and Accepted Masons, the grand lodge met at brother COPP's long rom, where the right worshipful James JACKSON, Esq. installed grand master of all masons in this state, to which office he had been previously elected.. The worshipful Sir George HOUSTON, deputy grand master, Thomas ELSE, Esq. senior grand warden, Samuel STIRK, Esq. junior grand warden..were likewise invested with the insignia of their offices.. The different lodges having joined the grand lodge, the most worshipful William STEPHENS, Esq. past grand master, received the thanks of the grand lodge for presiding..for two years.

(407) Charleston, January 29. Both branches of the legislature have agreed on giving leave to the honorable AEdanus BURKE, esq. to take his seat in the house of representatives of the United States, as a representative of the district of Beaufort and Orangeburg...

(408) Richmond, February 5. Yesterday 10 of the electors for this state met at the Capitol, for the purpose of electing a President and Vice-President; when upon examining the ballots, they stood as follows: President. General WASHINGTON, 10. Vice-President. John ADAMS, 5. George CLINTON, 3. John HANCOCK, 1. John JAY, 1.

(409) Arrived in Hampton Road, the Isabella, captain CURRY, from Greenock, who brings information of the premature exit of that favorite Scotch Bard Robert BURNS...

(410) Wilmington, February 19, 1789. Capt. SEVIER, who arrived here last week from Martico, left at that place the brig Nelly, Roger KEAN, master, belonging to Philadelphia, who had arrived there from Batavia, in the East-Indies, after a passage of 80 days, in want of provisions.

(411) The Commissioners of the Town of Wilmington for the year 1788, hereby publish a statement of their receipts and expenditures,..viz. January, 1788. Paid balance due W. NUTT, at settlement of accounts last year, L. 21 7 1.. Amount of A. RONALDSON's taxes for 85 & 86, omitted in return of uncollected taxes..L. 4 12 0 John

(411) (Cont.) ALLAN, his account to January 1st 1788, for work at the Market House-making wheel-barrows, and keeping the engine in repair L. 31 11 2.. William EWANS, balance his account for negro hire L. 7 15 0 L. MAC PHERSON, his account for nails supplied in 87 L. 0.19.3. Thomas CALLENDER, in part his account for iron 3.15.0 James WALKER, in full for bricks for Market-house 11.15.7. John CAMPBELL, in part of his account 1.12.0. Joshua POTTS and George HOOPER, to be laid out in reducing constitution hill. 50.0.0. Sedgick SPRINGS, in part of his account for iron work. 2.16.0. STEVENS and TELFAIR, in part their account for repairing the market wharf. 1.8.0. Paid James READ in part his demand for Negro hire. 2.10.0 Paid SPRINGS and HARRIS for smiths work. 3.18.0. Paid Charles JEWKES his account for lime, and for a bucket lost at a fire. 6.18.8. Paid Joshua POTTS for lumber. 1. 16.8. Paid Matthew JOHNSTON for Negro hire. 1.8.0 Paid John WALKER for Negro hire, per Captain KINGSBURY's order. 8.3.0. Paid H. TOOMER for Negro hire. 6.7.6. Paid EWAN's and M'CAUSLAN former balance. 1.4.0.

Received amount of taxes for the year 1787. L.298.12.3. Cash received of P. CARPENTER, in part of balance due to the Commissioners from him. 6.5.6... Wilmington, Feb. 16, 1789. By order of the Commissioners, William NUTT, T. Clerk.

(412) Irish Linens, Now Selling (for Cash) by the piece or quantity..by the subscriber, at the House of Capt. COOK. John FITZ GERALD. February 18.

(413) For Nantz, (In France) The Brig Nightingale, Joseph CLARK, Master, Will sail in three weeks..apply to the Captain on board, at William CAMPBELL's wharf. Feb. 19, 1789.

(414) Joshua POTTS, Has For Sale, Tobacco, Tar, Flour, Barrelled Pork, Sawed Lumber, Barrel Staves, Jamaica Rum, Indigo.. Also, For Sale, Part of a Lot of Land, in Wilmington... February 19.

(415) The Subscriber requests all those who are indebted to him..to call and pay their respective debts, on or before the First of May next... John CAMPBELL. February 19.

(416) The Subscribers, Executors of the last will of William HILL, Esq. deceased, and Administrators of the estate of Mrs. Margaret HILL, deceased, hereby require all persons who are indebted to either of the estates..to make immediate payment... John HILL, W. H. HILL. February 19.

(417) Was Stolen Out of the subscriber's store, on Monday evening last, by a Negro man, four Cotton Shauls, white ground and sprigged, with large flowery borders... A. JOCELIN. February 19.

(Vol. I.) Thursday, February 26, 1789. (Numb. 49.)

(418) Wilmington, February 26, 1789. The honorable Elbridge GERRY, is chosen a federal representative for the Middlesex county; and the hon. Benjamin GOODHUE, for the county of Essex, in the Commonwealth of Massachusetts. In the state of Connecticut the electors met on the day appointed at Hartford, when they gave seven votes for his excellency George WASHINGTON, five for his excellency John ADAMS, and two for his excellency Samuel HUNTINGTON, esquire.

(419) Ran Away From the subscriber, the latter end of January last, A Mulatto Wench, named KILLESTER, belonging to the estate of colonel SHAW, deceased... John KINGSBURY, North side Market-Street. Wilmington, Feb. 26, 1789.

(420) I intend to leave this state for France, in a few weeks. Jude BELLOC. Feb. 26, 1789.

(421) For Sale, A House and Lot, Situate in Princess Street... John ALLAN. Feb. 26, 1789.

(422) Ten Pounds Reward. Ran Away from the subscriber, a negro fellow, named SAM.. SAM is about 35 years old, five feet eight or nine inches high, lean person, thin face, and of a yellowish complection, speaks good English, can read and I believe write, and is much given to liquor.. Any person taking up the said slave, and delivering him to me in Newbern, or Mr. Edward JONES, in Wil____ (Remainder missing.) Richard ____ Newbern, Feb. ____

(423) Ran ____ From the Subs ____ In January ____ A Negro Fellow, named ALECK, formerly belonging to the estate of Parker QUINCE, esq.. A reward of Three Pounds currency will be given to any person who will deliver him to Mr. Lawrence DORSEY in Wilmington, or at Poplar-Grove on the Sound, to Francis CLAYTON. Feb. 26, 1789.

(Vol. I.) Thursday, March 5, 1789. (Numb. 50.)

(424) Richmond, January 21. Extract of a letter from Sullivan county, December 8. "Mrs. INGLES, who was taken about a year ago from German creek, is returned; she with four of her children were kept by a party of Cherokees in the mountains, a few miles from the Kentucke path, and near the ford of Cumberland river, for six months .. They then proceeded to the Wyandot towns on the Sandusky, with their plunder and prisoners: the latter they sold to that tribe, who are remarkably fond of increasing their numbers by adopting young prisoners. After some time, she, by the assistance of an Indian trader, was sent home with her youngest child. She gives an account that several of the northern tribes were about joining the Creek confederacy and that Alexander M'GILLIVRAY is to have the superintendance of the whole."

(425) Petersburg, February 12. Yesterday was celebrated in this town, the birth of his Excellency George WASHINGTON, Esq. In the morning thirteen cannon were fired, and at 12 o'clock the Dinwiddie Cavalry and Infantry, assembled, and were..joined by the Prince George Cavalry..they retired to Mr. Robert ARMISTEAD's tavern...

1795 - Filmed from originals in the University of North Carolina Library-July 3, 10, 17, 24, 31; August 7, 14 (Supplement), 20; September 5; October 1, 8, 22.

THE WILMINGTON CHRONICLE: and NORTH-CAROLINA WEEKLY ADVERTISER
3 Dollars per annum.
Friday, July 3, 1795. (No. 1.

(426) Open To All Parties, But Influenced By None.
Wilmington: Printed By James CAREY, At His Printing-Office, Corner of Market And Second Streets.

(427) New-York, June 6. The joint committee of the legislature, yesterday..closed the estimation of the votes given in this state, for governor, lieutenant governor, &c. The result furnished a majority for John JAY as governor-1,580. S. V. RENSSALAER, lieutenant governor-652...

(428) Philadelphia, June 8.-Friday last, the supreme court of the United States, which had been for some time past employed in trying those concerned in the late insurrection to the westward, adjourned. Philip WEIGLE and John MITCHELL were found

(428) (Cont.) guilty of treason, and condemned to be executed here on the 27th inst. The trial of James STEWART and captain WRIGHT was postponed till the next court. The others were acquitted.

(429) The senate of the United States this day assembled.. Present, John ADAMS, esq. president, and 24 members. The absentees were, Stephen R. BRADLEY, Vermont; Frederick FREYLINGHUYSEN, Jersey; John VINING, Delaware; John TAYLOR, Virginia; Pierce BUTLER, S. Carolina; and James GUNN, Georgia.

(430) Baltimore, June 10. Yesterday arrived in this port, the ship Ariadne, captain Philip GRAYBILL, 60 days from Dunkirk...

(431) Wilmington, July 3. For some weeks past a number of runaway negroes..have at night committed various depredations on the neighbouring plantations..they have added to their other enormities the murder of Mr. Jacob LEWIS, overseer to Alexander Duncan MOORE, esq. and have also wounded mr. William STEELY.-These continued outrages induced the magistracy to outlaw the whole of the banditti, in consequence of which a number of them have been shot...

(432) Advertisement. The enormities committed by the outlying Negroes, have induced the magistrates to outlaw the following Negro men, viz. MATHEWS, BACCHUS, CHRISTMAS, WILL, AUGUSTUS, and ROBERT: (the Two last-mentioned Negroes are said to belong to William HOWE esq. near Newbern.) A Negro woman, named HANNAH, likewise the property of mr. HOWE, is now in gaol-she was out with the above runaways.. Sixty Dollars is offered for each and every head of the above Negroes who were concerned in the murder of Jacob LEWIS... H. CAMPBELL, J. P., Wm. CUTLAR, J. P. Wilmington, July 2.

(433) To Be Sold, Or rented for one or more years, The house in Wilmington called The Lodge, with the lot adjoining.. And, to be leased for six years, 3000 acres of land, lying on Shallot River..in Brunswick County. Also for sale, That valuable plantation on CAULKIN's Neck, formerly the property of F. ALLSTON, esq. containing 1340 acres.. For terms apply to the subscriber, who is empowered to sell or rent the above. Sam. J. THURSTON. July 1, 1795.

Friday, July 10, 1795. (No. 2.

(434) New-York, June 12. On the 15th ult. died at Long-hill, Daniel COOPER, esq. On the 7th of May he was 100 years old; he was formerly one of the Judges of the county of Morris.. He has left a numerous race of respectable descendants; he had buried five wives, and had married the sixth, about four years ago.. A few weeks ago was buried at Morris Town, a mr. STILES, a German, about 50 years a resident in the county of Morris; he was about 107 years old.

(435) June 15. .. Yesterday arrived at this port, the ship Pennsylvania, captain TILLINGHAST, in 42 days from Bourdeaux.. On Thursday last captain T. fell in with admiral MURRAY's squadron, off Nantucket..and not withstanding the leaky condition of the Pennsylvania, he pressed from on board two Englishmen and two Americans, one of which (Angus M'DONALD) a New-Yorker born, these four being the only healthy men on board, except the officers.

(436) Charleston, June 29. Captain BURNHAM, on the 26th instant, in lat. 35.42. spoke a sloop, captain William ROBINSON, 27 days from Guadaloupe, bound to North-Carolina, had sprung her mast and lost her head.

(437) Boston, June 18. The proceeds of last Monday evening's performance, at the theatre, we are informed, amounted to 666 dollars, the whole of which sum mr. POWELL has generously deposited in the hands of his honour Moses GILL, president of the Massachusetts charitable fire society, as a donation to their funds.

(438) Philadelphia, June 17. This day was assigned for the execution of VOGEL and MITCHEL, the two persons under sentence for treason; but a respite from the supreme executive of the U. States has suspended the sentence until November next.

(439) June 25.-The Treaty Of Amity, Commerce And Navigation Between G. Britain And The United States Of America, Was Ratified Yesterday, By The Senate Of The United States.

(440) Wilmington, July 10. Outlying Negroes. Since our last, MATHEWS, belonging to general SMITH, was brought in and lodged in gaol.. WILL, another of the outlaws, belonging to mr. BRICE, was also brought in, tried and found guilty, on the clearest evidence, of having held Jacob LEWIS, whilst another of this gang shot him. He was executed at Gallows Hill, on Wednesday. PICKLE, belonging to Alexander Duncan MOORE, esq. although not outlawed, has been lodged in gaol, charged with having acted as a guide to the murderers of Jacob LEWIS...

(441) Wanted, About 40,000 Thin Heart Lumber, And 100,000 Good Shingles. Apply to Jas. LOCKWOOD. Wilmington, July 9, 1795.

(442) Charles LA PLACE, Watch-Maker, From Paris, Has the honour to inform the public, that he has taken the store lately occupied by Alexander YOUNG, in mr. JAMES's house; where he intends to carry on his business... Wilmington, July 9.

(443) For Sale, By William NUT, On Monday, the 20th July, instant, The goods and chattels of Samuel MOORE, deceased... Samuel LOWDER, administrator. Wilmington, July 9.

(444) University of North-Carolina. Notice is hereby given, that a special meeting of the trustees of the University of North Carolina, will be held at the seat of the University, on Monday the 13th of July next... Richard D. SPAIGHT, President.

(445) For New York, The Schooner Mark Anthony Captain DILLINO, master, Will sail on or before Wednesday next. For passage only, apply to A. Z. VERNON, who lodges at mr. J. JENNING's. Wilmington, June 9.

(446) For Sale, On Friday next, the 17th instant, The prize ship, Prince William Henry, Henry GHERARDI. Captain. Terms, Cash, on delivery. Wilmington, July 9.

Friday, July 17, 1795. (No. 3.

(447) From a late London paper. The old non-con. names, such as Praise-God BAREBONES, &c. are still kept up in North-America. In one of the New-York papers, a man of the name of Bethankful TIFFANY, warns the public against the mal-practices of Recompence TIFFANY, his wife.

(448) Senators of the United States. Voted for the Treaty. Samuel LIVERMORE, George CABOT, Caleb STRONG, Wm. BRADFORD, Theodore FOSTER, Oliver ELLSWORTH, Jonathan TRUMBULL, Elijah PAINE, Rufus KING, Frederick FRELINGHUYSEN, John RUTHERFORD, William BINGHAM, James ROSS, Henry LATIMER, John VINING, John HENRY, Richard POTTS, Humphry MARSHALL, Jacob READ, James GUNN. Voted against it. John LANGDON, Moses

(448)(Cont.) ROBINSON, Aaron BURR, Stevens Thomas MASON, Henry TAZEWELL, John BROWN, Alexander MARTIN, Timothy BLOODWORTH, Pierce BUTLER, James JACKSON.

(449) Wilmington, July 17. The sale of the prize ship Prince William Henry..will take place this afternoon, at five o'clock, on board said vessel. July 17. Errata in said advertisement. For Henry GHERARDI, captain, read James GHERARDI, captain.

(450) Since our last, two more of the outlawed negroes, namely AUGUSTUS and ROBERT (belonging to William HOWE, esq.), were lodged in our gaol...

(451) For New York, The Schooner Friendship, John KILBORN, Master, Will sail on Thursday next. For passage only, apply to BLAKELEY & VANCE. Wilmington, July 16.

(452) For Sale, To satisfy a judgment had at Brunswick court, A Likely Negro Wench... J. R. GAUTIER. Wilmington, July 15, 1795.

(453) Treasury Department. Revenue Office, April 10, 1795. The following abstract from documents on file in this office, is published for the information of the commanders of vessels in the trade of the United States. Doyle SWEENEY, principal clerk. -Cape Fear Light House is situated near Bald Head, a noted bluff on Cape Fear Island, at the mouth of Cape Fear River, on which river is built the town of Wilmington, in North Carolina. The iron lantern is 10 feet nine inches in diameter, and about 15 feet nine inches in height, from the floor to the top of the roof. It was first lighted on the night of the 23d December 1794.

(454) Boston, June 17. Arrived here in the ship Mary, Joaquim Joe DE BARROS, esq. vise consul of the United States at the Cape de Verd Islands.

(455) Pittsburg, June 13. On the 3d instant, the Indians killed James FINLAY and Barnabas M'CORMICK, on the farm of John HULING, eight miles from Cussewago, on French Creek.. And on the 5th, they killed James THOMPSON (one of the persons employed by captain POWERS, now surveying in that country)...

Friday, July 24, 1795. (No. 4.

(456) Philadelphia, June 29th, 1795. Sir, I have seen in your paper of this date an abstract of the late treaty between the United States and Great-Britain, which though not perfectly correct, is nearly so.. I send you herewith a genuine copy..for the purpose of giving to the citizens of America full information respecting this momentous business. I am, sir, your obedient servant, Sten. Thon. MASON. (One of the senators from Virginia.) To Benj. Franklin BACHE, Editor of the Aurora...

(457) Wilmington, July 24. By the Charleston papers..we learn, that the treaty between Great Britain and this country was generally reprobated in that city..on Thursday, the 16th, there was a general meeting of the inhabitants..where they resolved, as the best mode to make known their opinion of the treaty, that a committee of 15 gentlemen should be chosen by ballot, to take into consideration the..treaty..and to report their sentiments thereon to a meeting of the citizens..on Wednesday, the 22d instant. The following are the gentlemen chosen..-Christopher GADSDEN, John RUTLEDGE, David RAMSEY, Edward RUTLEDGE, Chas. C. PINCKNEY, Thomas T. TUCKER, AEdanus BURKE, William WASHINGTON, John MATHEWS, Thomas MORRIS, Thos. JONES, William JOHNSON, John B. HOLMES, John RUTLEDGE, jun. and John J. PRINGLE.

(458) Benjamin HAWKINS, of North Carolina, George CLYMER, of Pennsylvania, and Andrew PICKENS, of South Carolina, are appointed commissioners to hold a treaty with the Creek Indians.

(459) MATHEWS, one of the outlawed negroes..has since died of his wounds, and thereby prevented the interference of the public executioner.

(460) Apprentices Wanted. To the block, mast & pump-making business... Wm. SMEETON. Wilmington, July 23.

(461) Pro Bono Publico. In the month of February last I was induced, through the recommendation of mr. John JOHNSTON, of this town, merchant, to consign to Frederick LACHMAN, of Charleston, a quantity of prime bacon, with directions for him to vend the same, immediately, for cash; he infcrmed me, by letter, that 2½d per 16. was the price.. I requested him to send the bacon back to me, without selling any of it.. he did not comply.. After which I consigned to him a quantity of pork and beef, and one barrel of lard. His delinquency, after repeated requests to make remittance, induced me to go to Charleston..found my bacon in a wretched way, owing to his negligence. The barrel of lard I gladly received back..mr. JOHNSON claimed the barrel of lard, and proved the same to be his..I had received it in lieu of my own. Therefore I consider it a duty incumbent on me to inform my friends, that they may shun the rock which I have split upon. Alexr. YOUNG. Wilmington, July 22.

(462) For New York, The Brigantine Mary, Hugh WYER, Master, Has excellent accomodations for Passengers..apply to the Master on board, or to John CALHORDA & Co. Wilmington, July 23d, 1795.

(463) Post-Office, Wilmington. List of letters remaining in the Post-Office, Wilmington, which if not taken up before the first of October next will be sen to the General Post-Office. B. Master BAUDUY. John BRANSBERRY. James BROWN. Captain Samuel BRIGHT. John BARRETT. Samuel BUCKSTON, 2. C. Clerk of the Superior Court. Joseph CURTIS. D. John DICKENSON, 2. Citoyen DUSSAN. E. Elizabeth EARL, 2. Edward EASTON. James EISTMAN. F. Daniel FERGUSON. James FLOWERS. Captain FOOTERY. James FLEMING. G. James GILLESPIE, 3. William GORDON. William GRAHAM. H. Jeremiah HAND. Jo. HENDS. Captain Robert HOMES. Solomon HAMER. J. Charles JEWKES, 2. Mathew JOHNSTON, 2. Peter JOHNSTON. Benjamin JACOB. K. John KENNEDY. John KERR. L. John LEE. Margaret LAMB. Henry LYNDON. Colin LINDSAY. M. Alfred MOORE, 2. Peter MALLETT. Michael MOLTON. Miss MEARES. Wm. MOSELY. Margaret MOPOON. Frederick MILLER. John MOTHERALL. Peter MAXWELL. Patrick MURRAY. Peter M'BRIDE. Jo. M'CUN. Daniel M'KINNON. David M'COLLARE. Jo M'LAUGHLIN. Elizabeth M'LAINE. Peter M. MILLER. Mr. M'VAUGHTIN. Mrs. M'KINNON. John M'KENZIE. Mr. M'NORTON, Donald M'ALISTER, Archibald M'NEIL. N. Alexander NEILS. Elizabeth NICHOLS. Abraham TAYLOR. P. Lewis PRICE. Captain Skeath POTTER. Peter PELHAM. Captain Jeremiah POTE. R. Captain Benjamin RICE. Mrs. RUNDLE, 2. Fanny RICHARDSON. James RICHARDSON. David REED. Bartholomew ROLLAND. Archibald RONANDSON. S. Sheriff of New Hanover, 2. Jeanett SPENDLOVE, 3. William SMITH, 2. Captain Samuel STANWOOD. Captain Stephen SPRAGUE. Duncan STEWART. William STRUDWICK. Samuel STRUDWICK. T. Amey TURNER. THURBER and LEE, 2. Mr. TOMPKINS. James TATE. V. Samuel VIRGIN. W. Doctor WHITEMORE. John WARNER. Abisha WOODWARD. William WINGATE. Elizabeth WILKINSON. John BRADLEY, P. M. Wilmington, July 22, 1795.

Friday, July 31, 1795. (No. 5.

(464) The following is the official letter referred to in the treaty of amity, &c. ... Philadelphia, September 5, 1795, Sir, ... Thomas JEFFERSON (To) Geo. HAMMOND, Esq.

(465) Philadelphia, July 10. Doctor James WOODHOUSE has been appointed professor of chemistry, in the university of Pennsylvania, in the room of dr. PRIESTLY, who had declined.

(466) Henry William DE SAUSSURE, of South Carolina, is appointed director of the mint, vice David RITTENHOUSE, resigned.

(467) Wilmington, July 31. Notice. The members of the Whistling Society are requested to meet at DORSEY's the first Tuesday in August, on business of consequence. By order of the president, John JOY, Sec.

(468) Corn For Sale. Two Thousand Bushels of Corn for sale at No. 7, mr. CAMPBELL's wharf..enquire at the store or at mr. J. JENNINGS's. July 30, 1795.

(469) Public Auction. This day, at 12 o'clock, will be sold, Before the subscriber's vendue-store, A General Assortment Of Dry Goods;..Bacon; Beef; Claret; White Wine; Crockery Ware; Furniture... Thos. FITZGERALD & Co. Friday, July 31.

(470) Advertisement. I Want to hire a single woman, of good character, who understands spinning and weaving wool, cotton, and flax; to have the superintendence and direction of four or five Negro women... J. BURGWIN. Hermitage, July 27, 1795. To be Let, The corner brick house where mr. William BROWNE lately kept store.. Enquire as above.

(471) For Philadelphia, The Schooner Harmony, E. P. DRAKE, Master, (Will sail in a few days) For passage only, apply to Charles JORDAN. July 30, 1795.

(472) Charleston, July 14. The Arrival Of The Treaty! It has been merely an arrival, as it has not yet been accepted.. The motion then was, "That an election by ballot be held at the Exchange this afternoon..and tomorrow morning..to choose 15 gentlemen as a committee, to take into consideration the impending treaty of amity, commerce, and navigation, between the United States and Great Britain, and to report their sentiments thereon to a meeting of the citizens..at St. Michael's church, on Wednesday next.."..and the following gentlemen were appointed managers: Thomas HALL, John MITCHELL, Joseph RAMSEY, and James SIMONS, esqrs. to receive the ballots..at the said election...

Friday, August 7, 1795. (No. 6.

(473) Knoxville, June 10. We learn, that on or about the 4th instant, a large party of Creeks..surrounded the Chickasaw towns..a skirmish had taken place..and several were killed on both sides. A distinguished Chickasaw chief, of the name of UNDERWOOD, is said to be among the killed.

(474) Knoxville. Sunday last left this place for New Orleans, Rawleigh HOGAN, in a boat of 20 tons burden, laden with whisky, bar and cast iron, bacon, lime,.. The same day left here four boats of 15 tons each, commanded by Alexander MOOR. They were laden with bar and cast iron, and a variety of articles belonging to the inhabitants of Mero district...

(475) Wilmington, August 7. For Sale, By The Subscriber, Muscovado sugar, in hhds. and barrels. Jamaica rum, in puncheons. And, A Likely Negro Fellow. Geo. DUNCAN.

(476) Iron, Of the best quality (by the ton), And a few hhds. Havanna Molasses, For Sale, by John SHUTER. August 6.

(477) Final Notice. Notwithstanding the former notice of suing all those whose bonds, notes, or book accounts have been long standing, both of the concern of John JOHNSTON and Co. and the subscriber's, many still remain unpaid;..every debt not paid

(477) (Cont.) ..previous to the first day of October ensuing, will be placed in the hands of certain attornies at law, for recovery..; as I am anxious to close the whole of my business in this state as speedily as possible. Jno. JOHNSTON. Wilmington (N. C.), Aug. 6, 1795.

Supplement to the Weekly Advertiser, No. 7.

(478) Agreeably to instructions from his excellency Thomas MIFFLIN, Governor of the State of Pennsylvania, we shall offer for Sale, the following Town and Out-Lots, of Erie, Waterford, Franklin and Warren..to be disposed of in the City of Philadelphia, will commence on Monday the 25th day of July next. That portion..to be disposed of at Carlisle..on Wednesday the third day of August next..at Pittsburgh..on Monday the 15 day of August next... William IRVINE, Andw. ELLICOTT, George WILSON, Agents. Philadelphia, May 26, 1796. P. S. Plans of the above named Towns, may be seen by calling at Mr. ECKERTS Office in the Borough of Reading.

Thursday, August 20, 1795. (No. 8.

(479) Philadelphia, July 29.-In the ship Columbus, captain DILLON, arrived here, in 70 days, from Havre de Grace, came passenger that distinguished and persecuted Irish patriot, Archibald Hamilton ROWAN, esq.

(480) Baltimore, July 28. Saturday arrived at the fort, brig Paragon, captain George STORY, from Jeremie, 18 days.

(481) Real Estate Office, &c. The subscriber having been frequently applied to for the purpose of disposing of plantations, houses, slaves, and various other species of real and personal property, has..opened an office for the above purpose... Thos. FITZ GERALD. N. B. Vendue and Commission Business continued as usual. Wilmington, August 13, 1795.

(482) Bills, On New-York For sale. Apply to Thomas MURPHY. August 14, 1795.

(483) Notice. The partnership of DUNCAN & REARDON is, by mutual consent, dissolved. All persons indebted to said concern, are desired to make immediate payment to Geo. DUNCAN; and those having claims, will please present them for settlement. Geo. DUNCAN. August 9, 1795.

(484) Advertisement. Peter WISS, Merchant-Tailor, From Paris, Wishes to inform the public in general, that he has commenced business in the house formerly occupied by doctor James FERGUS... Wilmington, August 13, 1795.

(485) Wilmington, August 20. Ran Away. Whereas my negro fellow ABRAHAM, a Carpenter, hath for some time past made it a practice to go about at nights fiddling and drinking, whereby he has contracted a loose idle habit, and much injured his health. -He has lately eloped from my service, and is now supposed to be lurking about..I.. offer a reward of 10 Dollars to..deliver him to me at my plantation near Wilmington.. He is about five feet 10 inches high.. I intend to out-law him, if he is not taken in 10 days. C. BURGWIN. Hermitage, 17th August, 1795.

(486) Public Auction. This day, at 10 o'clock, will be sold, Before the subscriber's vendue-store, Wine..Rum, Porter, Bar-Iron, Nail-Rods, Household Furniture, &c. &c. T. FITZ GERALD & Co.

(487) Found, A Few days ago, some Bank Notes.-The owner may have them again, on

(487) (Cont.) proof of property... A. JOCELIN. Wilmington, August 19, 1795.

(488) Sherry, Port, Porter, Iron, Rum, &c. For sale, by John JOHNSTON. Aug. 20, 1795.

(489) For Sale, A Few Puncheons Jamaica Rum. Apply to Charles JORDAN.

The Wilmington Chronicle Extraordinary.-Saturday, September 5, 1795.

(490) The President's Reply To The Opposers Of The Treaty. The committee appointed by a general meeting of the citizens of Philadelphia, the northern liberties, and the district of Southwark, to sign and to transmit to the president of the United States, the..sentiments of the meeting, in relation to the treaty negotiated between mr. JAY, and lord GRENVILLE, have received by the hand of dr. SHIPPEN, jun. the following answer..for the information of their constituents. Thomas M'KEAN, Alexander J. DALLAS, Charles PETTIT, John SWANWICK, Moses LEVY, John HUNN, William COATES, Abraham COATES, John BARKER, Stephen GIRARD, Frederick A. MUHLENBERG, William SHIPPEN, Blair M'CLENACHAN. Philadelphia, August 14, 1795.

United States, 12th August, 1795. Sir, I have received your letter of the ___ of July, covering the memorial meeting in Philadelphia. As the answer, which I have given on? similar occasion to the select-men ___ Boston, is applicable to this memo I think it proper to transmit a co___ thereof to you. With due respect... G. WASHINGTON. (To) William SHIPPEN, jun. Ezra PRICE, Thomas WALLEY, William BORDMAN, Ebenezer SEAVER, Thomas? CRAFTS, Thomas EDWARDS, ___ LETTLE, William SCOLLAY, Jesse PUTNAM, esqrs. selectmen ___ the town of Boston. Gentlemen, ...

Thursday, September 24, 1795. (No. 13.

(491) Wanted Immediately, One or two white journeymen carpenters who understand framing; to such good wages will be given. Apply to John ALLEN.

(492) 50 Dollars Reward. Ran-Away from the subscriber, on Saturday the 5th inst. a likely Negro slave, named TONY. He is about 24 or 25 years old; in height 5 feet 4 or 5 inches; was born in New Providence, and speaks English well... Captain James GHERARDI. Sept. 17.

(493) Advertisement. State of North Carolina. Brunswick County. Notice is hereby given, that the cargo of the schooner Mary and Helen, (stranded on TUBE's Beach, near Shalotte Inlet)..will be sold..on Thursday, the 24th inst... James ALLEN, Captain. Jno. JOHNSTON, Shipper. September 14, 1795.

(494) Lands For Sale. On the sixth day of the term of the next superior court to be held in Wilmington..will be offered for sale the following tracts..of land, to wit, 640 Acres lying in Brunswick county, on the south west side of the north west branch of Cape Fear River and on the south side of LIVINGSTON's Creek, being the same land granted by patent the 22d day of May, 1772, to J. CARTER, Heir to Edward CARTER, deceased. 400 Acres situate in Duplin county, on the Beaver Dam Branch of Limestone, formerly possessed by one Morgan SWEENY. 148 Acres situate in New Hanover county, on the west side of the north east branch of Cape Fear River, joining the upper side of Benjamin EVANS's land; on the WELCH tract where John WRIGHT and Francis DRUMGOLD formerly lived; being the same land which was conveyed by Arthur BENNING to Andrew THOMSON. 600 Acres,..situate in the last mentioned county, on Black River, formerly possessed by Achilles ROAN, and the possession thereof lately recovered from J. DEVANE, by the trustees of the university of North Carolina. Also, one water lot,..

(494) (Cont.) in the upper part of..Wilmington, lying between the lots whereon mr. J. LOUDON and mr. W. CUTLAR now live;..being the lot which Robert ELLIS formerly conveyed to one Henry M'CULLOCH... The persons last seized of the foregoing lands dying without lawful heirs, the same lands became escheated, and were granted by the general assembly of the state to the trustees of the university of North Carolina... W. H. HILL; Attorney for the trustees of the university.

(495) Negroes' Coarse Shoes: 40 Dozen Pair To Be Sold Cheap, For Cash. W. NUTT. September 15, 1795.

(496) The subscribers have imported a general assortment of Medicines..will..wholesale or retail upon reasonable terms. R. & W. CUTLAR. Wilmington, 3d Sept. 1795.

(497) Just imported, by the subscribers, From Aux Cayes, And for sale, Molasses.. Coffee..Tinto Wine... F. FONTAINE & Co. September 9.

(498) For Private Sale, White & Red Wine..Bottled Porter, Peach Brandy. Also, a Well-Toned Bell, fit for a church for a large plantation with negroes. Apply to T. FITZ GERALD. Wilmington, Aug. 6, 1795.

(499) Philadelphia, September 10. In the Holland, from Hambourgh, came passenger, colonel James Napper TANDY, a citizen of Dublin.

(500) Philadelphia, September 10. On Sunday, the 23d of August, Absalom JONES, a free African, was ordained minister of the African church lately established in this city, by the right reverend bishop WHITE...

(501) Wilmington, September 24. On Thursday the 3d instant, captain N. CROCKER, of the schooner William Henry, of Wilmington, spoke with the schooner Illinois.. all well.

(502) The executors of Francis CLAYTON, deceased..concluded to sell the Rocky Point plantation, belonging to that estate..at public sale, on the third or fourth days of November term, in the town of Wilmington.-It consists of 1920 acres..about 16 miles from town, and bounded in part, by the North East branch of Cape Fear... Henry URQUHART, Henry TOOMER, Surviving executors of Francis CLAYTON.

(503) To Be Sold, At Public Vendue, The First Tuesday In October, Two parcels of land, supposed to contain about 1000 acres; levied upon, by two writs of fieri facias, at the suit of administrator of Godwin ELLITSON and administrator of Josiah RICHARDSON, against John Porter GRAINGE. This land is situated upon the East side of the North West River..near the line that divides the counties of Bladen and New Hanover-was advertised to be sold on the 19th inst. but a claim having been set up for it, by John HALL, the sale is postponed... Thos. WRIGHT, sheriff. September 23, 1795.

(504) To Be Sold, Cheap, For Cash Or Indian Corn, One, two, or three Negro Men, field slaves.-For particulars inquire of the subscriber, at his plantation on NESSY's (or NEFFY's) Creek near to Wilmington. John HILL.

(505) The subscriber informs those who were owners of carriages that did not make entry and payment of the duties last year, that unless they come forward and pay for the same..during the present month, that he will be under the necessity of returning their names to the attorney of the United States, to be sued without distinction. Mr. Archibald CUTLAR, in Wilmington, will receive the same. Kenan LOVE, Collector of Revenue.

(506) Five Dollars Reward, Ran-Away, about six weeks since, from the subscriber, at the Sound, a Negro named BEN.. He is about 19 or 20 years of age; five feet four or five inches high; stout and well made. Peter MAXWELL. Sept. 23, 1795.

(507) Taken Up, by the patrol of Wilmington, the 19th inst. a likely Negro man, who calls himself JACOB, and says he ran away from Archibald ROBERTSON, of Beaufort,.. He also declares, that he intended to go to Charleston, to his right owner, captain Joseph JENKINS, from whom he was plundered last war, by captain ANTHONY, off Charleston bar, out of a fishing boat. The fellow appears to be about 26 years old, near six feet high... Wm. JACKSON, jailor. Wilmington, Sept. 23, 1795.

Thursday, October 1, 1795. (No. 14.

(508) To Be Rented, Or Leased For 3 Or 5 Years, The subscriber's wharf, and the corner brick store, lately occupied by mr. James LOCKWOOD, deceased. Possession will be given on the 15th December, or sooner if wanted... John LONDON. September 26, 1795.

(509) A Brick-Maker, who is master of his business, may meet with good encouragement by applying at the Hermitage, or in Wilmington, to John BURGWIN.. A Millwright may also hear of a good job, by applying as above. Hermitage, Sept. 24, 1795.

(510) Public notice is hereby given, That 250 shares in the Catawba and Wateree company are offered for sale.. Any persons willing to become owners of stock in this company, are requested to apply to colonel SENF, at Rocky Mount, on the Catawba River (where he is now engaged in opening the said navigation), to doctor David RAMSAY, in the city of Charleston, or to general SMITH, at Belvidere, near Wilmington, North Carolina... J. F. GRIMKE, president.

(511) Agreeable to the last will and testament of James H. KIRKBY, deceased, will be sold at public auction, all the personal property belonging to said estate..also a parcel of salt... John JOHNSTON, John ALLEN, Executors. Wilmington, 29th September, 1795.

(512) To Be Let, And entered upon on the first day of December next..that pleasant and commodious House and Garden..lately occupied by Mr. James LOCKWOOD.-Enquire of John BURGWIN. September 28th, 1795.

(513) Notice is hereby given to all persons concerned, that the subscriber has qualified as an administrator to the estate of James LOCKWOOD, late of Wilmington, merchant, deceased... Simeon BELDEN, administrator. Also, Will be sold in Wilmington, On the 19th day of October next..The personal estate of the said deceased..merchandize, household furniture, one half of the schooner Fancy, &c. &c... Wilmington, Sept. 28, 1795.

(514) Notice. The trustees of the University of North Carolina will receive proposals (..at Raleigh, on the second Monday in November next), for building a house at the seat of the University, about 120 feet long, by 50 wide, and three stories high, of brick... R. D. SPAIGHT, president. Newbern, August 29.

(515) Wilmington, 1st of October, 1795. This is to request all persons, indebted to the estate of the late Thomas VICKEARS, by bond, note, or open account, to make speedy payments... Mary VICKEARS, sole executrix.

(516) Just Imported, In the brig Eliza, Timothy WHITE, master, from New-Haven, And

(516) (Cont.) for sale..St. Croix Rum,..Sugar..Molasses..Cheese, Butter, Onions and Potatoes, Cyder.. Enquire of the master, on board, at BRADLY's Wharfe. September 30, 1795.

(517) United States. Collectors' Office, Wilmington, N. Carolina, 25th Sept. 1795. Proposals, in writing, will be received at this office, until the 24th of October, for furnishing, by contract, all rations, quarter masters' supplies, and medical assistance, that may be wanted for the troops at this post, during the year 1796... James READ, Collector.

Thursday, October 8, 1795. (No. 15.

(518) For Sale, Excellent London Porter..Wanted-100 Live Hogs. BLAKELY & VANCE. October 6, 1795.

(519) Notice is hereby given, to forewarn all persons from bargaining or trading in any ____ whatsoever, with Elizabeth SIMPSON, the wife of Charles SIMPSON. Charles SIMPSON. Oct. 2?, 1795.

(520) United States of America. North Carolina District. Whereas Benjamin WOODS, esq. district attorney for the United States for North Carolina district, has exhibited his libel to the hon. John SITGREAVES, the district judge of the United States..setting forth that James READ, esq. collector of the port of Wilmington, on the 11th day of July, 1795..did seize, as forfeited to the United States, a..schooner, called the John..for that between the first day of January, 1795, and the time of said seizure, a certain writing, purporting to be a copy or certificate of an enrollment or record..not being then actually entitled to the benefit thereof..his honour has appointed the first Monday in November next..where he will hear the said libel and decree thereon. Abner NEALE, Clerk, October 5, 1795.

(521) To Be Sold, Very Cheap, for cash, part of a lot of land, in this town, 33 feet front, on Front-street, and 66 feet back; adjoining Peter CARPENTER's. For particulars, apply at the collector's office, to Thomas ROBISON. Wilmington, October 8.

(522) Eight Dollars Reward. Ran-Away from the subscriber, an apprentice to the printing business, named James PAXTON. He is near 18 years of age, middling stature, thin face and person, complexion remarkably pale, dark eyes, a down look... Benj. Franklin BACHE. Aurora Office (Philadelphia). Aug. 14.

(523) Paris, July 6. The American ambassador, James MONROE, celebrated the 4th of July, by a brilliant fete; the foreign ministers, many deputies of the convention, and 300 persons, were present. Thomas PAINE shone particularly among the society...

(524) Notice. The subscribers wish to inform..that they have opened a store, at the East End of the New Court-House, and intend doing business in the vendue and commission line... A. TOOMER & HOLT. Wilmington, Oct. 3.

Thursday, October 22, 1795. (No. 17.

(525) The Sheriffs of the different counties composing the district of New Hanover ..to take notice, that if the monies due from their respective counties, as taxes for building the district court house in Wilmington, for the year 1795, is not paid by ____ember ensuing, judgment will be taken on their heads, in behalf of the commissioners. James WALKER, Treasurer to the commissioners. ____ 10, 1795.

(526) Will be offered for sale, at public auction..the 5th day of the superior court at Wilmington, in November, that valuable plantation known by the name of Grovely; situate and laying on Town Creek, about eight miles from Wilmington-It contains 640 acres of old patent land..likewise, 640 acres lying ___ to Grovely... James WALKER. ___ 10, 1795.

(527) For Sale By Auction, For the benefit of the underwriters, _____ and DEAN's Warehouse, on BRADLEY's Wharf, Monday next, 12 o'clock, The Hull of the brig Polly, as she ___ lies stranded on Long Bay Beach... W. NUTT, auctionier. Oct. 12.

(528) Stolen Or Strayed, From the pasture of Richard DOSIER, in Brunswick, on the 22d instant, a sorrel horse.. A reward of 10 dollars..to any person who will deliver him to Mr. Lee SULLIVAN, of Duplin; and five dollars if delivered to captain Thomas LEONARD, in Brunswick, or the subscriber in Smithville, or Wilmington. Robt. HARLEY. Smithville, Sept. 24, 1795.

(529) Charleston, October 10. On Thursday was tried, at the court of sessions, Sally ARDER, known by the name of Spanish SALL, for the murder of John KEITH, she pleaded pregnancy, to stay judgment..the court then passed sentence of death on her, to be hanged on Monday, the 19th instant.

(530) Wilmington, October 22. Married, a few days since, mr. Philip SPAULDING, to the amiable and accomplished miss Margaret FERGUS.

(531) The subscriber being in want of an apprentice, wishes to engage a smart lad, of a good disposition.-To such an one, if well recommended, every encouragement will be given, and all means used to instruct him, as well in any other art the subscriber may be able to teach as the silver smith's business... D. LAMBERTOZ. Wilmington, October 20, 1795.

(532) Notice. Some time between the ninth and the eleventh of May last, my wife Elizabeth thought proper to withdraw herself from my house-I therefore give notice,.. that I will pay no debt which the said Elizabeth shall contract after this date. Laurence A. DORSEY. Wilmington, Oct. 21, 1795.

(533) Wanted To Rent, A House for the accomodation of captain M'RAE's Recruits. One as near as possible to the court house would be preferred.. Apply to BLAKELEY & VANCE, Contractors at this rendezvous. Wilmington, October 21, 1795.

(534) United States. Custom-house, Wilmington, Oct. 17, 1795. The commissioner of the revenue of the United States having directed me to contract for the stakeage of the channel of Cape Fear river... James READ.

1796 - Filmed from originals in the University of North Carolina Library-January 21, 28; February 11; May 5. From Harvard University Library-February 4; April 14; August 4. From Louis T. MOORE, Wilmington, North Carolina-May 5. (Photostat in the University of North Carolina Library.)

THE WILMINGTON CHRONICLE; AND NORTH CAROLINA WEEKLY ADVERTISER.

(535) Wilmington: Printed By John BELLEW, At His Office, Corner Of Market And Second Streets. Three Dollars per annum.)

Thursday, January 21, 1796. (Vol. II. No. 2.

(536) Public Auction. On Saturday the 23d instant will be sold..for the benefit of the underwriters, the hull and lower masts of the brigantine Governor Pinckney... T. FITZ-GERALD, V. M. Wilmington, 13th January, 1796.

(537) Advertisement. State of N. Carolina, Brunswick county. Notice is hereby given that the hull of the schooner Mary and Helen, as she lays on TUBE's Beach, near Shalotte Inlet, will be sold there at public auction, on the 25th instant... John JOHNSTON. 1_ January, 1796.

(538) The subscribers have for sale..Muscovado Sugar, of superior quality.-Also, some Coarse Salt... POTTS & GIBBS.

(539) For New-York, The Sloop Two Brothers, Captain CONKLING..will sail in a few days.-For passage, only, apply to the master on board; or Charles JORDAN...

(540) Lands For Sale, Two tracts, patented in the year 1758; one of 400, the other of 500 acres, lying on the White Marsh on Waggamaw Swamp, in Bladen county.. Apply to Edward JONES, attorney at law, who has the original patents in his hands.

(541) State of N. Carolina, Wilmington district. In Equity-November term, 1795. Exors. Bishop DUDLEY, vs. Matthew GREEN. It appearing to the court, that former order of publication   May term last past, has been complied with, it is again ordered to be published three weeks in the Wilmington Chronicle, that defendant put his answer in this office, at or before..the 13th May, 1796, or complainant's bill will be taken pro confesso. Witness, Thomas DAVIS, C. M. E. Wilmington (N. C.), 15th Dec. 1795.

(542) State of N. Carolina. Wilmington. In Equity-November term, 1795. Henry TOOMER, vs. William BLOUNT. It appearing to the court, that the former order of May term, last past, of publication in this cause has been complied with, ordered that the bill be taken pro confesso, that three months' notice be given to the defendant, by three weeks' successive publications in the Wilmington Chronicle, that the testimony of Jane DUBOICE, Allice HERON, Ann STUCKEY, and others, will be taken before the master in equity, for the district of Wilmington..on the first Monday in March next. Certified to be a true copy from the minutes. Thomas DAVIS, C. M. E. of said district.

(543) As the subscriber intends leaving this state as soon as possible, he requests all those who have demands against him to render in their accounts for settlement.. J. JOHNSTON. At the same time he wishes to inform his friends, that he will sell his remaining stock of goods..consisting of dry goods, wines, porter, grind-stones, lumber, shingles, &c. J. JOHNSTON.

(544) Cash, or Goods given for Auditors Specie-Certificates-Apply to John JOHNSTON. Wilmington (N. C.) Jan. 13, 1796.

(545) Advertisement. To be sold..for Cash, 500 acres of land, on a point of Broad and Green River, Santee..apply to Mrs. Elizabeth RICHARDS, in Wilmington. Jan. 13, 1796.

(546) Wilmington, January 21. Died. On the 3d ult. after a few minutes illness, David M'NIEL, esq. of Cumberland county; a gentleman universally lamented.

(547) Public Auction. On Monday, the 25th instant, will be sold..148 barrels kiln-dried Indian Meal, 50 barrels Flour; red oak and white oak Hogshead Staves..part of

(547) (Cont.) the brig Governor Pinckney's cargo. T. FITZ-GERALD, V. M. 15th January, 1796.

(548) For Private Sale. Eight Pipes Madeira Wine... T. FITZ-GERALD. 20th January, 1796.

(549) Notice. The sale of the schooner Mary And Helen..is postponed until Saturday the 30th instant. T. FITZ-GERALD, V. M. 20th January, 1796.

(550) WHEATON, TISDALE, & Co. Informs their customers..that they have removed their store to the one formerly occupied by Mr. James LOCKWOOD, deceased, at the S. E. corner of the New Market... Wilmington, January 20, 1796.

(551) Land For Sale, Three hundred and twenty acres in Bladen county, on the North West River; being one half of the tract formerly called Perlemberg.-For terms apply to the subscriber, who is authorised to sell. F. BRICE. Wilmington, January 20, 1796.

Thursday, January 28, 1796. (Vol. II. No. 3.

(552) Notice is hereby given to all persons concerned, That Sarah E. M'CALISTER and Richard QUINCE, jun. have obtained letters of administration on the goods, chattels, &c. of James M'CALISTER, late of Brunswick county, deceased... Sarah E. M'CALISTER, Admx. Richard QUINCE, Jun., Admr. Wilmington, 15th January, 1796.

(553) Notice is hereby given to all persons concerned, that the subscriber has qualified as an executor to the last will and testament of Mrs. Mary M'CALISTER, late of Brunswick county, deceased... Benjamin MILLS, Exr.

(554) Augusta, December 5. We hear from good authority, that on the 6th ultimo, two Indians, one named GEORGE, a Creek, and son of the HALLOWING KING, and the other, his uncle, a Cherokee, were treacherously murdered at Fort Washington, Franklin county, by two of those soldiers who were enlisted for the defence of this state.

(555) Charleston, December 11. Three men..came to a farmer's about mid-day, procured some refreshments for themselves and horses, and were observed to pay an uncommon attention to different parts of the house, and then departed with thanks for their kind reception. The farmer, suspicious of some design, invited a few of his neighbors to stay with him. About midnight the three men returned, and made violent attempts to break the doors and windows open, but in vain; they then..got the bolt of the lock off; but an iron bar having been previously laid across the door, one of them thrust his arm through the logs to remove it. The people within, being unarmed, laid hold of his arm, drew his body to the logs, and made it fast with a cord..they let him remain 'till day, when they went out and found his throat cut, from ear to ear, his associates having absconded; which was the only expedient the remaining two had to prevent a discovery. The person so murdered is supposed to be one Joel MOORE, a notorious villain.

(556) Wilmington, January 21. Died) In this town, captain Charles LAPHAM, of the brig Dolphin, after a short illness. A gentleman much regretted.

(557) The subscriber, intending leaving this state in the course of a few weeks, requests those who have any demands against him, to bring in their accounts for payment; and those indebted, to make immediate payment... Spafford DRURY. Jan. 26, 1796.

(558) Fire Insurance Company. The president and directors of the Massachusetts Fire Insurance Company hereby give notice, That they shall not in future, confine their business to the four Eastern States, but will receive proposals at their office, in State street, and make insurance for any citizens of the United States, on dwelling houses, stores, and all other buildings; and on goods, wares and merchandize... By order of the board of directors, Samuel CABOT, Sec. Boston, Nov. 21, 1795.

Thursday, February 4, 1796. (Vol. II. No. 4.

(559) Charleston, December 23. On Saturday evening last, as mr. James JAFFRAY, of this city, merchant, mr. John ADAMS, of Edisto-island, and three negroes, were crossing Edisto-river, in an open boat, she was overset by a slaw of wind; soon after the mast breaking the boat righted, and they pailed her out, but having neither sails or oars, she was driven about by the tide for several hours before they got on a marsh. Mr. ADAMS, and one of the negroes perished with the cold in a few hours after the accident. Mr. JAFFRAY got on the marsh, and survived till 10 o'clock on Sunday morning, when he died.. Both mr. JAFFRAY and mr. ADAMS have left wives and families to lament this their untimely fate.

(560) Wilmington, February 4. From a London paper, of November 6, we learn, that the much celebrated Thomas PAINE is dead-that he died at the house of the American minister at Paris, of an abscess in his right side.

(561) Ran-Away, From the subscriber's plantation, last week, a Negro Fellow named ALLICK. He is about five feet four inches high; about 30 years old.. He formerly belonged to colonel DUDLEY, at Fayetteville..five dollars reward... John BURGWIN. Hermitage, 2d Feb. 1796.

(562) To Be Rented, For Three Years, from the first of March next, A Valuable Plantation in Bladen county, six miles from the North-West ___ containing 640 acres... T. FITZ-GERALD, Guardian. Wilmington, 2d Feb. 1796.

Thursday, February 11, 1796. (Vol. II. No. 5.

(563) POTTS & GIBBS Have for sale French Brandy, Apple Brandy, and Cheese.

(564) Congress of the United States. House of Representatives. Monday, January 4. (Letter to) P. A. ADET, minister plenipotentiary of the French republic, on his presenting the colours of France to the United States... G. WASHINGTON. United States, January 1st, 1796. True copy, George TAYLOR, Jun. Chief clerk in the dep. of state.

(565) Nassau, December 22. On Saturday last arrived here a Bermuda built sloop, laden with tar and staves, from Wilmington in North Carolina, bound to France, but cleared for Hamburg, brought in by three Bahama negroes, who were taken in April last by the ship Hennique, captain ALLAINE.. The sloop was a British vessel, owned and commanded by a captain COX, of Bermuda, but taken by a French privateer, and carried into North Carolina, where she was sold, and purchased by mr. LANGDON, a merchant there, who loaded the vessel with the above cargo, and..sold the same to one James or Giacomo GHERARDI, third lieutenant of the above mentioned privateer ship.. GHERARDI having kept possession of three Bahama negroes named Anthony SANDS, Cyrus FISHER, and James ALEXANDER, formed the plan of going to France..and shipped an American master, Gilbert SHERWIN, for the purpose of covering the property, together with two American lads, William WADE and George NICKSON..sailed from Wilming-

(565) (Cont.) ton.. On the 23d of last month, supposed near Bermuda, the negroes ..in a scuffle with GHERARDI,..over powered him, and, it is supposed, threw him overboard. They then compelled the American master to shape his course for this port.

(566) Wilmington, February 4. Married) Mr. Samuel MORGAN, of this place, to Miss Elizabeth TORRINS, of Duplin county, a young lady of the most gentle and engaging manners.

(567) Died) Last week, Mr. Thomas DAVIS, of this town-a gentleman universally esteemed and much regretted. His remains were attended to the church, by a large assemblage of the memebers of the Wilmington Lodge of Free-masons, where the funeral service was performed, and from thence to the waterside, amidst a crowd of citizens of all ranks. From the wharf the body was taken across the river, and conveyed to the place of interment at Rock Hill.

(568) For Sale. Sugar and Molasses... Charles JORDAN. Feb. 11, 1796.

(569) Wanted, On Freight or Charter, To load for Grenada, A Vessel of about 500 barrels burthen..of produce. Geo. HOOPER & Co. Feb. 11, 1796.

(570) Wanted to Charter, A Vessel From 120 to 150 tons burthen. Apply to Spafford DRURY. Feb. 11, 1796.

(571) An advance of cash will be made, all the bricks found, and six years' use of the premises will be given to any person, who will put such brick buildings on the large lot opposite to Mr. DORSEY's, as will correspond with a plan in the hands of WARD & LANGDON. Who will..give seven years' lease on a large body of Land, near William GAUSE, esquire's, in Brunswick county... Wilmington, 11th Feb. 1796.

(572) Newark, December 30. A few days since, a most horrid and inhuman act was committed by Mathias CUTLIP, at Newton, in the county of Sussex, on the body of his wife,.. CUTLIP had been butchering some beef for a neighbour, and returned home something intoxicated, and says to his children, I have been butchering cattle today, and now I intend to butcher your mother! The cries of the children, the intreaties of the wife, who was six months advanced in pregnancy, would avail nothing; the wretch! The monster in human shape, seized her, and gave her three separate stabs, one of which was mortal!.. He then attempted to make his escape, but was apprehended and is confined in the prison of that place...

Thursday, April 14, 1796. (Vol. II. No. 14.

(573) On the fourth day of the ensuing superior court, will be sold at public vendue, in the town of Wilmington, the following lands, belonging to the subscriber, viz. 640 acres on the forks of Long Creek, patented by Rufus MARSDEN, esq. &c. 360 acres on the north side of Long Creek, joining lines of John SWANN and Armand DE ROSSETTE, esqrs. deceased, &c... Alice HERON. April 6, 1796.

(574) Tuition. The Rev. W. MEREDITH, wishing to employ his leisure hours while in Wilmington, intends opening a seminary for useful literature where the Latin and English languages will be taught grammatically...

(575) Notice. Those indebted to the late co-partnership of DUNCAN and REARDAN by bond, note, or open account, are requested to make payment to the subscriber on or before the 20th instant... Geo. DUNCAN. April 6, 1796.

(576) From the New-York Diary. The subscriber is authorized to inform the merchants and the public in general, that there is established a Post-Office at Hamburgh, called the "American post expedition, for the convenience and safe correspondence between America and Europe."... James ZWISTER.

(577) Notice is hereby given to all persons concerned, That the subscriber has obtained letters of administration upon the estate of GHERARDI, dit GUIRARD, deceased ... F. FONTAINE, Admr. Wilmington, April 5th, 1796.

(578) Advertisement. Will be sold at public auction, on Saturday the 23d instant, at Mr. POTT's store, in the town of Smithville..a valuable Frame of a Boat... Charles BETTS. April 6, 1796.

(579) India Sugars. A quantity of excellent and very fair Calcutta Sugars for sale... John SHUTER.

(580) Wilmington, April 14. To the Electors of the town of Wilmington. Fellow citizens, Desirous to serve the country in which from my infancy I have been, and.. expect to be resident, I offer myself a candidate to represent you in the ensuing general assembly... James WALKER, Nephew of Major WALKER, in order to distinguish.

(581) The Rev. W. MEREDITH intends opening school on Tuesday April the 19th, at the house where Mr. HAMILTON now teaches. April 13.

(582) Notice. The subscribers having qualified as executors to the last will and testament of Charles JEWKES, deceased, request all persons indebted..to make immediate payment... P. MALLETT, Jos. G. WRIGHT, Exrs. April 11, 1796.

(583) Will be sold, on Monday next, the 18th instant, 25 or 30 casks of Merchantable Rice, And about 1000 bushels of rough Rice..the property of James M'CALLISTER, of Brunswick county, deceased, by R. QUINCE, Jun. Admr. April 13, 1796. N. B. The above mentioned produce will be sold at Belville.

(584) Notice. The subscriber, in addition to his advertisement in May, 1792, gives this final notice to all those indebted to the estate of Wm. EWANS, deceased, to settle and pay up to him..their respective accounts, on or before the 1st day of July next, otherwise..be sued... John MARTIN, Admr. Wilmington, 4th April, 1796.

Thursday, May 5, 1796. (Vol. II. No. 17.

(585) Notice. The subscriber expected to have had it in his power to close his business in this state and move to the Northward, before this period.-But the backwardness of many..still frustrates his design..he is therefore obliged to continue in this state..continues doing business... John JOHNSTON. Wilmington (N. C.) March 23, 1796.

(586) Advertisement. Charles LA PLACE, watch-maker, after having left this town, wrote to me, requesting me to redeem a certain Gold Watch, the property of a person who had put it in his hands..to be repaired, but whose name he could not recollect... Apply to P. MANGEON. March 23, 1796.

(587) For Sale, Gun powder of the first quality, lately received. John SHUTER. April 20, 1796.

(588) For Liverpool, The Ship Edward, Isaac HOWLAND, Master,..-For passage only

(588) (Cont.) apply to mr. Jeremiah DONOVAN, or to the captain on board. April 17, 1796.

(589) Washington Canal Lottery, No. 1. Whereas the state of Maryland has authorised us the underwritten to raise 26,250 dollars, for the purpose of cutting a canal through the city of Washington, from the Potomac to the Eastern Branch Harbour. The following is the Scheme of No. 1... Such prizes..not demanded in six months after the drawing is finished, shall be considered as relinquished for the benefit of the canal... (Signed) Norley YOUNG, Daniel CARROLL, of D., Lewis DEBLOIS, George WALKER, W. M. DUNCANSON, Thomas LAW, James BARRY. City of Washington, Feb. 9, 1796.

(590) Wilmington, May 2, 1796. Scheme of a Lottery, For the disposal of a variety of articles of merchandize... T. FITZ-GERALD, Proprietor.

(591) New-York, March 29. Yesterday the brig Eliza, captain Sweny WILSON, arrived from the Downs, in 34? days...

(592) Wilmington, May 5. On Thursday last came on the annual election for members of assembly for Brunswick county, when general SMITH was chosen senator and W. E. LORD, and Abraham BEZANT, esqrs. were chosen commoners. At the same time and place was held an election for a representative in congress. The state of the poll is as follows. William Henry HILL, 99. James GILLESPIE, 11. James KEENAN, 00. Gabriel HOLMES, 00.

(593) For Sale, 625 acres of land, upon the north-east side of the North-West River, in Bladen county, lying between Thomas BROWN and Samuel ASHE, esqrs'. land... John JOHNSTON. Wilmington, 4th May, 1796.

(594) Saddle and Harness making. George REED, Respectfully informs the public, that he intends declining business in the course of the summer, on account of..backward payments... Wilmington, May 4, 1796.

(595) London, January 23. Admiralty Sessions. Murder. Francis COLE, George COLLEY, Michael BLANCHE, and Emanuel BETHER were indicted, for that the aid COLE on the 28th of October last, about ___ leagues from the Isle of Wight, on the high seas, in a certain merchant's ship called the American Eagle, did assault William LITTLE, formerly the master of the said ship, and the said Villiam, upon the thigh and left groin, did strike, stab, penetrate, and wound with a knife-Also, that the said Francis COLE did giv_ the said William LITTLE three several morta_ wounds, of the depth of three inches, and the breadth of one inch; that the said Francis COLE feloniously, maliciously and with malice forethought did also strike and beat the said William LITTLE upon the head, back, belly, _ide, stomach, and groin, with an iron tea-kettle; of which he the said William LITTLE did then and there die; that the said George COLLEY, Michael BLANCHE, and Emanuel BETHER, were maliciously and feloniously aiding, abetting, assisting, and maintaining the said Francis COLE, in the murder so then, and there committed... A jury was impannelled to try Francis COLE and George COLLEY only, because the other two prisoners, Michael BLANCHE and Emanuel BETHER, not being subjects of his majesty (Spaniards.)

Sir William SCOTT, counsel for the prosecution, stated, that on the 15th of September last, the..American Eagle, sailed from Virginia, bound to Havre de Grace, with a cargo of tobacco.. The first witness, was Samuel DEARBON, an American, who deposed that he went on board the Eagle, in Newbury Port, on the 28th of June last..to Virginia.. There were then on board William LITTLE..Richard LITTLE, the mate, who was the captain's brother-John STIPNEY, John HARRIS, John CASSANDRA, Archibald HART, the

(595) (Cont.) four persons charged with the murder, and the witness. Soon after, Richard LITTLE, John STIPNEY, and John HARRIS died... (To be concluded in our next.)

Thursday, August 4, 1796. (Vol. III. No. 4.

(596) Proposals For printing by subscription, Sketches Of the History of the United States, From the peace of 1783, to the termination of the present session of congress, By Mathew CAREY... Philadelphia, February __, 1796.

(597) For Sale, On a credit of one and two years, two tracts of land-One of 640 acres, in New-Hanover county, on the west side of the north-east branch of Cape Fear River, on Turkey Creek,.. The other of 400 acres in Bladen county, on the Waccamaw Lake.. Conveyances will be made by the subscriber, under a power of attorney. Thos. WRIGHT. June 1st, 1796.

(598) A few copies of IREDELL's Revisal For sale at BLAKELEY and VANCE's, For cash only.

(599) Notice. As the co-partnership of TELFAIR and KIDDY has for some time been dissolved, this is..to request all those who may have claims to render in their.. accounts... John TELFAIR. Wm. KIDDY. Wilmington, 18th May, 1796.

(600) List of Letters remaining in the Wilmington Post-Office. A. Monsieur AUBINAU, James ANCRUM, John ARNOLD. B. James BRIAN, Ezekiel BRYANT, Thomas F. BATES, Gooden BOWEN, A. BARTLETT, Mrs. BEAUMEZ, Thomas BURKE, John BROWN. C. Gorton CHASE, Wm. COOPER, 2, Sam. CORNING, 3, Clerk of New Hanover, Monsieur CAUDRIN. D. Capt. W. DAVIS, Ozias DANFORTH, Joseph DEAN, Monsieur DE LAMOTTE, Mrs. Mille DEAL, mrs. DELL, monsieur Martin DUCOLOMBIE. F. Mr. FESTENS, mrs. FLUMING, 3. Andrew GREER, Henry GRIGGS, Needam GOSS. H. Sam. HALL, Henry HALSEY, mr. HERRIN. J. Capt. Thos. JONES, David JONES, S. R. JOCELYN. K. Wm. KELLY, Wm. KEDDIE, M. KEENON, John KENNEDY. Monsieur L'HOMAEA, 2, Eugene LCEET?, 5. M. Norman M'LEOD, mr. MANSFIELD, at mr. HOOPER's, Abijah MASON, Peggy M'PHERSON, Sam. MARCHANT, James M'GUFFORD. N. John NICHOLS, Thomas NEALE, Robert NIXON. P. William PARKER, monsieur PAISSON, capt. PEPPER, James PRICE. S. Lemuel STANWOOD, H. F. STRUDWICK, the Sheriff of New Hanover, 3, John SIMPSON, 2, Sam. SHAW, capt. SLOCUM. T. Nancy THOMAS, capt. Dan. TUBBS, David TUMAN, mr. TARBET, James TAYLOR. U. Mr. VICKERS, Henry URQUHART. W. WALKER & ANDERSON, John WARNER, Willis WHITFIELD, Benjamin WILLIAMS, Constant WOODMAN, William WINGATE. R. BRADLEY Asst. P. M.

(601) At home..We hear that Simeon DE WITT is appointed surveyor-general of the United States. We are happy to hear that an history of Connecticut by Benjamin TRUMBULL, is offered to the public, upon subscription, including its affairs from 1630 to 1712, in one octavo volume.

(602) Wilmington, August 4. To the Electors of the town of Wilmington. Fellow citizens, At the request of a number of respectable inhabitants of this town, I am induced to declare myself a candidate for the honor of representing you in the next general assembly... Henry URQUHART. July 11, 1796.

(603) To the Citizens of the town of Wilmington. Gentlemen, It appearing necessary ..that I should declare my sentiments thus publicly, to request your suffrages for the appointment of your representative in the next general assembly-I..offer myself as a candidate for that honor... William GREEN. August 4th, 1796.

(604) The Brigantine James & Margaret, is hourly expected in here From New-York, and

(604) (Cont.) will then take in freight for the above port. John SHUTER. August 3d.

(605) Public School. Thomas D. HAMILTON, Respectfully informs the inhabitants of Wilmington..that he intends opening a school here about the beginning of October.. teaching..Latin... Wilmington, August 3, 1796.

(606) To Be Let, That pleasantly situated house, lately occupied by general SMITH. Enquire of John BURGWIN. Wilmington, July 24, 1796.

(607) For Private Sale, On Consignment,..Soap..candles..Tea..Chairs, Ginger..Shot, Men's Fine Hats, Nails, assorted. T. FITZ-GERALD. July 27, 1796.

(608) For Sale, Cheap for Cash or Produce. Antigua Rum..New-England, do..French Brandy..Prime Sugars... Apply to Charles JORDAN. Wilmington, July 27, 1796.

(609) Tavern and Boarding-House. The subscriber takes the liberty of informing the public and his friends that he has opened a House of Entertainment, in that large and commodious building lately occupied by mr. SPALDING... James CARR. Wilmington, July 27, 1796.

(610) 4000 bushels of excellent St. Ubes Salt, and a few hogsheads of Prime Tobacco. Apply to WHEATON, TISDALE, & Co. July 21.

(611) Advertisement. To be sold by private sale, the plantation in Duplin county, known by the name of The Old Court House, whereon mr. Keenan LOVE lately lived. .. Also, 300 acres of land in said county, just above Rock Fish, and 300 acres in New Hanover, on HARRISON's Creek. For terms apply to James PRICE, on Topsail Sound, or to Archibald CUTLAR, in Wilmington.

1797 - All issues missing except for the following from Harvard University Library-February 9, 16; March 2, 23, 30; April 6, 20; June 8; September 7, 14, 21, 28; October 5, 12, 26; November 3. From the University of North Carolina-August 24.

HALL'S WILMINGTON GAZETTE.
(No. 6.) Thursday, February 9, 1797. (Vol. I.)

(612) On Friday the 24th instant, will be sold, for the benefit of the underwriters, The brig Neptune, and all her materials... Wm. NUTT, Auct'r.

(613) The subscribers have 500 Casks Flax Seed, which they wish to Freight to Ireland. Geo. HOOPER & Co. January 19.

(614) 100 barrels Pork, and Bills on Boston at 30 days sight, for sale by R. LANGDON. February 2.

(615) Excellent London Porter in bottles, for sale by BLAKELEY and VANCE. Feb. 2.

(616) For Sale, Twenty hhds. 3d proof St. Croix Rum. Also 10 quarter casks of excellent Dry Lisbon Wine. M. R. WILLKINGS. January 12.

(617) Best London Particular Madeira, Fayal, Teneriffe, Lisbon, and Port Wine.. Cordage..other articles, for sale by John CALHORDA. January 5.

(618) Notice. The subscribers to the University are informed, that their last payments become due this day.. Warrants will be issued and suits brought against those

(618) (Cont.) who do not..pay their subscriptions in a short time. R. BRADLEY. January 3.

(619) The subscribers intend opening a Grocery Store, on the first of March next, opposite DORSEY's Hotel. DORSEY and MARTIN. February 2.

(620) To The Public. The subscriber intends to leave this state as soon as his affairs can be settled.. All those who have still remaining in his shop, Watches, Silver work or Jewelry, are particularly requested to call or send for the same... D. LAMBERTOZ. February 2.

(621) VOSBURGH & CHILDS. (Windsor Chair-Makers, from New-York) Respectfully inform the citizens of North-Carolina, that they have commenced the above business on the south side of Dock-street, near the wharf...

(622) Boot and Shoe Manufactory. The subscriber respectfully informs..that his business will be carried on in every branch... G. CHACE. February 2.

(623) I will be obliged to those persons who borrowed the undernamed books, to returned them speedily: The first volume of the Bon Ton Magagine, for..1791;..the second volume of Elegant Extracts, in prose, printed in London, 1794. Robert HARLEY. February 2.

(624) University of North-Carolina. Whereas William HILL, Esquire, late attorney for the Trustees in the district of Wilmington, has lodged with the subscriber all those bonds taken by him, for the sale of escheated property.. Notice is hereby given to all concerned, that unless full payment be made at the store of Walter and Gavin ALVES, on Little-river, by the first day of April next, on all bonds..then.. due, suits will be..commenced... Gavin ALVES, Treasurer. January 1.

(625) Republican Livery stables. The subscriber informs..that he has prepared himself with Livery stables for keeping horses, at the Garden of Eden, three-quarters of a mile from town... David DUDLEY, Who has for sale..Leather, makes men and women's Saddles, and will furnish Chair and Coach Harness, and Carriage Trimmings on the shortest notice. Wilmington, January 19.

(626) Wilmington, January 26. Scheme of a Lottery. For the disposal of sundry articles of Merchandize... T. FITZGERALD, J. MUMFORD, Proprietors.

(627) Public Notice Is hereby given, that the subscribers have qualified as executors of the last will and testament of John JOHNSTON, merchant, late of this town, deceased... Henry HOSKINS, Francis FONTAINE, Ex'rs. January 12.

(628) Notice. The subscribers have qualified as executors of the last will and testament of the late Doctor Henry KINGSBURY... Philip SPAULDING, Joseph DEAN, Ex'rs. January 5.

(629) Norfolk, January 26. Yesterday arrived here the brig Betsey, Captain T. BAKER 21 days from St. Martins. Came passenger in the brig Betsey, Capt. John HALL, of the sch'r Rebecca of Baltimore, (captured and carried into St. Martins)..was plundered of every thing he had, by the prize master and crew..part of his crew put on board a prison ship, who..work in the day time, and at night were put in irons.

(630) Wilmington, February 9. Court of Hymen. On Thursday evening last Mr. John CALHORDA was married to Miss Sarah MARSHALL, both of this town.

(631) Public Auction. This Day, at 12 o'clock, Before the subscriber's Auction-room, Will Be Sold, 100 hogsheads St. Ubes and Liverpool Salt. Thomas FITZGERALD, Auctioneer. February 9.

(632) For Private Sale. A Negro wench and child... Apply to Thomas FITZGERALD.

(633) Take Notice. Came to the subscriber's plantation, on the Sound, on the 29th of January, a negro fellow who says his name is LEWIE, that he belongs to a man in the West Indies, and ran away from a vessel which left this port about three months ago.. He is a Guinea negro..about five feet four inches high, slender built, and very black. Joseph ROBINSON. February 9.

(634) For Sale, A tract of Land in Chatham county, on Haw-river, consisting of 450 acres, finely timbered and watered, with a good house, and out-house, stable, and a good flat at a valuable ferry, commonly called CLARK's Ferry, on the main road from Fayetteville to Hillsborough. It has a natural fine mill seat, the race about half done, the dam and floodgate finished, timber for the sawmill is hewed and at the spot, some of the grist mill timber is got, and 30,000 bricks at the place.. For particulars apply to Henry Lewis LUTTERLOH, Chatham county, or to Edward JONES, Esq. Attorney at Law, Wilmington. February 9.

(635) Twenty Dollars Reward Will be paid to any person who will apprehend and bring to me, at the Hermitage, in New-Hanover county, a negro fellow named YORK, who ran away last Tuesday, without the least provocation. He is a likely able-bodied negro, about five feet 9 or 10 inches high.. The said fellow is outlawed... John BURGWIN. Hermitage, 4th February.

(636) List of Letters remaining in the Post-Office at Wilmington. Governor ASHE, ALGEE. Timothy BLOODWORTH, Madam BROWN, George BUCHANNAN, Charles BLACKBURN, Thomas BURK, Thomas F. BATES, Amhert BARTLETT, Mary BALLANTINE. Captain S. CORNING, 2, John COLVIN, Tobias COBB, Hugh CRAMMER, John CHADWICK, James COXETER, Jacob CHADWICK, Lydia CRANDLE. Ozias DANFORTH, Mr. DATE, French taylor; Captain William DAVIS, 2. Doctor Robert DICKSON. William T. ELSWORTH, John ERWIN. Nicholas FENNEL. William GUTHERIE, Henry GEDDES, William GORE. John HALL, Henry HOSKINS, Captain John HARTLEY, Daniel HARTWELL, Jonathan HUNTINGTON, Mr. HARTMAN, Mr. HUMMOND, Ezra HUBBELL, Henry HERVEY, Robert HENDERSON, Eman HOLLINSWORTH. Samuel JONES, 4, Thomas JONES, Edward JONES. Doctor H. KINGSBURY, Captain Zeph. KINGSLEY, John KELLY, Miss Anna LONG, Margaret LAMB. Auly MACNAUGHTON, John MILNE, 2, Joseph MILNE, 2, John MARSHALL, Samuel MARCHANT, John MAGILL, George M'CULLOCH, Dugald M'DUFFIE, George M'DONALD, Neil M'KAY, Archibald M'CALLUM, James M'HENRY, Peter MALLET, MANGEON and LALANE. Solomon NORTON, 3, William NEW. Hans PATTEN, William PARKER, 5. Mrs. QUIGLEY, Charles QUANDRILL. William ROBERTSON, Amos RICHARDSON, Mrs. ROBINS, Guios ROW. Mrs. STRUDWICK, Francis SMITH, Mildred SWANN, Moses SMITH, John SIMPSON, Peter SULL, The Sheriff of New-Hanover. John TELFAIR, John THOMPSON, James TAYLOR, Captain George TURNER, 3, David TUMAN, 4. William WILKINSON, 3, Henry WARD, William WALLIS, Henry WATTERS, James WALKER, John WILLKINGS, Willis WHITFIELD, Captain Thomas WALKER, John WILLIS, Benjamin WILLIAMS. R. BRADLEY, Ast. P. M. January 24.

(637) Fifty Dollars Reward. Stolen from the subscriber, in Wilmington, North-Carolina, on Sunday the first instant, a light grey Horse..-likewise a saddle, bridle, and a brown camblet great coat, lined with green baize, and has claret coloured basket buttons. The person who carried away the said horse, &c. passes by the name of Davis ALE, otherwise Davis ALLEN; he is about 26 years of age, 5 feet 11 inches high, well made, passes for a school and singing-master... J. R. ROBINSON. He has passed by Tarborough for Edenton.

(638) Ten Dollars Reward. Ran away from the subscriber, a negro fellow named TOBY ..will probably attempt to get off in some vessel, and pass as a freeman by the name of ELLISS... A. B. TOOMER. January 26.

(No. 7.) Thursday, February 16, 1797. (Vol. I.)

(639) A. HALL has for sale, WRIGHT's new and complete Life of Jesus Christ,.. A Case respecting British Debts.. A Supplement to IREDELL's Revisal..MARTIN's Justice.. A description of Occacock Inlet.. Address from Robert Goodloe HARPER to his constituents... Printing-Office, Feb. 16.

(640) John CALHORDA, In addition to his former stock of Wines, has received by the late arrivals, Sherry in quarter-casks and Tent Wines.. Also a fresh assortment of Dry Goods... February 16.

(641) Wilmington, February 16. Extract of a letter from a merchant in New-York, to his correspondent here, dated the 27th January. "In consequence of the depredations made on our trade by the French, an Embargo is much talked of..reports say it is now under consideration in the Senate..."

(642) From the Baltimore Telegraphe. Messrs. CLAYLAND, DOBBIN, & Co. I have just been presented with the enclosed letters and send you a copy, (the originals are in the hands of Mr. James CALHOUN).. Yours, &c. Joshua BARNEY, Brigadier General in the service of France. Baltimore, January 20.-Charleston, January 3, 1797. Mr. James CALHOUN, Sir, A French armed vessel called the Vengeance, took from on board a vessel of ours, coming from Jamaica, a hogshead of Jamaican rum, and gave the captain an order upon a Mr. ___, of your place, to pay the amount, (on account of Captain BARNEY)... W. & E. CRAAFS.-At sea, 12th December, 1797. Sir, Having met the schooner Sally, bound to Charleston, Captain John LEICH,..finding myself in want, I took with the consent of the Captain, one hogshead containing 109 gals. rum which I pray you to pay for..and place it to the account of Captain BARNEY, my owner... Your humble servant, L'EVEILLE. Mr. ___, merchant, Baltimore.

(643) The New-Hanover Troop of Cavalry are requested to attend parade properly Equipped, at the usual place in Wilmington, on Wednesday the 22d instant. T. HILL, Capt.

(644) Just received from Liverpool, and for sale by the subscriber, 1000 bushels Salt, and a number Crates Ware. Richard LANGDON. February 16.

(645) For Sale, On board the schooner Amity, Benjamin SHAPLEY, master, lying at the Market-Wharf, or at mr. LANGDON's store, Jamaica Rum..Gin..Wine..Salt..Window Glass 8 by 10 and 7 by 9... February 16.

(646) For Sale, Two Tracts of Land upon Town creek, in Brunswick county.. Apply to Mr. James WALKER, or the subscriber. Mary A. WALKER. Wilmington, Feb. 16.

(647) Notice. Ordered, by the Commissioners of the town of Wilmington, That all persons having any masts, spars, logs, or lumber of any kind, laying in the public docks, or streets of the town, remove the same from thence in five days from the date hereof... By order of the Board, J. BERNARD, T. Clk. February 13.

(648) Dancing School. Richard COLEMAN Presents his most respectful compliments to the ladies and gentlemen of Wilmington and its vicinity, and informs them that his Dancing school will again commence on Monday the 20th instant, at Mr. James CARR's... February 16.

(649) Henry LATIMER, Esquire, is re-elected Senator of the United States, by the Legislature of the state of Delaware, for six years, commencing the first of March next.

(No. 9.) Thursday, March 2, 1797. (Vol. I.)

(650) 20 Dollars Reward. Ran away from the subscriber, on the 10th inst., a negro fellow named SCIPEO, formerly the property of George DAVIS, Esquire... Richard QUINCE. February 23.

(651) At a meeting of the Commissioners of Pilotage and Navigation for the Port of Wilmington, Ordered, That all vessels arriving in this Port shall be strictly examined by the pilot who may bring such over the main bar or New-Inlet, and if any sickness be on board..such vessel or vessels..shall not proceed farther than Battery-Island, and if at the New-Inlet..not farther than Five Fathom Hole.. Ordered, That all vessels from the West-Indies and Bahama Islands, that may not be stopped at Battery-Island or Five Fathom Hole..shall be brought to at the Dram-Tree..shall remain until report be made by the pilot and permission given by the health officer in writing..under the penalties set forth in the Quarantine Law. Published by order of the Commissioners, William NUTT, Clerk. February 23.

(652) Taken up by the subscriber's people, a ships Boat... Benjamin SMITH. Belvedere, February 21.

(653) Wilmington, March 2. Public Auction. To-Morrow, at 12 o'clock, Before the subscriber's Auction-room, Will Be Sold, Two large Scale Beams with Weights..Axes.. Skillets and Spiders..Whip and Mill-Saws... William NUTT, Auctioneer. March 2.

(654) To Be Sold, A high post fluted Mahogany Bedstead with cornishes; a complete set of new Bed Curtains of fashionable yellow ground Chintz, with the fringes, lace, lines, rings, leads, tassels and pins thereto appertaining.. The above to be had new as from the Upholsterer's, and for the cost, say 185 dollars. Inquire of Francis FONTAINE. March 2.

(655) James I. THURSTON formerly acting partner in the Company of WHEATON, TISDALE & Co. of this place, having lately left said business, it will in future be carried on under the firm of WHEATON, TISDALE & Co. as aforesaid, and conducted by Robert BALL, present acting partner, who has for sale, 35 casks Old Sherry Wine..Port..Madeira..Glass Ware..Tea..Salt. Wilmington, March 2.

(656) By virtue of a writ of Fieri Facias to me directed, at the suit of Robert HOWE, as the admr. of James M'ALISTER, will be sold for ready money, on Saturday the 18th of March next, at the ferry opposite Wilmington, Five Negroes, viz. PRENTER, AZZURE, ADONIAS, COLEY and SAM. Thomas LEONAREL, Sheriff. Bladen county, February 28.

(657) Notice. The subscriber having qualified as admr. to the last will and testament of the late Thomas JAMES, of Duplin county, requests all persons indebted to the estate..to make payment... John JAMES, Adm'r. South Washington, Mar. 1.

(658) Notice. The subscriber having qualified as adminx. to the last will and testament of the late Sampson MOSELY, requests all persons indebted to the estate..to make payment... Sarah MOSELY, Adm'x. March 2.

(659) For Charleston (To sail immediately) The Schooner Betsey, (Charleston Packet,) John M'ILHENNY, master... March 2.

(660) For New-Providence, (To sail in 10 days) The Brig Nancy, of Washington, Samuel SLOCUM, Master... February 23.

(661) For Sale. A quantity of barrel Pork and Beef; Hogs Lard, and Butter..; black eyed Pease; Deer Skins.. Also, Peach Brandy by the barrel and 100 barrels Flour. Apply to Isaac J. PATTERSON. February 23.

(No. 12.) Thursday, March 23, 1797. (Vol. I.)

(662) Boston, February 27. Saturday morning about half past eight o'clock, this town was alarmed at the cry of Fire, occasioned by the copper of the tar house belonging to Messrs. TYLER and CASWELL, boiling over, which instantly caught some hemp ..the ropewalks of TYLER and CASWELL, John WINTHROP, Esq. JEFFERY and RUSSEL, and four dwelling houses, were consumed...

(663) Wilmington, March 23. By the schooner Polly, Stephen CONNICK, which arrived last week, from New-Providence the printer has received the Bahama Gazette...

(664) We are just favored with the following..by Capt. Archibald CUNNINGHAM, of the ship Nancy, belonging to this port, who left Bristol on the 22d of December, and had a tedious passage of 69 days.-On his arrival on this coast, he was boarded off Charleston, on the 2d inst..by the Republican schooner privateer Pouline, Alexander BOLCHOS, master, who took possession of his ship and cargo as a prize, for being from a British port, and took out William MURRAY, chief mate, Henry WILLIS, second mate, six seamen, and shaped a course for some Spanish port in East Florida.. On the 10th inst. they arrived off St. Augustine bar.. The Governor..told them that he had no orders to permit any American vessels to be brought in as prizes, that he wished to befriend both the French and Americans. After lying there four days, the captain of the privateer proposed to capt. CUNNINGHAM to give him up his ship and cargo for the sum of 2250 dollars, who acceded thereto..and mr. Wm. COOK, a merchant of Savannah, being there, advanced him the money by giving bills upon his owner...

(665) To Be Hired By the month, quarter, or half year, two good black Carpenters... T. HILL. March 23.

(666) For Sale, A few hds. St. Croix Sugar, by George DUNCAN. March 23.

(667) For Sale, A few neat Saddles, Saddle Bags and Bridles.. Also, Boots and Shoes made as usual. Gorton CHACE. March 23.

(668) The subscriber having taken that commodious house opposite the Church, lately occupied by Joseph FRILICH, intends keeping a house of Entertainment... William MITCHELL. Newbern, March 17.

(669) Ten Dollars Reward. Ran away from my plantation, on Wednesday evening last, a negro lad about 18 years old..-he served his time to mr. Peter HARRIS, blacksmith, in Wilmington..says he has a wife, a negro girl belonging to mr. VANCE, named LUCINDA... John BURGWIN. Hermitage, 17th March.

(670) Three Dollars Reward. Ran away from the subscriber's plantation at the sound, a mulatto Girl named NANCY, about 16 years of age... Peter MAXWELL. March 23.

(671) To Be Sold, That part of Lot No. 5, in the town of Wilmington, which was sold by David FLOWERS to the subscriber, bounded on the east by Front-street, on the south by ground formerly Wm. EWAN's, now belonging to John MARTIN, on the west by

(671) (Cont.) ground which the said David FLOWERS sold to James FLEMING, and now belongs to Wm. CAMPBELL, and on the north by ground belonging to Peter MALLET.. For further particulars apply to Mr. Richard BRADLEY, or to the subscriber, who has also for sale several Lots in Fayetteville, particularly The Houses and Lot possessed by Col. DEKEYSER. The Houses and Lot possessed by Samuel WILSON, on the north side of court-house square. The Houses and Lot possessed by Joseph HAYS, opposite to Mr. ADAMS's store. Several unimproved Lots..100 acres and upwards adjoining the town, between Grove street and Lewis BARGE's brick house. 70 acres..at the back of James M'CRACKAN's, and on both sides of Ramsay street. 150 acres..above Haymount, within a mile from town. 640 acres joining and above Malcolm MACKAY's on the drains of Cross Creek, about 4 miles from town. 640 do. on do. adjoining the last mentioned 640 acres. 640 do. on the north east side of Cape-Fear, about 5 miles above MOORE's ferry..below Thomas JONES's lands. 200 do. back of do. 200 do on Flat swamp, joining Nathaniel HOLTON's lands. 150 do..between lands of Jesse POTTS & William LORD. 500 acres..on Cedar creek..formerly the property of Sylvanus WILSON, about 8 miles below BLOCKER's ferry. 200 acres formerly Charles MACNAUGHTON's, on Brown Marsh, Bladen county. 100 ditto in the Great Marsh, formerly GOODWIN's in Robeson county. 100 do. in do. do. do. county. 100 do. on Bear's creek, Moore county. 250 do. on Waggon branch, waters of Deep river, in said county. 1333 1/3 acres on STONE's river, in the state of Tennessee. 11,881 do. of R. HENDERSON and Company's Grant from the Assembly of North-Carolina, in POWER's valley and on Claret river. 2822 do. of R. HENDERSON & Company's Grant from the Assembly of Virginia, in Kentucky. Apply at Hillsborough, to James HOGG. March 23.

(672) Notice. The subscriber intends leaving this place shortly..all persons having any demands against him,..bring in their accounts... Jonathan AVERY. March 9.

(673) Wanted A good house Wench, and a Negro Boy about 12 or 13 years of age, to attend in a family. Enquire at Mr. VORRIER's?. March 16.

(674) Notice. All persons having accounts unsettled with WHEATON, TISDALE and Co. while Samuel I. THURSTON was acting partner, are requested to..settle the same..make immediate payment to Robert BALL, present acting partner... Daniel WHEATON. March 16.

(675) The subscriber intends leaving Wilmington about the middle of April next, requests those indebted to him, to make speedy payment... William SMEETON. March 16.

(676) Notice. The Copartnership of SPAULDING and DEAN being this day, by mutual consent, dissolved, all persons having accounts unsettled with them, are requested to call on Joseph DEAN, at Mr. Samuel LOWDER's store, for settlement... Philip SPAULDING, Joseph DEAN. March 6.

(677) Notice. The copartnership of HARRIS and SPRINGS is by mutual consent, this day dissolved; those whom they may have running accounts with, are requested to render them for settlement... Peter HARRIS, Sudgwick SPRINGS. March 9.

(No. 12.) Thursday, March 23, 1797. (Vol. I.) EXTRA.

(678) Philadelphia, March 7. An account of the inauguration of our new President and Vice-President.. On Saturday at 12 o'clock..John ADAMS, as President of the United States attended in the chamber of the house of representatives, to take his oath of office.. On his entrance as well as on the entrance of the late President, and of Thomas JEFFERSON, the Vice-President, loud and reiterated applause involuntarily burst from the audience.

(679) George BUCHANAN Respectfully informs the people of Wilmington..that he has opened Store second door from Captain JOCELYN's, east of the new court-house, and has for sale, the following Goods: Spirits..Coffee..Sugar, Raisins; Cinnamon; Cloves, Nutmegs... March 16.

(No. 13.) Thursday, March 30, 1797. (Vol. I.)

(680) New-York, March 6. Spoliation. At a meeting of the underwriters in this city, affected by spoliations on American commerce, held at the Tontine coffee house, on Friday the 24th of February, Messrs. William NEILSON, Isaac GOUVERNEUR, and John B. COLES, were appointed a committee for the purpose of adopting such measures as they may deem necessary, for obtaining compensation for vessels and cargoes which have been taken by the belligerent powers.. The committee..have appointed Mr. John FERRERS as their agent...

(681) Philadelphia, March 7. The following resolution was laid on the table of the house of representatives of the United States. Whereas it is stated to this house in the report of the secretary of the treasury of the 15th of February, "That the accounts of Edmund RANDOLPH, esq. late secretary of state, for monies advanced to him for foreign expenditure, still remain unsettled..."

(682) Wilmington, March 30. Extract of an act entitled "An act concerning the Circuit Courts of the United States" approved March 3, 1797.. Timothy PICKERING. Secretary of State. North-Carolina. In obedience to the foregoing act, notice is herby given..that the stated District Courts..will hereafter be holden at Newbern.. Given under my hand at Edenton, this 15th day of March, 1797. Michael PAYNE, Marshal of North-Carolina District.

(683) Division Orders. The Brigadier-General of the third and fourth brigades will issue the necessary orders for the purpose of having their respective brigades reviewed by regiments.. As these reviews are ordered for the purpose of ascertaining the force and condition of the militia of the division.. It is requested that the Brigadier-Generals with their Brigade Majors, will attend the reviews of their respective brigades, in order to make proper arrangements on the force of rank. Thomas BROWN, Major-General of the 2d D. of N. C. M. March 30.

(684) For New-Providence, (To sail the 4th of April) The fast sailing Brig Salacia, Elihu NOYES, master. For passage apply to the master on board, or to Robert MUTER. March 30.

(685) Notice. The subscriber has been appointed Land Entry-Taker for the county of New-Hanover. R. HARLEY. March 30.

(686) Oratorical Chamber. On Monday Evening, 3d of April, Mr. WALL will exhibit at the Theatre, for the last time, a Theatrical Dish Of All Sorts, consisting of Prologue, Epilogue and Song, with Music on the Guitar. Tickets 1-2 dollar may be had of Messrs. ISAACKS & LEVY, and at Mr. James PRICE's.

(687) For Sale,..A Boat, built of Live Oak and Cedar, 65 feet keel, 14 feet beam.. enquire of Charles & P. BELHAM, who have for sale, A few hhds of sweet scented Tobacco. March 30.

(688) For Sale By the subscriber, cheap for Cash, About 37 M feet of merchantable Lumber. Anthony B. TOOMER. March 30.

(689) For Sale, On moderate terms, Best French Rappe Snuff. LEGRO, In the aliy near mr. CARR's. March 30.

(690) Notice. The subscribers have qualified as executors to the last will and testament of Mrs. Margaret BELOATE, late of Wilmington, deceased... Joseph G. WRIGHT, Samuel R. JOCELYN, Ex'rs. March 30.

(691) Notice. The subscriber having qualified as sole executor of the last will and testament of Mary and Thomas VICKARS, late of Wilmington, requests all persons indebted to said estate to make speedy payment... Edward RUSSEL. March 30.

(No. 14.) Thursday, April 6, 1797. (Vol. I.)

(692) Allmand HALL Has for sale, at his Book & Stationary Store, corner of Market and Second-streets.. Also, Maps of Kentucky, Tennessee, and the West-Indies...

(693) The subscriber, D. LAMBERTOZ, having on hand sundry articles of Silver Plate, Jewelry, &c. intends to dispose of them by the following Scheme of a Lottery... Wilmington, April 6.

(694) Twenty Dollars Reward. Ran away some time ago, a mulatto fellow named ELIJAH, about 5 feet 7 or 8 inches high.. The above reward..to any persons that will deliver him to Doctor HILL in Wilmington, or the subscribers at Rockey Point. W. DAVIS, T. MOORE. April 6.

(695) New-York, March 15. Yesterday arrived here the schooner Little John, captain Henry KING, from Port au-Prince...

(696) Wilmington, April 6. Appointments-By Authority. Joel BARLOW, of Connecticut, consul general for the city and kingdom of Algiers. John GAVINE?, consul for the port of Gibraltar, in the room of James SIMPSON, appointed consul for Morocco. Procople? Jacinto POLLOCK, of Pennsylvania, consul for the port of New Orleans. Frederick FOLGER, of Maryland, consul for the port and district of Aux Cayes, St. Domingo. Charles JACKSON, of Georgia, district attorney. David LENOX, of Pennsylvania, agent to reside in the kingdom of Great Britain, for the relief and protection of American seamen Vice John TRUMBULL, appointed fifth commissioner, under the British treaty.

(697) Theatre, By Particular Desire. To all lovers of Wit, Satire, Character and Sentiment, Llewellyn L. WALL, Comedian, will exhibit on Saturday Evening the 8th of April, An elegant Lecture on Heads..also perform on the Guitar..tickets..may be had at Messrs. ISAACKS and LEVY's store, and Mr. Jas. PRICE's, for half a dollar each... April 6.

(698) For the accomodation of the Poor. Any person disposed to undertake the building a house in the town of Wilmington..60 feet by 16, divided into four apartments, with two stacks of brick chimneys, will give their proposals in writing to John MACLELLAN, Treasurer. April 6.

(699) The subscriber is a qualified Executor of the estate of Thomas CUNNINGHAME, deceased; and is in readiness to settle any legal accounts relative to the same. Joshua POTTS, Ex'r. Wilmington, April 6.

(700) Robert ADAM & Co. Have for sale, Best London Porter in bottles; ditto Brown stout..Peach Brandy..Queen's Ware..Refined Sugar-small loaves..Flour & Dry Goods.. April 6.

(701) For Sale, In hogsheads and barrels, Apple Brandy, Cherry Rum, and Molasses... John SHUTER. April 6.

(702) Lost or stolen from the subscriber, at the house of George LOGAN, on the 21st of March last, a Black Pocket Book, containing the following papers: PEABODIE and LEARCHER's obligation for six months rent of the lower part of George LOGAN's house; Roger CUTLER's note of hand for 9 dol's. payable to Duncan M'RAE; two bills of sale from Wm. G. M'DANIEL to the subscriber, for two horses..handsome reward... William COOPER. April 6.

(703) Ten Dollars Reward. Ran away from the subscriber, a negro man called ANDREW, he is a stout thick set short fellow, about 24 years of age..was raised at the plantation that Mr. M'GUIRE lived at, on the North-West and it is possible he will harbour between that and Gen. BROWN's, as he has a negro woman of the General for a wife... John HILL. April 6.

(No. 16.) Thursday, April 20, 1797. (Vol. I.)

(704) Wilmington, April 20. Mr. HALL, Saw in your paper of the 23d ult. a paragraph which reflected on my conduct as late mate of the ship Nancy, A. CUNNINGHAM master... James MURRAY.

(705) For Sale, The House and part of the Lot in Smithville, formerly belonging to J. R. GAUTIER, Esquire. Also a considerable quantity of good Bricks, which may be delivered at Belvedere or Wilmington. Apply to Benjamin SMITH. April 20.

(706) To Be Sold Cheap for Cash. My Saw and Grist-Mill on VAUGHAN's Creek, near the ferry on LIVINGSTON Creek.-Also will be Sold a team of Six Oxen. William HOOPER. April 20, 1797.

(707) Dancing School. Mr. COLEMAN..informs..that he purposes teaching three afternoons in each week, for one month, to commence on Monday next... April 20.

(708) Fifty Dollars Reward. Ran away on Monday the 10th day of the present month, from the subscriber's Belvedere plantation..a country-born negro fellow named TONEY- he is about 40 years of age, 5 feet 7 or 8 inches high, thick set, has a round face, and stutters. Ten dollars..for..him at the above plantation. If harboured by a slave, 15 dollars for such delivery and conviction.. If harboured by a free person, 20 dollars.. If harboured on board a vessel..with an intent to carry him out of the state, the reward of 50 dollars will be paid..by Benjamin SMITH.

(709) Five Dollars Reward. Ran away from me..a negro wench named SABINA.. She will endeavour to pass as in the service of General SMITH. William CLAYPOOLE. Wilmington, April 20.

(710) To Be Sold,..at the court-house in Wilmington, on the 16th day of May next, A Tract of Land in Bladen county, lying on the north east side of North-West River of Cape-Fear, containing 525 acres, adjoining the river on the space between the lands of his Excellency Samuel ASHE, and those of William Davis KELLY... F. FONTAINE, Henry HOSKINS, Ex'rs. Wilmington, April 4.

(711) Ten Dollars Reward. Ran away from the subscriber, two men slaves,..by the names of BUCK and PARKER. The former is a black, of about 30 years of age, 5 feet 8 or 9 inches high.. The latter is a yellow or mulatto colour, one or two inches higher than the former..by trade a cooper and tolerable house carpenter. He was

(711) (Cont.) purchased some years ago from captain James BRADLEY in Bladen county, near Elizabeth... Peter MAXWELL. April 13.

(712) Forty Dollars Reward. Ran away from the Hermitage, last night, two Negroes. One of them named FRANK, a cooper..about 5 feet 4 inches high, has remarkable thick lips.. The other named NED, who served his time with Messrs. HARRIS and SPRINGS, blacksmiths, in Wilmington.. NED is a tall slender made boy, with a good countenance .. And as I have reason..to believe, that my negro fellow YORK (advertised in this paper) has been harboured by some evil disposed person, I will give a reward of 30 Dollars to..give me information of such harbouring, on conviction.. The said three fellows are outlawed, and may be shot, unless they return to me in 10 days. John BURGWIN. Hermitage, April 12.

(No. 23.) Thursday, June 8, 1797. (Vol. I.)

(713) Petersburg, May 30. On the 22d inst. at the Federal Court at Richmond, the Grand Jury for the District of Virginia, made the following presentment: "We of the Grand Jury of the U. States, for the District of Virginia, protest as a real evil the circular letters of several members of the late Congress, and particularly..with the signature of Samuel J. CABELL?."

(714) June 2. Accounts from Paris mention, that Thomas PAINE left that city about the 1st of March, on his return to America.

(715) Wilmington, June 8. Errata. Under the head of Deaths, in last week's Gazette, for Mr. John TELFAIR, read Mr. William A. ATKINS, who died at the house of Mr. TELFAIR.

(716) Notice. That the subscriber has for sale the following Tracts or Parcels of Land lying in Duplin county, formerly the property of Joseph and Walter BLAKE, Esqrs. viz. 400 acres on the north-east and south sides of Cypress creek swamp, patented by John NORRIS, and by him conveyed to Thomas HICKS, &c. 320 acres, being part of 640 acres granted to John POCOCK in 1737, beginning at a branch near the mouth of a small branch running into Rock-Fish creek. 100 acres on the north side of Goshen swamp, at the mouth of Cowshole-swamp, bordering on the land formerly James TAYLOR's. 250 acres on Lime Stone on the west side of the North-east river, above the Dutch Landing, formerly Plunket BALLARD's; 60 acres on Long Branch, joining RIVENBERG's, surveyed for Peter YOUNG, and from him conveyed to John THULLY, &C. 56 acres on the Northwest side of the North-east branch of Cape-Fear, formerly the property of William BURTON, above said BURTON's home place. 300 acres on the north side of Rock-Fish creek, within half a mile of Rock-Fish bridge, formerly CASE's land. 100 acres on the north side of STEWART's creek, below the Great-Road. 200 acres on MAXWELL's swamp, near Thomas KEENAN's old place. 100 acres on Long Branch, being a branch of Rock-Fish creek, conveyed from RIVENBERG to John FOLK, &c... John BURGWIN. Hermitage. June 5.

(717) Notice. The drawing of Edward RUSSELL's Lottery will commence on Wednesday next... Edward RUSSELL. June 8.

(718) For New-York, (To sail in six days,) The Schooner William, Captain CLIFFORD.. For passage apply to the Master on board, or to Charles JORDAN. June 2.

(719) Good Fresh Flour, and Corn Meal, For Sale, by F. FONTAINE & Co. May 18.

(720) Forty Shillings Reward. Ran away from the subscriber, a negro fellow named

(720) (Cont.) ALICK, about 20 years of age..has..I am informed, been lurking about the plantation of Mr. John HILL, to whom his mother belongs. Samuel VANCE. June 8.

(721) United States. Custom-House Wilmington, North Carolina, 31st May 1797. The Commissioner of the Revenue of the United States having directed me to contract for the Stakeage of the channel of Cape-Fear river, persons desirous of undertaking the same, are requested to deliver their proposals in writing on or before the 19th day of June... James READ, Collector.

(722) Valuable Lands For Sale, 2000 Acres about eight miles from Wilmington, nearly opposite the flats, on the east side of Cape Fear river.. Also, Seven miles of Bank Land south of Cabbage-Inlet.. For terms apply to Mr. James WALKER, or to the subscriber. William MOSELEY. June 1.

(723) Notice. Agreeably to an act of the General Assembly,..in 1794..will be exposed to sale, at the court-house in Duplin, on the 18th of October next, for the payment of the taxes, the following lands, viz. 640 acres on the east side of the North-east river. 640 acres on the west side of the North-east river. 3000 acres on the north-east marsh, joining Thomas BARFIELD's. The above lands are the property of Samuel JOHNSTON, Esq. of Edenton. Thomas WRIGHT, Sheriff. Duplin county, May 25.

(724) Five Dollars Reward. Ran away from the subscriber, on the 31st day of March, 1796, a Negro fellow named SAMPSON, about 50 years old, 5 feet high.. He is Guinea born, speaks bad English, is a fortune teller and conjurer.. Since he has been in this country, he has lived about Muddy-creek, in Duplin county, and is well known by the name of PICKET's SAMPSON... Jinkin AVIRETT. Onslow county, May 30.

(725) To Be Rented, The dwelling House, ware Houses, and Wharf, occupied by Mr. Richard LANGDON. For terms apply to Joshua G. WRIGHT. June 1.

(726) The subscribers give notice, that the bonds given, for purchases made at the sale of the personal estate of Hugh CAMPBELL, are now due, and that payment will be expected in the course of the present month. Thomas CALLENDER. Joshua G. WRIGHT. June 1.

(727) Will shortly be published By PRICE and STROTHER, A Complete Map of the state of North-Carolina,..from an actual survey.. They have been upwards of four years laboriously engaged in making the surveys..and..can now venture to open subscriptions for the same, which will be received by Allmand HALL, in Wilmington, and in Newbern, by William JOHNSTON and Jonathan PRICE, at four dollars a copy.. They will also publish immediately, at Newbern, A complete Chart of the Sea-coast, from Cape Henry to Cape Roman... Wilmington, May 4.

(728) For Sale, Two thousand acres of Land on the North-West, 640 of which is an excellent Mill-Seat, the best on the river, it joins HOOD's creek..terms by applying to the subscriber, or to General Benjamin SMITH. Elizabeth HOWELL. May 11.

(729) Five Dollars Reward, Absented herself on the 3d of January last, the day on which she was hired, a Negro woman named FANNY, about 23 years of age, the property of Miss QUINCE, she worked for the last two years at Doctor HILL's plantation, and before that with Mr. JENNINGS, of Wilmington... James CARSON. Clarendon, May 8.

(No. 35.) Thursday, August 24, 1797. Vol. (I.)

(730) Wilmington, August 24. Returns of the Election for Members of the next General Assembly of North-Carolina. For the County of <u>New-Hanover</u>, John HILL, for the senate; A. D. MOORE and Samuel ASHE, for the Commons. For the town of Wilmington, William Henry HILL. <u>Craven.</u> Senate-William M'CLURE, commons, Wm. BLACKLEDGE, Henry TILLMAN. Town of Newbern, Edward GRAHAM.

(731) For Sale or Charter, The Schooner Polly, Lying at Jos. DEAN's Wharf. For terms apply to MACLELLAN & LORD. August 24.

(732) To Be Rented, A Brick Ware-House with the privilege of a Wharf. Also a convenient Dwelling-House. For terms apply to the subscriber, or to Henry YOUNG, at the store of Mr. WILKINGS. Jos. G. WRIGHT. August 24.

(733) United States. Recruiting Service. Healthy, able-bodied young men, who are fond of living easy and honorable, will meet with great encouragement by applying to Philip WILLIAMS, Sergt. Artillerists ___ Engineer. Fort Johnston, 14th August, 1797.

(734) Ran Away, A Mustee fellow named JOSH, the property of CRAIK's estate, well known in town as a fidler.. Also, A Wench, named HANNAH, the property of CLAYTON's estate, who has two children with her, and was hired this year by Richard QUINCE, Esq.... James CARSON. Clarendon, 8th August, 1797.

(735) Fayetteville, August 12. On Wednesday last a public dinner was given by the inhabitants of Fayetteville, to the Honourable William Barry GROVE, the representative in Congress, from Fayetteville district, at Colonel DEKEYSER's Hotel...

(736) Inspector's Office. Fayetteville, July 22. Offices of inspection will be open in each county of the first survey, during the month of September.. Owners of carriages, and retailers of wines and foreign distilled spirits, will apply to the following collectors or their auxiliary officers. Stephen CAMBERLING of Newbern, for Craven; Benajah WHITE of Jones, for Jones, Lenoir and Wayne; Samuel HALLIDAY of Glasgow, for the said county of Glasgow; Thomas M'REYNOLDS of Moore, for Sampson & Johnston; Andrew M'INTIRE of Duplin, for Onslow and Duplin; Robert MUTER of Wilmington, for New-Hanover; John STORM of Lumberton, for Brunswick, Bladen and Robeson; Duncan M'REA of Fayetteville, for Cumberland; and John GILCHRIST of Moore, for Moore, Richmond and Anson.

(737) As the act for laying duties on carriages, is not understood by many persons interested, I subjoin for more general information, the 5th and 6th sections of the law... Thomas OVERTON, Inspector for the Revenue, for the first Survey, of the District of N. Carolina.

(738) Notice. On Monday and Tuesday, the 11th and 12th of September, I will attend at Mrs. LAMBERT's, on the North-east road, and on Friday and Saturday, the 15th and 16th..at Mr. John EDEN's, on the Newbern road, to receive entries of carriages and grant licenses to retailers of wines and foreign distilled spirits. The rest of the month I shall attend at Wilmington, agreeable to Col. OVERTON's notice. Robert MUTER, Collector of the Revenue for the County of New-Hanover. Wilmington, 22d August, 1797.

(739) The Subscribers having obtained an injunction from the Court of Equity, to restrain the purchasers of goods, &c. bought at public auction and old by Thomas MURPHY as the property of Thomas ANDERSON, late deceased..from paying the amount, or any part thereof to the said Thomas MURPHY..in the meantime, the subscribers are the only persons legally authorized to receive such payments. Geo. HOOPER, J. LIVINGSTON, A. JOCELIN. Wilmington, August 9, '97.

(740) Notice. The Subscriber intends to carry on the following business in its various branches, viz. Making and mending men and women's saddles, chair and coach harness, horse-men's caps, pistol holsters, sword scabbards and belts, portmanteaus and portmanteau trunks, fire buckets, mattrasses, band-boxes, ladies' artificial hips, craws, and body belts. David DUDLEY. Wilmington, August 9, '97.

(741) To Be Let, The Tenement and Store..at present occupied by Mr. Thomas MURPHY, adjoining Robert ADAM and Co.'s Store, near the market-house.. Please to enquire of Robert MUTER. Wilmington, 16th July.

(742) For Sale. 9000 Bushels best ground Liverpool Salt, and Queen's-ware..now landing at Mr. CAMPBELL's wharf... Robert ADAM, & Co.

(No. 37.) Thursday, September 7, 1797. Vol. (I.)

(743) New-York, August 22. By this vessel (not named), we have received the following information from James SIMPSON, the American Consul at that place (Gibraltar), which he handed to the captain the day he sailed...

(744) Philadelphia. August 23. The Inspectors of the Health Office inform their fellow-citizens that 15 new cases of the prevailing Fever have been reported to them since yesterday... By order of the Board, J. MILLER, Jun., Chairman.

(745) From a Fredericksburgh Paper. At a meeting of the People of Caroline county, at the court house, on Tuesday the 8th day of August, 1797..to consider whether the constitution of Virginia required revision and amendment.. Resolved unanimously, as the opinion of this county, That the said constitution is defective.. Signed by order of the meeting, James TAYLOR, Chairman. Attest, John PENDLETON, jun. Secretary.

(746) Petersburg, Sept. 1. Dr. Charles CALDWELL, in a lengthy publication on the fever of Philadelphia, attributes its origin to importation, and says that the infected neighbourhood extends from Spruce to South street, and from Front street to the water's edge...

(747) Wilmington, Sept. 7. Returns of the Election for Members of the next General Assembly of North Carolina. Brunswick. Senate, Gen. SMITH; commons, ___ WINGATE and George DAVIS. Bladen. Senate, Josiah LEWIS; commons, James BRADLEY and James MOOREHEAD. Sampson. Senate, Gabriel HOLMES; commons, ___ BRYANT & James THOMPSON. Robeson. Senate, John GILCHRIST; commons, RIGGING and WOODS. Anson. Senate, James MARSHALL; commons, Isaac JACKSON and Donald ROSS. Richmond. Senate, Robert WEBB; commons, William ROBINSON and James SANDFORD. Rowan. Senate, Basil GATHER; commons, Matthew BRANDON and Thomas CARSON; Town of Salisbury, John NEWNAN. Chatham. Senate, George LUCAS; commons, Thomas STOKES and ___ DABNEY. Halifax. Senate, Colonel Stephen CARNEY; commons, Colonel James TABB and Wood J. HAMLIN. Town of Halifax, Thaddeus BARNES. Northampton. Senate, John BINFORD; commons, Benjamin WILLIAMS and Nicholas EDMONDS. Nash. Senate, Archibald GRIFFIN; commons, Archibald HUNTER and R. BUNN. Tyrrel. Senate, John GUTHER; commons, Henry WARRINGTON & James FOSTER. Beaufort. Senate, Hans PATTEN; commons, F. GRICE and T. ELLISON. Hyde. Senate, H. SILBY; commons, Simon ALDERSON and J. WATSON. Jones. Senate, John HATCH, commons, Amos JOHNSTON and W. BUSH. Onslow. Senate, Christopher DUDLEY; commons, Joseph S. CRAY and Nathaniel LOOMISS. Wake. Senate, Tignal JONES; commons, William HENTON and Solomon ROGERS. Johnston. Senate, Samuel SMITH; commons, Matthias HANDY and John WILLIAMS. Cumberland. Senate, Hestor M'ALLISTER; commons, Neil SMITH and Daniel M'LEAN. Town of Fayetteville, James DICK.

(748) For New-York, The Schooner Margaret, James DAVIS, Master, Will sail in a few days..apply..to Charles JORDAN, Who has for sale St. Croix Rum and Sugar..Also New-England Rum... September 7.

(749) Metallic Substances. For Sale, A few sets of Doctor PERKINS's celebreted Metallic Substances-extremely useful in removing pains and inflamations incident to the human body.. Apply to WHEATON, TISDALE & Co. September 7.

(750) North Carolina. Treasury-Office, Sept. 1, 1797. On the sixth day of October next..it will become the indispensible duty of the public Treasurer to proceed against all persons who shall be found then in arrear to the state... John HAYWOOD, Public Treasurer.

(751) A Caution. Whereas my wife Elizabeth SIMPSON hath eloped from my bed and board without any cause or povocation whatever. These are to caution all persons from crediting her on my account, as I shall not pay for her contracts. Charles SIMPSON. Sept. 1.

(752) Will Be Sold, On Saturday the 9th of September next, at the Brick House opposite Wilmington, Sundry Likely Negroes. Sold at the instance of James FERGUS vs. the administrators of James M'ALESTER. Thomas LEONARD, Sheriff. Brunswick county, August 26.

(753) For Sale, Cheap For Cash, A Fayetteville Boat, that carries about 55 hogsheads. Inquire of F. FONTAINE & Co. August 31.

(754) Ran away from the subscriber about eight days past, a Negro fellow by the name of JOHN who calls himself John GARDENER-he is a short active well set fellow, and is by trade a Blacksmith.. He would be known in Fayetteville by Mr. GROVE's negroes, in Wilmington by Mr. D. MOOR's, in Chatham by Mr. MALLETT's.. I will give 50 Dollars to ..secure..him... W. NASH. N. B. A fellow by the name of ROBIN, belonging to Mr. Garrot GOODLOE, went off with him... W. N. Caswell county, July 17.

(No. 37.) Thursday, September 14, 1797. Vol. (I.)

(755) Wilmington, Sept. 14. Returns of the Election for Members of the next General Assembly of North Carolina. Pitt. Senate, Sam. SAMPSON; commons, Holland JOHNSTON and William GRIMES. Edgcombe. Senate, Nathan MOYO; commons, Frederick PHILIPS and ____ GILBERT. Martin. Senate, William M'KINZIE; commons, Jeremiah SLADE & John HYMAN. Franklin. Senate, Henry HILL; commons, Britain HARRIS and John FOSTER. Chowan. Senate, Lemuel CREECY; commons, Richard BENBURY and Benj. COFFIELD. Town of Edenton, Thomas JOHNSTON. Perquimans. Senate not known; commons, John SKINNER and Joseph WHITE. Bertie. Senate, Francis PUGH; commons, George OUTLAW and James B. JORDAN. Pasquotank. Senate, Thomas BANKS; commons, Wm. FARANGE & Baily JACKSON. Camden. Senate, Mr. TORKLEY; commons, Enoch DALEY and Z. BURGESS. Currituck. Senate, ____ PHILIPS. Stokes. Senate, Matthew BROOKS; commons, Wm. HUGHLET and Charles BANNER. Mercklenburg. Senate, Robert IRWIN; commons, Nathaniel ALEXANDER and James CONNER. Town of Hillsborough, Absalom TATOM. Granville. Senate, Wm. LITTLE; commons, Thomas TAYLOR and Tho. PERSON. Warren. Senate, Solomon GREEN; commons, James CALLIER and Wm. PERSON. Gates. Senate, Joseph RIDDICK; commons, James GATLING and ____ HUTCHINGS. Hertford. Senate, Tho. WYNNS; commons, Robert MONTGOMERY and Jas. JONES.

(No. 38.) Thursday, September 21, 1797. Vol. (I.)

(756) Wilmington, Sept. 21. Court of Hymen. On Monday last Capt. Richard BOSTWICK was married to Miss Ann JONES, of this town.

(757) Smithville. At a meeting of the Commissioners of Smithville, at the house of citizen GUMACHE, on Monday the 4th of September, 1797, They took into consideration the propriety of altering the plan of the Town... By order of the Commissioners, Joshua POTTS, Clerk.

(758) Notice is hereby given To the purchasers at the sales of the estate of the late Sampson MOSELY, deceased, that from the urgent demands exhibited against said estate, the administratrix is under the indispensable necessity to call for immediate payment... Sarah MOSELY, Adm'x. N. B. The bonds and notes will be lodged in the hands of W. H. HILL, Esq... September 21.

(759) Alexandria, August 18. Gentlemen, I observe in your paper of the 14th instant a piece of news, said to have been brought by me from Rotterdam, which has not been reported to you in its true light... John TOWERS, Master of the ship Saratoga. (To) Messrs. YUNDT and BROWN.

(No. 39.) Thursday, September 28, 1797. Vol. (I.)

(760) Baltimore, Sept. 4. On Wednesday last was arrested and brought before George BUCHANAN, esq. for coining of counterfeit dollars, a person who calls himself Richare HARPER, and said he was from Philadelphia. On his examination he confessed a certain DORSEY of this city was concerned with him. He was instantly committed to prison. A warrant was issued against DORSEY, and yesterday he was also taken and committed.

(761) Baltimore, September 7. This morning, precisely at 9 o'clock, at the navyyard of major STODDER, the builder, was launched the United States Frigate Constellation..no man on a similar occasion, acquitted himself with more honor and ability, than did major Benjamin STODDER.

(762) Wilmington, Sept. 28. On Sunday last Mr. Wm. M'KERRELL was married to Miss Fanny PURVIANCE.

(763) Notice. The subscriber has qualified as Executrix to the last will and testament of Caleb NICHOLS, late of New-Hanover county, deceased... Unity NICHOLS, Ex'x. Wilmington, 28th Sept.

(764) On Saturday the 14th day of October next, at the Sound, on the plantation of Caleb NICHOLS, late dec., formerly Thomas LOPER's will be sold, the perishable property of said Caleb NICHOLS... Unity NICHOLS, Ex'x. September 28.

(765) Lansingburgh, August 29. Indian Treaty. A treaty with the six nations is about being held at Big-Tree, on the Genesee river in Ontario county-General SHEPHERD, of Hampshire, Massachusetts, Col. WADSWORTH, of Hartford, Connecticut, and Mr. BAYARD, of New-York, have been appointed..commissioners on the part of the United States to hold this Treaty. The principal object..is a relinquishment of the Indian title to the lands in the Massachusetts pre-emption, owned by Robert MORRIS, Esq. and others...

(No. 40.) Thursday, October 5, 1797. Vol. (I.)

(766) Wilmington, October 5. From the Alexandria Gazette. To the Editors of the

(766) (Cont.) Columbian Mirror. Gentlemen, In your paper of the 7th inst. is inserted a paragraph..which states that the differences in the western country, betwixt Spain and the United States, were settled..the probability of its truth is further to be questioned.. I can easily conceive how the information came. If I am not mistaken, it was brought by one Thomas POWER... I am, sirs... Francis BAILEY. Sept. 13, 1797.

(767) Notice. The Copartnership betwixt George HOOPER and John INGRAM, merchants, was dissolved on the 7th of July last, by the event of the death of the latter..the firm of George HOOPER and Co... The stock of Dry Goods on hand..are for sale-as also the Brig Fair American.. Apply to George HOOPER, Surviving Copartner. Wilmington, Oct. 5, 1797.

(768) List of Letters remaining in the Post-Office at Wilmington, N. C. Col. Samuel ASHE, Andrew ADAMS. William BURN, care of Mr. GIBBS; Joseph BLAND; Captain Robert BOGG. Benjamin CHURCH, care of Mr. WILLKINGS; Peter CARPENTER, Josiah CLOAGE, Elisha CALLENDER, John COOKE. Captain E. DYER, Thomas DODD, Mons. Demous DERBIGNY. Henry ENONET?, John FARGSON, Edmund FISH. James GREEN, Mr. GAMOCHE. Henry HOLDEN, John HALL, Louis HOUSSET, Richard HERRING, Bright HERRING, A. Thomas HEATTY, William HOOPER. Edward JONES, Mrs. Mary E. JONES, Matthew JOHNSTON, Martin JORIS. Duncan LEVINGSTON, Captain LEVINGSTON. William M'CONDRAY, Edward MORGAN. Captain John M'FARLANE, James MURRAY, Benjamin MILLS, J. B. MOORE, Archy M'COLLUM, Captain Stephen MINOR. George REED. William SNELL, Sedgwick SPRINGS, Jonathan STANDLEY, Isaac SIMS. Captain Joseph TATOM. Anthony B. TOOMER, William TUTON, Wm. TURNER. Henry URQUHART. VOSBURGH and CHILDS. James WALKER, James WALKER, jun., Capt. Harvey WINCHESTER, Henry WOOD. R. BRADLEY, Ast. P. M. October 3r_

(769) Found on the Newbern road, about 15 miles from Wilmington, two large Charts of North America..apply to William PENROSE, on Harrison's Creek. Harrison's Creek. Oct. 4, 1797.

(770) Ten Dollars Reward. Ran away from the subscriber on Saturday last, a black Negro fellow named TRIM, about 20 years of age, 4 feet 8 or 10 inches high.. He was raised by Doctor Isaac GUION, of Newbern, and since belonged to Mr. Peter MANGEON, of Wilmington, from whom he was last purchased. I have great reason to suppose he was concerned in a daring robbery..in my house last night... Margaret M'KEAN. South Washington, October 2.

(No. 41.) Thursday, October 12, 1797. Vol. (I.)

(771) Philadelphia, Sept. 21. Yellow Fever. Drs. Samuel DUFFIELD and Edward STEPHENS, Physicians to the City Hospital, have reported to the Inspectors of the Health Office, that, since the commencement of the institution, there has been 169 patients admitted, 69 of whom have died, 31 cured and discharged, 8 eloped, and 61 still remaining, of whom 14 are upon the recovery.

(772) Baltimore, Sept. 30. Last evening arrived ship Becky, capt. CUNNINGHAM, 60 days from Liverpool; bale goods-WILSON and MARIS, & others. Also, snow Eliza. P. BENSON, 42 days from Liverpool; bale goods S. SMITH & BUCHANAN.

(773) Norfolk, Sept. 28. By a gentleman passenger in the Danish ship Christians Haven, capt. Patrick CORRAN, arrived yesterday in 43 days from Teneriffe...

(774) Wilmington, October 12. On Sunday last arrived here Mr. Wm. SWANSON, one of the crew of the brig Hull Packet, belonging to this port, which foundered at sea on

(774) (Cont.) the 8th ult. between Cape-Fear and Charleston. She was from Falmouth in England bound home...

(775) Married on Wednesday the 27th inst. Mr. David ANDERSON merchant of Fayetteville to Miss Ann JONES, of New-Hanover County.

(776) Died on Saturday last, the Rt. Worshipful John BLAKELEY, master of St. Tammany's Lodge in this town. On Wednesday last Capt. Stephen CONNICK.

(777) Port of Wilmington. Entered. Ship, William & Henry, James CUSCADEN, New-York. Brig, Sheerwater, Joseph ROBERTSON, New-Providence. Brig, Two Brothers, Alexander FORRESTER, Charleston. Schooner, Friendship, John DAVIS, Charleston. Sloop, Catharine, John BLAIR, Baltimore. Cleared. None.

(778) For Sale, On board the Sloop Catharine, Capt. John BLAIR, lying at Mr. BURGWIN's Wharf..Flour..Castings, consisting of Pots, Ovens and Skillets..Bar Iron..Molasses, Salt..N. E. Rum.. Apply to the master on board, or R. ADAM & Co. Wilmington, October 12.

(No. 43.) Thursday, October 26, 1797. Vol. (I.)

(779) New-York, October 7. Copied from the log book of the schooner Nancy, of Savannah, John M'ALLASTER, master, from St. Croix. Sept. 14, at 10 P. M. saw a brig close under our lee..after passing us she hove about and fired a shot.. She ordered out our boat and the captain on board with the papers.. The boat returned with the captain of the brig and four of his men..their particular object was for plunder.. making prize of everything they laid their hands on, in particular our stock and provisions.. The honest thieves belonged to the brig Caesar of 12 guns and 120 men ..commanded by GUOY, a Frenchman; the brig belonged to Mr. MORE.

The 7th (September), the ship Superb of Philadelphia, captain John BOYDE, bound to the Havannah, plundered her..having on board an American as master in speaking vessels in English, one Samuel BARNES of Portsmouth, New-Hampshire.

(780) Alexandria, October 5. We announce with much pleasure..that the Marquis DE LA FAYETTE and Family have been liberated from confinement in the prison of Olmutz. His son, who is now at Mount Vernon, will take passage to that part of Europe...

(781) Wilmington, October 26. French Fraternity, With Additions & Amendments.. The English ship Aracabessa, Capt. STOREY, bound from Jamaica to London, which put into this port in distress, having carried away his mizen & main masts..was yesterday Burnt in Five Fathom Hole, by a French..pirate.. On Monday..Mr. John CALHOUN, went down to the ship with provisions..and dined on board with capt. STOREY.. About two o'clock, Mr. HUFFEY (or HUSSEY) the pilot coming in,..observed her all in flames, her larboard side burnt to the water's edge, her decks burnt and fallen in, ..no living person on board...

(782) General Orders. The Detachment of 7,268 Men, to be drawn from the Militia of this State, are to be arranged into Two Brigades, commanded by a Major General and two Brigadiers: Major General William R. DAVIE, is appointed to take Command of the Detachment drafted under my orders of the 1st of Sept. last, and Brigadier General Martin ARMSTRONG, and Brigadier General Stephen MOORE will consider themselves as appointed on duty... Samuel ASHE, Captain General and Commander in Chief in and over the state of North-Carolina. Roger MOORE, A. D. C. Raleigh, Oct. 12, 1797.

(783) Imported From London, And for Sale at the Store lately occupied by George HOOPER & Co..A very General Assortment of Goods, Suited to the Season... B. W. THACKER. Wilmington, Oct. 26.

(784) Public Auction. The subscriber proposes to do some business the ensuing season, in the Vendue and Commission line... A. JOCELYN. October 25.

(785) A Warning. A Practice has existed for several years, of cutting and carrying away, without permission, from the lands of my Hillton plantation, fire-wood, hoop-poles, and timber of every kind.. I am constrained to give notice to my neighbors.. that this practice will no longer be allowed... W. H. HILL. October 26.

(786) Found By a negro woman under my house on Sunday last the 22d inst.; a new double skirted saddle, faced with velvet. The owner may have it by proving property, paying the expence of this advertisement and giving a small reward to the finder. Christopher DUDLEY. Wilmington, 26th October.

(787) Bargains. To be Sold by Public Auction, at the Court House in Wilmington, on the 2d. day of the ensuing Term of the Superior Court, the following described Valuable Lands, formerly the property of John ROWAN, Esq. deceased,-Viz.-640 Acres on the North side of the North-west River, joining lands formerly owned by Goodwin ELLETSON, decd. 291 Acres joining the above and below, on lands of John HALL, Esq. 320 Acres on the South side of the River joining the same, on John P. GRATY. 400 Acres joining the same, beginning at the mouth of WOOD's Creek and running down the river. 500 Acres on Alegator branch, between the North-west Road and River. 500 Acres joining the above, and near Mrs. WILLIAMS's on WOOD's Creek. Also, the Mill-Lands, Containing 2120 Acres by Patents and Deeds... Benjamin SMITH. Oct. 26.

(788) To Be Sold, On the First day of January next..Eight valuable country born Negroes, belonging to the Estate of the late Col. SWAN.. The family of negroes are at present hired to Messrs. ISAAKS and LEVY in Wilmington, and may be seen there. Mildred SWAN, Adm'x., Fred. JONES, Adm'r. Oct. 26.

(789) HAYWOOD's Reports, Proposals For Printing by Subscription, A Volumn of Reports of Cases adjudged in the Superior Courts of North-Carolina, from the year 1789, to the present time. By John HAYWOOD, one of the Judges of the Superior Courts of Law and Equity... Halifax, Sept. 1797.

(790) Notice. On Saturday the 19th day of November next, will be sold at Public Auction, Several Negroes, part of the personal estate of Mrs. Margaret BELOAT, deceased... S. R. JOCELIN, J. G. WRIGHT. Ex'rs. Wilmington, Oct. 19.

(791) The Co-partnership of BLAKELEY & VANCE Was dissolved on Saturday the 6th inst. by the death of the former... Samuel VANCE, Surviving Co-partner. Wilmington, Oct. 13.

(792) Ran away from the subscriber, on the 7th instant, a tall Black Negro Man, by the name of HARRY..he is about 40 or 45 years of age, and is left handed-has large white eyes, can read & write indifferently-was raised in Maryland..he is a Ditcher by trade... James WRIGHT. N. B. Two Dollars reward, if in this state, Ten if in any other, provided I get him. Duplin County, Oct. 13.

(No. 44.) Thursday, November 3, 1797. Vol. (I.)

(793) Boston, Oct. 12. Extract of a Letter from Mr. Unite DODGE, merchant in Cape

(793) (Cont.) Francois, to a merchant in this town, dated Sept. 15, 1797...

(794) Washington (Penn.) Sept. 19. Robert ODLIN and Alex. CRAWFORD, apprehended at Lancaster in June last, for passing counterfeit dollars, have received sentence, one to suffer 12, the other 16 years imprisonment to hard labor.

(795) Richmond, Oct. 18. Mr. SCULL, The information in your last paper of an insurrection among the inhabitants at Natchez is not correct. It is at Kaskaskias.. that the French settlers have been instigated by Spanish and French emissaries to throw off their alliegance to the United States and erect the standard of the French Republic. General WILKINSON is on his march with a strong detachment of Federal troops to suppress the insurgents.. It gives us great uneasiness to learn that three Frenchmen who passed through this place..have been addressing themselves to CORNPLANTER's Indians and telling them..they were oppressed...

(796) Charleston, October 7. Extract of a letter from Capt. Edward JOHNSON, of the sloop James, belonging to Messrs. BLAKE and MAGWOOD, of this city, dated Nassau, Sept. 20...

(797) Wilmington, Nov. 2. For Sale, On the Third Day of next Superior Court; a Plantation on the mouth of LOOKWART's Folly River, Brunswick county..containing 1100 acres of Land-400 of which is very good for the culture of Indigo.. For terms apply to P. AUBINAUD. Wilmington, Nov. 3.

(798) Notice. All persons Indebted to the Subscriber, by Note, Bond, or open Account, are requested to make immediate payment, to Archibald CUTLAR in Wilmington, or Hugh STALLIONS in South Washington... Samuel BLOODWORTH. Nov. 3.

(799) The Subscriber has for Sale, Cheap for Cash Rum, Sugar, Teas, Gun-Powder in kegs, Bottled Porter, Flour, &c. &c... T. F. GERALD. Wilmington, Nov. 2.

(800) Savannah, Sept. 29. On Monday the 25th inst., were arrested by a warrant from John GLAN, Esq. mayor of this city, John MOSSAY (or MOFFAY) of the state of Maryland, and William COWELL of the state of North-Carolina, citizens of the United States, (who were picked up at sea with three other whites, and 35 blacks, by capt. CALLAGHAN, of the schooner Exuma); having been on board the British armed ship, General Nicholls, of Grenada, they were brought before doctor John LOVE, one of the aldermen of this city, for examination, when it appearing Joseph MOSSAY had shipped himself voluntarily on board the said armed ship, he was committed to the federal jail for his trial; but it appearing that William COWELL, on the oath of two of the crew of said armed ship, was picked up at sea in a boat with capt. EWING, late master of the schooner Grace, of Washington, North-Carolina, Mr. ARMOUR, the owner, an apprentice boy, Edward POTTER, of North-Carolina, and Charles LANGLEY, a boy of Boston, with two blacks; that cap. Michael MORRISON, of the said armed ship, had permitted the captain, owner, apprentice and the two blacks to go on board of an American schooner, but had detained by compulsion the said William COWELL, Edward POTTER and Charles LANGLEY, on board; and that at Nassau, on his arrival there, he placed a number of blacks to guard the said COWELL and LANGLEY to prevent them getting away from his ship, (for POTTER had jumped into the boat of the Quebec frigate at sea, after exchanging a shot first with her by mistake at night)-he was in consequence discharged by alderman LOVE.

END OF VOLUME I

INDEX

As the spelling in this time period was phonetic, it is strongly recommended that any name be checked for all possible spellings.

ABBOT, Henry 244
  Stephen 243
ADAM, R. 778
  Robert 700,741,742
ADAMS,
  Andrew 768
  John 179,374,408,418,429,
    559,678
  Samuel 144
ADET, P. A. 564
ADGATE, Matthew 199
AKINS, Jonathan 199
ALDERSON, Simon 747
  Thomas 244
ALE, Davis 637
ALEXANDER, Abraham 163
  Adam 163
  Alexander 345
  Chas. 163
  Ezra 163
  Hez. 163
  John M'Knit 95
  John Mc'Knitt 163
  Nathaniel 755
  R. 244
  Robert 290
ALGEE, ___ 636
ALISON, Francis 155
ALLAINE, ___ 565
ALLAN, John 388,411,421
ALLEN, Davis 637
  Drury 200
  H. 244
  James 493
  John 491,511
  Nathaniel 244
  Richard 244
ALLISON, Robert 244
ALLON, Thomas 78
ALLSTON, F. 433
  Francis 332
ALVES, Gavin 624
  Walter 624
AMIS, Thomas 228

ANCRUM, ___ 52,109,114,171
  James 600
  John 101,161
ANDERSON, ___ 600
  David 775
  James 244
  John 244
  Thomas 739
ANTHONY, ___ 507
APTHORP, Charles W. 386
  Maria 386
ARDER, Sally 529
ARENOT?, Abraham 199
ARMISTEAD, Robert 425
ARMOUR, ___ 800
ARMSTRONG, ___ 95
  James 311,321
  John 243
  Martin 782
  Thomas 244
ARNETT, S. W. 322
ARNOLD, Benedict 291
  John 600
ASH, Harriet 368
ASHBY, ___ 229
  Solomon 342
ASHE, ___ 636
  John 129,148,193
  John Baptist 117
  John Baptista 7
  Samuel 117,148,193,243,
    593,710,730,768,782
  Samuel, Jr. 243
ATKINS, William A. 715
AUBINAU, ___ 600
AUBINAUD, P. 797
AUSTIN, Daniel 73
AVERY, Jonathan 672
  Waitstill 163
AVIRETT, Jinkin 724
B OWNJOHN, ___ 26
BACHE, Benj. Franklin 456,
  522
BACHOP, Peter 159

BACON, Jacob 164
BACOT, Peter 237
BAILEY, Francis 766
BAIN, Donald 193
BAKER, T. 629
  William 244
BALCH, Hez. J. 163
BALCOUR, Peggy 243
BALL, Robert 655,674
BALLANTINE, Mary 636
BALLARD, Plunket 716
BANCKE, Abraham 199
BANE, Donald 323
BANKS, Thomas 755
BANNER, Charles 755
BANNERMAN, Robert 150
BARBER, William 164
BARCLAY, Thomas 340
BAREBONES, Praise-God
  447
BARFIELD, Thomas 723
BARGE, ___ 131
  Lewis 62,298,671
BARKER, John 490
BARLOW, Joel 187,696
BARNES, ___ 186,320
  Elias 244
  George 94
  Samuel 779
  Thaddeus 747
BARNEY, ___ 213
  Joshua 642
BARNHILL, ___ 52
BARRETT, John 463
BARRINGER, George H. 244
BARRIT, James 272
BARRY, James 589
  Richard 163
BARTLET, ___ 349
BARTLETT, A. 600
  Amhert 636
BASS, Gillam 371
BASSET, Richard 324,349
BAST, Andrew 244

BATES, Thomas F. 600,636
BATTLE, Elisha 244
BAUDUY, ___ 463
BAY, John 199
BAYARD, ___ 765
  William 27
BEALE, Joseph 243
BEAUMEZ, ___ 600
BELDEN, Simeon 513
BELHAM, Charles 687
  P. 687
BELL, Bithel 244
  James 55
  John 90,243
BELLEW, John 535
BELLOC, Jude 420
BELOAT, Caesar 243
  Margaret 790
BELOATE, Margaret 690
BENBURY, Richard 755
BENFORD, John 244
BENNING, Arthur 98,494
BENSON, Egbert 270
  P. 772
BERNARD, I. 399
  Isaac 190,219,388,400
  J. 647
  John 343
BETHELL, William 244
BETHER, Emanuel 595
BETTS, Charles 578
BEZANT, Abraham 592
BIGGLESTON, J. 87
BINFORD, John 747
BINGHAM, William 448
BLACKBURN, Charles 636
BLACKLEDGE, Wm. 730
BLACKMORE, ___ 76
  Herrall 74
BLAIR, John 244,777,778
BLAKE, ___ 796
  Joseph 716
  Walter 716
BLAKELEY, ___ 451,533,
  598,615,791
  John 776
BLAKELY, ___ 518
BLANCHE, Michael 595
BLAND, Joseph 768
BLEAKLY, John 308
BLOCKER, ___ 671
BLOODWORTH, James 201,244
  Samuel 798
  Timothy 244,247,329,448,
  636

BLOUNT, Edmund 244
  John G. 244
  William 542
BLYTH, ___ 158
  James 92
BOARDMAN, Jonathan 243
BODDINGTON, William 122
BOGG, Robert 768
BOGLE, Robert 391
BOLCHOS, Alexander 664
BONDS, John 244
BONNER, James 244
BOON, Joseph 244
BORDEN, Joseph 27
BORDMAN, William 490
BOSTWICK, Absalom 244
  Richard 756
BOSWELL, James 244
BOWDOIN, ___ 341
BOWEN, ___ 172,201,228,
  234,299
  Gooden 600
  T. B. 345
BOWLAND, Robert 243
BOWLER, Metcalf 27
BOYD, ___ 67,154,388
  A. 54,121,126,132
  Adam 50,58,71,85
BOYDE, John 779
BRACKSDALE, Susannah Frances 357
BRADFORD, Wm. 448
BRADLEY, ___ 527
  Ann 281
  James 362,711,747
  John 171,228,243,347,463
  R. 600,618,636,768
  Richard 70,671
  Stephen R. 429
BRADLY, ___ 516
BRAMHALL, Mathew 261
BRANAN, James 304
BRANCH, John 244
BRANDON, James 244
  John 226
  Matthew 747
BRANSBERRY, John 463
BRANSBY, John 267
BRENAN, Patrick 277,304
BRETTELL, John 32
BREVARD, Eph. 163
BRIAN, James 600
BRICE, ___ 114,440
  F. 392,551
  Francis 377

BRIDGES, William 244
BRIGHT, Samuel 463
BROCAS, Richard 108
BROOKS, Mathew 244
  Matthew 755
BROUARD, J. B. 312
BROWN, ___ 173,636,703,
  759
  David 3
  Francis 164
  Jacob 154
  James 463
  John 164,244,324,448,
  600
  Neil 244
  Thomas 96,244,593,683
BROWNE, William 470
BROWNETT, ___ 112
BRUYN, Jacobus S. 199
  Johannes 199
BRYAN, George 27
  J. H. 244
  John 244
  N. 244
BRYANT, ___ 747
  Ezekiel 600
BUCHANAN, ___ 772
  George 679,760
BUCHANNAN, George 636
BUCKLEY, William 252
BUCKSTON, Samuel 463
BUFORD, John 82
BUNN, R. 747
  Red. 244
BURDEN, William 244
BURGESS, Z. 755
BURGWIN, ___ 104,323,
  778
  C. 485
  J. 89,331,470
  John 15,75,93,102,111,
  134,169,177,225,296,
  509,512,561,606,635,
  669,712,716
BURK, Thomas 636
BURKE, AEdanus 356,407,
  457
  Thomas 600
BURKIT, L. 244
BURN, William 768
BURNHAM, ___ 436
BURNS, Robert 409
BURNSIDE, James 378
BURR, Aaron 448
  Thadeus 396

BURTON, William 716
BUSH, W. 747
BUTLER, James 154
  Pierce 398,429,448
  Thomas 244
CABARRUS, ____ 244
  Stephen 244,322
CABELL?, Samuel J. 713
CABOT, George 448
  Samuel 558
CADE, John 244
CAHALT, Daniel 80
CAIN, ____ 180
  John 244
  Samuel 244
  William 196
CAINE, Christopher 49
  John 181
CALDWELL, Charles 746
  David 95,244
CALHORDA, John 462,617,
  630,640
CALHOUN, James 642
  John 781
CALLAGHAN, ____ 800
CALLENDER, ____ 184
  Elisha 768
  T. 275
  Thomas 295,348,353,371,
    411,726
CALLIER, James 755
CAMBERLING, Stephen 736
CAMPBELL, ____ 116,468,742
  Farquahard 129
  H. 432
  Hugh 726
  John 95,201,294,347,348,
    388,411,415
  John A. 244
  John Ablen 207,404
  W. 259
  William 122,173,347,413
  Wm. 671
CANNON, David 243
CANTINE, John 199
CAPEHART, Jacob 352
CAREY, James 426
  Mathew 596
CARLETON, ____ 146
CARMAN, Stephen 199
CARMICHAEL, Maurice 391
CARNEY, Stephen 747
CARPENTER, P. 411
  Peter 521,768
CARR, ____ 689

CARR (Cont.)
  James 609,648
  Joseph 243
CARRAGAN, Hugh 243
CARREL, John 244
CARROL, Charles 349
  Mitchell 143
CARROLL, D. 589
  Daniel 589
CARSON, James 729,734
  Thomas 244,747
CARTER, Edward 494
  J. 494
CARY, ____ 26
CASE, ____ 716
CASSANDRA, John 595
CASWELL, ____ 662
  Richard 129,322
CAUDRIN, ____ 600
CAULKIN, ____ 433
CHACE, G. 622
  Gorton 667
CHADWICK, Jacob 636
  John 636
CHALDWELL, ____ 41
CHAMBERS, Maxwell 95
CHASE, Gorton 600
CHILD, Francis 228
  Sylvester 243
CHILDS, ____ 621,768
CHRISTMAS, Thomas 244
CHURCH, Benjamin 768
CIG, William 154
CLARK, ____ 242,634
  Daniel 4
  Ebenezer 199
  Joseph 81,413
CLAYLAND, ____ 642
CLAYPOOLE, William 709
CLAYTON, ____ 109,734
  Francis 423,502
CLEAVES, Nathaniel 164
CLENDENNING, Matthew 243
CLEOD, ____ 196
CLIFFORD, ____ 718
CLINTON, ____ 199
  Geo. 246
  George 363,408
  James 199
  Richard 108,244
CLOAGE, Josiah 768
CLYMER, George 354,458
CO____, James 158
COATES, Abraham 490
  William 490

COATS, William 29
COBB, Tobias 636
COBHAM, ____ 84,174
COCHRAN, Robert 118
COFFIELD, Benj. 755
COGDELL, R. 160
COGSWELL, James 375
COLE, Francis 595
COLEMAN, ____ 707
  John 210
  Richard 648
  Samuel 239
COLES, John B. 680
COLLET, ____ 66
COLLETT, John 141
COLLEY, George 595
COLLINS, John 182,243
  Josiah 244,311,321
  Thomas 81
COLSON, James 200
  John 334
COLVIN, John 636
COMEE, Joseph 164
CONKLING, ____ 539
CONNELY, Nuton 243
CONNER, Dempsey 321
  James 755
  Mary 105
  Morris 105
CONNICK, Stephen 663,776
CONNOLLY, Ann 180
CONNOR, Demsey 311
CONSTABLES
  BROWN, Jacob 154
  BUTLER, James 154
  CIG, William 154
  CROOK, John 154
  FREDERICK, William 154
  FRYIC?, Jonathan 154
  HOUSMAN, John 154
  KING, Michael 154
  ME____, William 154
  SOUTHERLAND, William
    154
  WARD, Daniel 154
CONWAY, ____ 245
COOK, ____ 412
  Samuel 164
  William 313
  Wm. 664
COOKE, John 768
COOPER, Daniel 434
  Joseph 137
  William 702
  Wm. 600

COOR, James 129
COPP, ___ 406
CORNELL, ___ 81
  Samuel 81
CORNING, S. 636
  Sam. 600
CORRAN, Patrick 773
CORRELL, Mitchell 131
CORRIE, ___ 34
CORTLANDT, Philip V. 199
COTTERELL, John 243
COTTON, John 28
COUNCIL, James 298
COVINGTON, Benjamin 244
  John 342
COWARD, ___ 372
COWELL, William 800
COX, ___ 565
  J. 244
COXE, Tenche 354
  William 8
COXETER, James 636
CRAAFS, E. 642
  W. 642
CRAFTS, Thomas? 490
CRAIK, ___ 734
CRAIKE, ___ 371
  Thomas 141,147
CRAMMER, Hugh 636
CRANDLE, Lydia 636
CRANE, Josiah 199
  Thaddeus 199
CRAWFORD, Alex. 794
CRAY, Joseph S. 747
CREECY, Lemuel 755
CROCKER, N. 501
CROOK, John 154
CROPTON, Charles 222
CRUDEN, John 83,125
  John, Jr. 125
  John, Sr. 125
CRUGER, John 27
CUMMING, Henry 220
CUNNINGHAM, ___ 125,772
  A. 704
  Archibald 664
CUNNINGHAME, Thomas 699
CURRIE, John 243
CURRY, ___ 409
CURTIS, Joseph 463
CUSCADEN, James 777
CUTLAR, Archibald 505,611,
  798
  R. 496
  W. 494,496

CUTLAR (Cont.)
  Wm. 432
CUTLER, Roger 702
CUTLIP, Mathias 572
CUYLER, Jacob 199
DABNEY, ___ 747
DALAND, Benjamin, Jr. 164
DALEY, Enoch 755
DALLAS, Alexander J. 490
DALTON, Tristram 349
DANFORTH, Ozias 600,636
DANIEL, S. 253
DATE, ___ 636
DAUGE, Peter 244
DAVIDSON, John 163
  Robert 155
  Wm. 163
DAVIE, ___ 244
  William R. 244,782
DAVIS, ___ 164
  Devotion 244
  George 650,747
  Greffit 254
  J__s 81
  James 748
  Jehu 286
  John 368,777
  Thomas 205-207,339,404,
    541,542,567
  W. 600,694
  William 26,636
DAWSON, John 324
  W. J. 322
  William J. 244
DAY, John 80
DAYTON, Henry 381
DE BARROS, Joaquim Joe 454
DE LA FAYETTE, ___ 780
DE LAMOTTE, ___ 600
DE NANCREDE, P. J. G. 397
DE ROSSETTE, Armand 573
DE SAUSSURE, Henry William
  466
DE WITT, John 199
  Simeon 601
DEAL, Mille 600
DEAN, ___ 527
  Jones A. 254
  Jos. 731
  Joseph 600,628,676
  Thomas 401
DEARBON, Samuel 595
DEBBING, ___ 99
DEBLOIS, Lewis 589
DEKEYSER, ___ 112,671,735

DELANCEY, Ja. 290
DELL, ___ 600
DERBIGNY, Demous 768
DERBY, ___ 316
  Elias Hasket 316
DEVANE, J. 494
  Thomas 244,247
DEW, Spencer 81
DEXTER, Knight 265
DICK, James 747
DICKENSON, John 463
DICKINS, Robert 244
DICKINSON, John 27
DICKSON, ___ 273
  Henry 116
  Robert 99,636
DIGS, R. 244
DILLINO, ___ 445
DILLON, ___ 29,479
DIXON, ___ 120
  Jonathan 243
  Robert 99
  William 244
DOBBIN, ___ 642
DOBINS, William 244
DOBSON, ___ 30
DODD, David 244
  Thomas 768
DODGE, Jordan 194
  Unite 793
DONELSON, Stokely 244
  William 244
DONOVAN, Jeremiah 588
DORAM, Travis 77
DORSEY, ___ 388,400,467,
  571,619,760
  Elizabeth 532
  L. 326
  L. A. 326,344,347
  La. 326
  Laurence A. 532
  Lawrence 243,423
  Lawrence A. 350
DOSIER, Richard 528
DOUD, Corn. 244
DOUGAN, Thomas 244
DOUGGAN, Thomas 334
DOUGLAS, Joseph 244
DOUGLASS, ___ 273
  Robert 254
DOWNS, Henry 163
DRAKE, E. P. 471
DRAYTON, William 345
DROMGOOLE, Alexander 364
DRUMGOLD, Francis 494

DRURY, Spafford 557,570
DRY, ___ 200
DU BOIS, John 10,12,63
DUANE, James 182,199,263
DUBOICE, Jane 542
DUBRUTZ, ___ 312
  Gabriel 206
DUCOLOMBIE, Martin 600
DUDLEY, ___ 561
  Agatha 236
  Bishop 541
  Christopher 747,786
  David 625,740
  G. 283
DUFFIELD, George 155
  Samuel 771
DUKES, George 81
DUNBIBIN, Jonathan 113
DUNCAN, ___ 382,575
  Alexander 39,171
  Geo. 475,483,575
  George 666
DUNCANSON, W. M. 589
DUNKIN, John 244
DUNN, ___ 320
  John 137,226
  Robert 249
DUPRE, Cornelius 288
  Lewis 288
DUPREE, Lewis 244
  Sterling 244
DUSSAN, ___ 463
DYAR, Eliphalet 27
DYE, Martin 203
  Thomas C. 176
DYER, E. 768
EACHRAN, Duncan 243
EAGEN, Elizabeth 17
EAGLES, ___ 57
EARL, Elizabeth 463
EASLEY, Daniel W. 361
EASTER, John 254
EASTON, Edward 463
EBORNE, John 244
ECCLES, John 223
ECKERT, ___ 478
EDEN, John 738
EDMONDS, Nicholas 747
EDWARDS, Isaac 129
  John 93
  Thomas 490
EISTMAN, James 463
ELKINS, ___ 316
ELLERY, Christopher 293
ELLETSON, Goodin 174

ELLETSON (Cont.)
  Goodwin 787
ELLICOTT, Andw. 478
ELLIOT, George 244
ELLIS, Evan 4
  James 337,339
  Robert 494
ELLISON, T. 747
ELLISSON?, Goodin 244
ELLITSON, Godwin 503
ELLSWORTH, O. 349
  Oliver 317,448
ELMER, Jonathan 349
ELSE, Thomas 406
ELSWORTH, William T. 636
EMMET, James 48
ENGLISH, Joseph 33
ENONET?, Henry 768
ERICHSON, Severin 183, 205,267
ERWIN, James 88
  John 190,636
EVANS, Benjamin 494
  Thomas 244
EVEREGAIN, Edward 244
EWANS, ___ 158
  William 411
  Wm. 584,671
EWING, ___ 800
FARANGE, Wm. 755
FARGSON, John 768
FARMER, Nathaniel 164
  William 244
FAUCETT, James 254
FAYETTE, ___ 256
FELT, Joshua 164
FENNEL, Nicholas 636
FEREBEE, Joseph 244
  William 244
FERGUS, James 484,752
  Margaret 530
FERGUSON, Daniel 463
FERRERS, John 680
FESTENS, ___ 600
FIGURES, Matthew 334
FIGURS, Joseph 35
FINLAY, James 455
FISH, Edmund 768
FISHER, Hendrick 27
  Thomas 2
FITZ GERALD, John 412
  T. 486,498
  Thos. 481
FITZ-GERALD, T. 536,547, 548,549,562,590,607

FITZGERALD, T. 626
  Thomas 631,632
  Thos. 469
FLAHAVEN, Roger 80
FLEEMING, James 231,232, 308
FLEMING, James 463,671
FLENNIKEN, John 163
FLETCHER, James 244
  Stephen 342
FLINT, William 164
FLOWERS, ___ 308
  David 243,671
  James 463
FLOYD, William 270
FLUMING, ___ 600
FOLGER, Frederick 696
FOLK, John 716
FONTAINE, ___ 297
  F. 497,577,710,719, 753
  Francis 627,654
FOOTERY, ___ 463
FORBES, Arthur 244
FORD, Jacob 199
  John 163
FOREMAN, Caleb 244
FORRESTER, Alexander 777
FORSTER, ___ 114
  A. M. 244
  John 107
FORT, William 244
FOSDICK, Samuel 197
FOS?DICK, Samuel 243
FOSTER, ___ 14
  James 747
  John 755
  Theodore 448
FOY, James 220
FRANKLIN, Benjamin 165
FREDERICK, William 154
FRELINGHUYSEN, Frederick 448
FREY, John 199
FREYLINGHUYSEN, Frederick 429
FRILICH, Joseph 668
FROST, Samuel 164
FRYICK?, Jonathan 154
FULLARD, Andrew 99
FULLER, William 39
GADSDEN, Christopher 27, 457
GAGE, ___ 140,146
  Thomas 144

GAILLARD, John 72
GAINS, James 244
GALLOWAY, Charles 244
  James 244
  Joseph 290
GAMOCHE, ___ 768
GANSEVOORT, P., Jr. 199
GARDNER, Isaac 164
GARRETTSON, Richard 254
GATES, Horatio 152
GATHER, Basil 747
GATLING, James 755
GAUSE, William 571
GAUTIER, J. R. 452,705
  Joseph 244
GAVINE?, John 696
GEDDES, Alexander 243
  Henry 636
GEEKIE, James 186
GEER, Gilbert 243
GEFFORD, Robert 243
GELLESPIE, James 243
GEORGE, John 180
GERALD, T. F. 799
GERRY, Elbridge 418
GHERARDI, ___ 577
  Giacomo 565
  Henry 446,449
  James 449,492,565
GIBB, John 395
GIBBONS, Thomas 266
GIBBS, ___ 57,538,563,768
GIFFARD, Alexander 243
GILBERT, ___ 755
GILCHRIST, John 736,747
GILL, Mordecai 345
  Moses 437
GILLESPIE, Daniel 244
  James 463,592
GIRARD, Stephen 490
GLAN, John 800
GLASGOW, James 311,322
GOLD, ___ 382
GOLDTHWAIT, Ebenezer 164
GOODHUE, Benjamin 418
GOODLOE, Garrot 754
GOODWIN, ___ 671
  Drury 81
GORDON, James 199
  William 463
GORE, William 636
GOSS, Needam 600
GOUDY, William 244
GOULD, Daniel 244
GOUVERNEUR, Isaac 680

GRAHAM, Edward 730
  John 290
  M. Joseph 244
  William 463
  Wm. 163
GRAINGE, John Porter 503
  Thomas 124
GRANDY, Charles 244
GRANGE, John 227,383
GRANT, John 207,404
GRATY, John P. 787
GRAVES, John 244
GRAY, Etheld. 244
  Thomas 129
  William 129
GRAYBILL, Philip 430
GRAYSON, William 324,349
GREAVES, ___ 129
GREEN, ___ 187
  James 195,768
  John 81,281
  Joseph 228
  Matthew 541
  Solomon 755
  William 281,603
  Wm. 238
GREENLEAF, Thomas 199
GREENLEE, James 244
GREER, Andrew 600
GREGG, Frederick 12
GREGORY, Isaac 244
  James 244
GRENVILLE, ___ 490
GRICE, F. 747
GRIFFIN, Archibald 747
  Cyrus 324
GRIGGS, Henry 600
GRIMES, ___ 273
  John R. 290
  William 755
GRIMKE, J. F. 510
GRISWOLD, Matthew 188,396
GROVE, ___ 754
  William B. 173
  William Barry 244,735
GROVES, Ephraim 355
GUERARD, John 243,351,362
GUION, Isaac 770
GUIRARD, ___ 577
GUMACHE, ___ 757
GUNN, ___ 30
  James 429,448
GUOY, ___ 779
GUTHER, John 747
GUTHERIE, William 636

H_KE, John 173
HADLEY, Samuel 164
  Thomas 164
HADLY, Thomas 18
HALL, ___ 64,704
  A. 639
  Allmand 692,727
  Durham 244
  John 227,383,503,629,
    636,768,787
  Sam. 600
  Thomas 472
HALLIDAY, Samuel 736
HALSEY, Henry 243,600
HAMER, Solomon 463
HAMILTON, ___ 581
  Alexander 182,199
  John 244
  Thomas D. 605
HAMLIN, Wood J. 747
HAMMER, Solomon 243,304
HAMMOND, Geo. 464
HANAGHAN, William 319
HANCOCK, John 144,156
  182,408
HAND, Jeremiah 463
HANDLY, ___ 270
HANDS, ___ 320
  John 225
HANDY, Matthias 747
HANLY, James 244
HARDIMAN, Thomas 244
HARDING, Joseph 254
HARGET, Frederick 244
HARING, John 199
HARLEY, R. 685
  Robert 623
  Robt. 528
HARNET, ___ 115
  C. 10
  Cornelius 12
HARNETT, ___ 109,320
  Cornelius 115,129,141,
    145,148,382
HARPER, Arthur 193
  James 193
  Richard 760
  Robert Goodloe 639
  William 199
HARRACKS, Thomas 369
HARREL, Samuel 244
HARRINGTON, Caleb 164
  Jonathan 164
HARRIS, ___ 411,712
  Britain 755

HARRIS (Cont.)
  James 163
  John 595
  Peter 669,677
HARRISON, ___ 63,611,769
  Benjamin 230
  Richard 182,199
HART, Archibald 595
HARTLEY, John 636
HARTMAN, ___ 636
HARTWELL, Daniel 636
HARVEY, John 44
  Thomas 244
HARVIE, David 303
HASELL, James 65
HATCH, John 747
  Lemuel 129
HATCHER, Edward 180
  Priscilla 315
HATFIELD, Richard 199
HAVENS, Jonathan N. 199
HAWKER, James 25
HAWKINS, Benjamin 458
  Wyatt 244
HAYNES, Deacon 164
HAYS, Joseph 671
HAYWOOD, Egbert 244
  John 750,789
HAZARD, George 243
HEATTY, A. Thomas 768
HEDG__, David 199
HEMMENWAY, ___ 164
HENDERSON, R. 671
  Richard 334
  Robert 636
HENDRE, Jean 243
HENDRY, William 243
HENDS, Jo. 463
HENRY, John 349,448
HENTON, William 747
HERIOT, Robert 101
HERNDON, Joseph 244
HERON, Alice 573
  Allice 542
HERON?, Benjamin 64
HERRIN, ___ 600
HERRING, Bright 768
  Richard 768
HERVEY, Henry 636
HICKS, John 164
  Thomas 129,716
HILL, ___ 694,729
  Elizabeth 306
  Henry 244,755
  Isaac 108

HILL (Cont.)
  John 81,108,327,416,
    504,703,720,730
  Margaret 301,327,416
  T. 643,665
  W. H. 327,370,416,494,
    758,785
  Whitm. 244
  Whitmil 311
  Whitmill 321
  William 13,416,624
  William H. 306
  William Henry 592,730
HILLHOUSE, Stephen M. Mit_
  356
HINES, Thomas 244
HINTON, James 244
HO__ER, ___ 164
HOAGLAND, Jerom 199
HOBART, John Sloss 182,199
HODGESON, Abby 243
HOGAN, Rawleigh 474
HOGG, ___ 116
  James 671
HOLDEN, Henry 768
HOLLAND, ___ 25
HOLLINSWORTH, Eman 636
HOLMES, Gabriel 592,747
  Hardy 244
  John B. 457
  Lewis 244
HOLT, ___ 524
  Joseph 81
  William 167
HOLTON, Nathaniel 671
HOMES, Robert 463
HOOD, ___ 728
HOOPER, ___ 181,600
  Geo. 613,739
  George 120,173,201,
    336,338,348,360,372,
    411,569,767,783
  Thomas 120
  William 91,129,148,
    706,768
  William, Jr. 217
HOPKINSON, John 212
HOSKINS, Henry 348,627,
  636,710
HOSTLER, ___ 241
  Alexander 139,388
HOUSE, R. B. 162
HOUSMAN, John 154
HOUSSET, Louis 768
HOUSTON, George 406

HOUSTON (Cont.)
  William 20,21,32
HOVEY, Samuel 276
  Seth 244
HOWARD, ___ 172,201,
  228,234,299
  James 164,243
HOWE, ___ 172
  Arthur 243,253
  Job, Sr. 145
  Robert 129,172,656
  William 432,450
HOWELL, Elizabeth 728
  John 211
HOWALND, Isaac 588
  William 366
HOWLEN, Daniel 405
HUBBELL, Ezra 636
HUFFEY, ___ 781
HUGER, Daniel 356
HUGHES, John 8,25
HUGHLET, Wm. 755
HULING, John 455
HUME, ___ 34
HUMMOND, ___ 363
HUMPHRIES, John 244
HUNN, John 490
HUNT, J. 244
HUNTER, Archibald 747
  Miles 358
  Robert 243
  Sarah 81
  Thomas 81,244
HUNTINGTON, Benjamin 356
  Jedediah 396
  Jonathan 636
  Samuel 182,418
HUSKE, John 201,218,
  382,387
HUSSEY, ___ 781
HUTCHINGS, ___ 755
HUTCHINSON, Thomas 127
HYMAN, John 755
HYRNE, Henry 97
INDIANS
  M'GILLIVRAY, Alexander
    424
  M'GILVERY, Alexander
    364
  OTISQUETTE, Peter 256
  CORNPLANTER 795
  FOOL WARRIOR 279
  GEORGE 554
  GREAT TASSEL 235
  HALLOWING KING 554

INDIANS (Cont.)
  HANGING MAW 279
  OLD ABRAHAM 279
  OLD TASSEL 279
  PONDIAC 23
  UNDERWOOD 473
INDIAN TRIBES
  Cherokee 136,279,364,424
    554
  Chickasaw 473
  Chicomageo 279
  Chuckamawgau 364
  Creek 270,365,424,458,
    473,554
  Wyandot 424
INGLES, ____ 424
INGRAHAM, ____ 201
INGRAM, John 767
INGRUM, ____ 173
IREDEL, James 244
IREDELL, ____ 598,639
  James 311,321
IRVINE, William 478
IRWIN, Robert 163,244,755
ISAACKS, ____ 686,697
ISAAKS, ____ 788
IVEY, Curtis 244
IZARD, Ralph 398
JACKSON, Baily 755
  Charles 696
  Isaac 747
  James 406,448
  Wm. 507
JACOB, Benjamin 463
JACOBS, George 281,334
  Henry 164
JAFFRAY, James 559
JAMES, ____ 130,442
  John 47,98,657
  Thomas 657
JASPER, James 244
JAY, ____ 490
  John 182,199,263,408,427
JEFFERSON, Thomas 464,678
JEFFERY, ____ 662
JENKINS, Joseph 507
JENNETT, Thomas 243
JENNING, J. 445
JENNINGS, ____ 729
  J. 468
  Thomas 243
JENSEN, Cornelius T. 199
JEWKES, ____ 392
  Charles 296,411,463,582
JOCELIN, A. 173,417,487,739

JOCELIN (Cont.)
  Amaziah 338,380
  S. R. 790
JOCELYN, ____ 679
  A. 784
  S. R. 600
  Samuel R. 690
JOHNSON, Charles 244
  Edward 796
  John 244
  Matthew 315
  Priscilla 315
  Samuel 244,373
  Samuel William 27
  W. S. 349
  William 457
JOHNSTON, ____ 81
  Amos 747
  Holland 755
  J. 543
  James 244
  Jno. 477,493
  John 461,477,488,511,
    537,544,585,593,627
  Mathew 463
  Matthew 411,768
  Peter 463
  Samuel 141,148,311,
    321,723
  Thomas 244,334,755
  William 81,727
  William S. 317
JONES, ____ 226,382
  Abraham 244
  Ann 756,775
  Betsy 377
  David 600
  E. 201
  Edward 185,204,240,247,
    422,540,634,656,768
  Fred. 788
  Frederic 174
  Frederick 97
  Jas. 755
  John 244
  John Paul 269
  Mary E. 768
  Nathaniel 103,244
  Rowland 243
  Samuel 199,270,636
  Silas 245
  Thomas 243,636,671
  Thos. 457,600
  Tignal 747
  Willie 244

JORDAN, Charles 471,489
  539,568,608,718,748
  James B. 755
  Josiah 180
JORIS, Martin 768
JOY, John 467
JUDGES
  COOPER, Daniel 434
  HAYWOOD, John 789
  OLIVER, Peter 127
JUSTICES
  CAMPBELL, H. 432
  CUTLAR, Wm. 432
  DIXON, Robert 99
KEAIS, Nathan 244
KEAN, Roger 410
KEDDIE, William 243
  Wm. 600
KEELY, John 258
KEENAN, James 592
  Jeremiah 53
  Thomas 716
KEENON, M. 600
KEITH, John 529
KELLY, John 636
  Mary 94
  William Davis 710
KENAN, Felix 81,103,154
  James 108,244
  Michael 108
KENNA, ____ 282
KENNEDY, Archibald 243
  George 81
  John 81,463,600
  Robert 76
KENNON, Wm. 163
KENON, ____ 241
KERR, John 463
KERSHAW, ____ 95
KIDDY, Wm. 599
KILBORN, John 451
KINCHEN, John 321
KINDAL, William 244
KINDRICK, ____ 26
KING, Henry 695
  Michael 154
  Rufus 448
  Thomas 244
KINGSBURY, ____ 248,294,
  411
  H. 636
  Henry 628
  J. 268,277
  John 419
KINGSLEY, Zeph. 636

KIRK, ___ 280
KIRKBY, James H. 511
KNICHEN, John 311
KNOX, Robert 345
   William 290
KOLLOCK, Jacob 27
L'EVEILLE, ___ 642
L'HOMAEA, ___ 600
L'HOMMEDIEU, Ezra 270
LA PLACE, Charles 442,586
LACHMAN, Frederick 461
LALANE, ___ 636
LAMB, Margaret 463,636
LAMBERT, ___ 738
LAMBERTOZ, D. 531,620,693
LANCASTER, William 244
LANE, Ephraim 81
   George 81
   Joel 244
   John 164,244
   Pearson 81
   Samuel 81
   William 81
LANGDON, ___ 565,571,645
   John 349,448
   R. 614
   Richard 644,725
LANGLEY, Charles 800
LANIER, ___ 95
   Burrell 108
   Lewis 244
LANSING, John 199
LAPHAM, Charles 556
LATIMER, Henry 448,649
LAW, Richard 396
   Thomas 589
LAWRENCE, Nathaniel 199
LAWSON, ___ 230
LCEET?, Eugene 600
LEACH, B. 259
LEAD?, ___ 164
LEAN, ___ 226
LEARCHER, ___ 702
LEDBETTER, George 244
LEE, ___ 463
   Charles 152,157
   John 463
   Nathaniel 254
   Richard Henry 324,349
LEECH, Joseph 244
LEFFERTS, Peter 199
EEGRO, ___ 689
LEICH, John 642
LENNON, Dennis 60
LENOIR, William 244

LENORE, ___ 329
LENOX, David 696
LEONARD, J. 253
   Jacob 244,253
   John 253
   Thomas 528,752
LEONAREL, Thomas 656
LETTLE, ___ 490
LEVINGSTON, ___ 768
   Duncan 768
LEVISTON, John 243
LEVY, ___ 686,697,788
   E. 262
   Moses 490
LEWIS, Howell, Jr. 244
   Jacob 431,432,440
   Josiah 747
   W. I. 321
LILLINGTON, Alexander 148
LINDSAY, Colin 463
LINLEY, Jonathan 244
LISPENARD, Leonard 27
LITTLE, Richard 595
   W. 244
   William 595
   Wm. 755
LIVERMORE, Samuel 448
LIVINGSTON, ___ 200,494,
   706
   Gilbert 199
   Henry 199
   J. 739
   James 199
   P. V. B. 151
   Philip 27
   Philip R. 199
   Robert R. 27,182,199
LLOYD, Caleb 24,30
LOBB, ___ 38
LOCK, ___ 329
   Burwell 244
LOCKWOOD, James 508,512,
   513,550
   Jas. 441
LOFTIN, W. 244
LOGAN, Benjamin 229
   George 702
LONDON, John 68,220,508
LONG, Anna 636
LOOKWART, ___ 797
LOOMISS, Nathaniel 747
LOONEY, David 244
LOPER, Thomas 764
LORD, ___ 731
   W. E. 592

LORD (Cont.)
   William 671
LOUDON, J. 494
   John 115
   Lydia 188
   Samuel 188
LOVE, John 800
   Keenan 611
   Kenan 505
LOVELL, Abner 184
LOW, Nicholas 182,199
LOWDER, Samuel 393,443,
   676
LOWLEY, Miles 24,29
LUCAS, ___ 241
   Francis 78
   George 244,747
   John 51
LUDLOW, Daniel 271
LUTTERLOH, Henry Lewis
   634
LUTTERLOW, Henry E. 243
LUX, William 405
LYNCH, Thomas 27
LYNCHE, ___ 226
LYNDON, Henry 463
LYON, ___ 191
   John 42,216,388
M'ALESTER, James 752
M'ALISTER, Donald 463
   James 656
M'ALLASTER, John 779
M'ALLISTER, Alexander 244
   Hestor 747
   John 244
M'ANNELLY, Charles 244
M'BRIDE, Peter 463
M'CAFFERTY, Jeremiah 95
M'CALISTER, James 552
   Mary 553
   Sarah E. 552
M'CALLISTER, James 583
M'CALLUM, Archibald 636
M'CARTER, ___ 21
M'CAULEY, William 244
M'CAUSLAN, ___ 411
M'CLENACHAN, Blair 490
M'CLEOD, ___ 196
M'CLODE, ___ 180
M'CLURE, William 730
M'COLLARE, David 463
M'COLLUM, Archy 768
M'CONDRAY, William 768
M'CORMICK, Barnabas 455
   Hugh 243

M'CRACKAN, James 671
M'CRADY, ___ 345
M'CULLOCH, ___ 181,233, 251
  George 636
  Henry 494
M'CULLOH, Henry Eustace 290
M'CUN, Jo. 463
M'DANIEL, Wm. G. 702
M'DONALD, Angus 435
  George 636
M'DOWAL, Charles 244
  Joseph 244
  Joseph, Jr. 244
M'DUFFIE, Dugald 636
M'FARLANE, John 768
M'GEACHY, Neil 203
M'GEE, John 95
M'GUFFORD, James 600
M'GUIRE, ___ 703
M'HENRY, James 636
M'ILHENNY, John 659
M'INTIRE, Andrew 736
M'INTOSH, John 81
M'KAY, Margaret 203
  Neil 636
  William 292
M'KEAN, Jos. B. 354
  Margaret 770
  Thomas 27,490
M'KENNA, Charles 378
M'KENNIE, Richard 244
M'KENZIE, John 463
M'KERRELL, Wm. 762
M'KINNON, ___ 463
  Daniel 463
M'KINZIE, William 755
M'LAINE, Elizabeth 463
M'LANE, ___ 273
M'LAUGHLIN, Jo 463
M'LEAN, Daniel 747
  Robert 81
M'LEOD, Norman 600
M'MANUS, James 226
M'MURPHEY, Daniel 236
M'NEIL, Archibald 463
M'NIEL, David 546
M'NORTON, ___ 463
M'PHERSON, Lewis 253
  Peggy 600
M'QUEEN, ___ 266
M'RAE, ___ 533
  Duncan 702
M'REA, Duncan 736
M'REYNOLDS, Thomas 736

M'VAUGHTIN, ___ 463
MC'CLURE, Matt. 163
MC CAIN?, ___ 113
MC CANN, Bartholamew 102
MC COMMACK, ___ 243
MC DONNELL, John 69
MC DOUGAL, John 56
MC DOWEL, Joseph, Sr. 329
MC FARLAND, Robert 243
MC FARLANE, John 243
MC GEE, John 334
MC INTIRE, James 106
MC IVER, Alexander 309
MC KAY, Donald 243
MC KENZIE, Andrew 243
MC KERNAN, Charles 402
MC KINNAN, Fingal 243
MC KINNIS?, ___ 129
MC LAREN, John 249
MC LEOD, ___ 83
MC MURPHEY, James 243
MC NEAL, Donald 243
MC VERRICK, William 243
MAC PHERSON, L. 411
MABSON, William 243
MACKAY, Malcolm 671
MACKENZIE, John 347
  William 244
MACLAINE, A. 118,131,173, 191,201,234,244
  Archibald 148,170,221, 240,244,388
  Thomas 198
  William 244
MACLAY, W. 349
MACLELLAN, ___ 731
  John 698
MACNAUGHTON, A. 201,250
  Auly 636
  Charles 671
MACNEILL, Archibald 135
MACON, ___ 244
  John 244
MADISON, James, Jr. 324
MAGILL, John 636
MAGWOOD, ___ 796
MALLET, Peter 636,671
MALLETT, ___ 754
  P. 582
  Peter 228,308,463
  Samuel 243
MANGEON, ___ 636
  P. 389,586
  Peter 770
MANSFIELD, ___ 600

MARCHANT, Sam. 600
  Samuel 636
MARIS, ___ 772
MARNS, William S. 244
MARSAULT, William 81
MARSDEN, Rufus 573
MARSHAL, William 244
MARSHALL, Humphry 448
  James 747
  John 636
  Sarah 630
MARTIN, ___ 141,147,158, 619,639
  Alex. 330
  Alexander 305,448
  Catharine 233
  Francois Xavier 339
  John 584,671
  Joseph 346
  Josiah 86,136
  Luther 176
  Samuel 163
  William 244
MASON, ___ 230
  Abijah 600
  Sten. Thon. 456
  Stephens Thomas 448
MASTERS, ___ 180
  John 196
MATHEWS, John 457
MAULTSLY, ___ 200
MAXWELL, ___ 401,716
  Peter 168,347,463,506, 670,711
MAY, John 244
MAY?, Joseph 300
MAYO, Nathan 244
ME___, William 154
MEADOWS, J. 226
MEADS, William 178
MEARES, ___ 463
MEBANE, ___ 321
  Alexander 244
  Wm. 244
MEEK, Mary 333
MEREDITH, W. 574,581
MERRICK, George 177
MIFFLIN, Thomas 478
MILES, James 164
MILLER, Frederick 463
  J. 243
  J., Jr. 744
  James 164
  Millington 162
  Peter M. 463

MILLER (Cont.)
  Robert 244
  William 122
MILLS, Benjamin 553,768
  James 219
MILNE, John 636
  Joseph 636
MING?, ___ 99
MINOR, Stephen 768
MITCHEL, ___ 438
MITCHELL, Elijah 244
  John 345,428,472
  William 668
MOFFAY, John 800
MOLTON, Michael 463
MONISON, Isaac 194
MONROE, James 523
MONTAGUE, Charles 43
  George 130
MONTFORT, Henry 244
MONTGOMERY, Robert 755
MOOR, Alexander 474
  D. 754
MOORE, ___ 384,671
  A. D. 730
  Alexander Duncan 431,440
  Alfred 243,370,463
  George 148,243,244
  George, Sr. 119
  Harry 26
  J. B. 768
  James 77,148
  Joel 555
  John 119,244
  Roger 782
  Samuel 443
  Stephen 278,782
  T. 694
  Thomas 122
MOOREHEAD, James 298,747
MOPOON, Margaret 463
MORE, ___ 779
MORGAN, Edward 768
  Samuel 566
MORIN, ___ 297
MORRIS, George Anthony 118,170
  James 170
  Joseph 118,170
  Lewis 199
  Richard 182,199
  Robert 292,310,316,349,765
  Thomas 457
MORRISON, Colin 243
  Michael 800

MORRISON (Cont.)
  Neill 163
  William 231
MORTON, John 27
MOS___, Thomas 7
MOSELEY, William 722
MOSELY, Sampson 658,758
  Sarah 658,758
  Wm. 463
MOSSAY, John 800
  Joseph 800
MOTHERALL, John 463
MOUAT, William 16
MOYE, Richard 244
MOYO (see MAYO, Nathan 755
MUHLENBERG, Frederick A. 490
MULLER, A. A. 365
MUMFORD, J. 626
  R. 402
  Robertson 334
MUNRO, Revel 13
MUNROE, Ebenezer 164
  Jedediah 164
  Robert 164
  Timothy 164
MURDOCK, William 27
MURGATTOYD, John 115
MURPHEY, Patrick 92
MURPHY, Thomas 482,739,741
MURRAY, ___ 72,435
  James 704,768
  Jo. 88
  John 109
  Patrick 463
  William 664
MUTER, Robert 684,736,738,741
MUZZY, Isaac 164
NASH, W. 754
NATHAN, ___ 180
  Abraham 196
NEALE, Abner 520
  Thomas 600
  Thomas, Jr. 227,383
NEFFY, ___ 504
NEGROES
  ALEXANDER, James 565
  ASHLEY, Joseph 384
  EASTERBROOKS, Prince 164
  ELLISS, ___ 638
  FISHER, Cyrus 565
  GARDENER, John 754
  JONES, Absalom 500
  SANDS, Anthony 565

NEGROES (Cont.)
  Abraham 82,485
  Adonias 656
  Aleck 423
  Alick 720
  Allick 561
  Andrew 703
  Augustus 432,450
  Azzure 656
  Bacchus 432
  Belly 174
  Ben 506
  Betty 6
  Boston 11
  Buck 362,711
  Carlos 101
  Charles 186
  Christmas 432
  Coley 656
  Cuffe 403
  Cuffee? 145
  Elijah 694
  Fanny 729
  Frank 61,712
  George 72
  Hannah 432,734
  Harry 289,403,792
  Hector 101
  Jacob 370,507
  Jamey 77
  Jerry 61
  John 754
  Josh 734
  Killester 419
  Lewie 633
  Lucinda 669
  Mathews 432,440,459
  Nancy 670
  Ned 712
  Parker 362,711
  Peter 103,241
  Phillis 334
  Pickle 440
  Prenter 656
  Qua 241
  Richmond 52
  Robert 432,450
  Robin 754
  Sabina 709
  Sam 422,656
  Sampson 403,724
  Scipeo 650
  Sylvia 72
  Toby 638

NEGROES (Cont.)
  Tom 253
  Toney 708
  Tony 174,492
  Trim 770
  Valentine 78
  Will 72,384,432,440
  William 51
  York 635,712
NEILS, Alexander 463
NEILSON, William 680
NESSY, ____ 504
NEW, William 636
NEWNAN, John 747
NEWTON, Constantine 81
  Sarah 124
NICHOLS, ____ 316
  Caleb 763,764
  Elizabeth 463
  Ichabod 264
  John 600
  Unity 763,764
NICKSON, George 565
NICOLL, Francis 199
NICOLLS, ____ 26
NIXON, Richard 244
  Robert 600
NORRIS, John 716
NORTON, Solomon 636
NORWOOD, John 244
NOYES, Elihu 684
NUT, William 443
NUTT, John 224
  W. 411,495,527
  William 175,411,651,653
  Wm. 612
OCHLETREE, D. 163
ODLIN, Robert 794
OGDEN, David 290
  Robert 27
OLIVER, Andrew 244
  Francis 244
  Peter 127,128
OOTHOUDT, Henry 199
ORMOND, Thomas 81
ORNSBY, Clement 215
OTIS, James 27
OUTLAW, George 755
  Ludowick 81
OVERTON, ____ 738
  Thomas 737
OWEN, ____ 173
  Thomas 244
PAGE, Mann 324
PAINE, Elijah 448

PAINE (Cont.)
  Thomas 523,560,714
PAISSON, ____ 600
PALMER, George 4
PARHAM, Stith 254
PARKER, George 11
  Jonas 164
  William 600,636
PARKS, William 319
PARRAT, J. 136
PARRATT, J. 86
PARSONS, ____ 329
  Samuel 81
PARTRIDGE, Oliver 27
PATERSON, James 309
PATRICK, Alexander 243
PATTEN, Hans 636,747
PATTERSON, Isaac J. 661
  William 95,349
PATTON, Benj. 163
PAUL, Robert 254
PAXTON, James 522
PAYNE, James 244
  Michael 244,322,682
PEABODIE, ____ 702
PEALE, ____ 405
PEARSON, T. 244
PEEBLES, Robert 244
PEIRCE, Benjamin 164
  Solomon 164
PELHAM, Peter 463
PENDERGRAS, ____ 180
PENDERGRASS, William 196
PENDLETON, Edmund 189
  John, Jr. 745
PENROSE, William 769
PEPPER, ____ 600
PEPPEREL, W. 290
PERKINS, ____ 273,749
  James 355
PERSON, Tho. 755
  Thomas 244
  Wm. 755
PETTIT, Charles 490
PEYRINNAUT, F. 313
PHIFER, Caleb 244,273
  John 163
PHILIPS, ____ 755
  Frederick 755
PHILLIP, ____ 395
PHILLIPS, Abraham 244
  James 244
PICKENS, Andrew 458
  David 244
PICKERING, Timothy 682

PICKET, ____ 724
PIERCE, ____ 288
  Aaron 243
  Evert 244
PIMENTAL, Aaron 206
PINCKNEY, Charles 398
  Chas. C. 457
  Thomas 166
PINKSTONE, Thomas 361
PL____, Edward 357
PLATT, Zephaniah 199
PLUMMER, Aaron 298
  Joshua 197
PLUNKET, ____ 382
POCOCK, John 716
POLK, Ezekiel 163
  Thomas 163
POLLOCK, Procople? Jacinto 696
POLLY, William 164
PORTER, Azael 164
  David 243
  John Swan 117
  William 244
PORTERFIELD, ____ 201
  James 244,334
POSTMASTERS
  BRADLEY, John 243,463
  R. 600,636,768
POTE, Jeremiah 463
POTT, ____ 578
POTTER, Edward 800
  Skeath 463
POTTS, ____ 538,563
  Jesse 671
  Joshua 309,411,414,
    699,757
  Richard 448
POWEL, William 382
POWELL, ____ 437
POWER, ____ 671
  Thomas 766
POWERS, ____ 455
PRENTICE, James 243
PRICE, Ezra 490
  James 600,611,686
  Jas. 697
  Jonathan 727
  Joseph 81
  Lewis 463
PRIDGEN, David 244
PRIESTLY, ____ 465
PRINGLE, John J. 457
PROVOOST, ____ 386
  Samuel 263

PUGH, Francis 755
PURVIANCE, ___ 93
  Fanny 762
PURVIENCE, ___ 36
PUTMAN, Henry 164
PUTNAM, Israel 152
  Jesse 490
  Nathaniel 164
  Perley 164
PYLES, ___ 129
QUANDRILL, Charles 636
QUEARY, John 163
QUIGLEY, ___ 636
QUINCE, ___ 293,308,325,729
  Parker 129,353,423
  R., Jr. 583
  Richard 45,61,650,734
  Richard, Jr. 552
RABORG, Christopher 405
RAFORD, ___ 362
RAMSAY, ___ 245
  David 510
RAMSEY, Ambrose 244
  David 457
  Joseph 472
RAMSDELL, Abednego 164
RANDAL, William 244
RANDOLPH, Edmund 681
RAWLINGS, Asahel 244
RAYMOND, John 164
READ, ___ 173
  George 324
  Jacob 448
  James 411,517,520,534,721
READING, Thomas 244
REARDAN, ___ 575
  D. 261
  Dennis 211
REARDON, ___ 483
REDDICK, Joseph 244
REED, ___ 149
  David 463
  George 164,349,594,768
REESE, David 163
REGAN, John 244
REID, ___ 310
  Thomas 284
RELFE, Enoch 244
RENSSALAER, S. V. 427
RHODES, J. 243
RICE, Benjamin 463
RICHARDS, Elizabeth 545
  H. J. 221,320
RICHARDSON, ___ 226
  Amos 636

RICHARDSON (Cont.)
  Fanny 463
  Josiah 503
  William 122
RIDDICK, Joseph 755
RIDGE, ___ 382
RIGGING, ___ 747
RINGOLD, Thomas 27
RIPLEY, Eliphalet 337
RITTENHOUSE, David 466
RIVENBERG, ___ 716
ROADS, ___ 161
  Henry 129
ROAN, Achilles 494
ROBBINS, John 164
ROBE, John 118
ROBERTS, George 244
ROBERTSON, Archibald 507
  Joseph 777
  William 636
ROBESON, John 80
  Thomas, Jr. 5
ROBINS, ___ 636
ROBINSON, J. R. 637
  Joseph 633
  Moses 448
  William 436,747
ROBISON, Thomas 521
  William 382
RODDY, James 244
RODNEY, Caesar 27
ROGERS, ___ 33,180,294
  Isom 81
  John 37
  Michael 81
  Solomon 747
  William 196
ROLLAND, Bartholomew 463
ROME, George 290
RONALDSON, A. 411
RONANDSON, Archibald 463
ROOSEVELT, Isaac 182,199
ROOT, Jesse 356
ROSS, Alexander 14
  David 59
  Donald 747
  James 448
  John 243
  Robert 252
ROUKES, ___ 41
ROW, Guios 636
  James 243
ROWAN, ___ 200
  Archibald Hamilton 479
  John 129,243,787

ROWAN (Cont.)
  Robert 129,221,283
ROWAND, William 138
ROWLAND, David 27
RUGGLES, Timothy 27,28
RUNDLE, ___ 463
  Richard 115
RUSSEL, ___ 271,662
  Edward 289,691
  Samuel 243
RUSSELL, Edward 717
  Jason 164
  Seth 164
RUTHERFORD, Griffith 244
  John 243,448
  Thomas 379
RUTHERFURD, Thomas 129
RUTLEDGE, Edward 457
  John 457
  John, Jr. 457
RUTLIDGE, ___ 27
RYERSS, Cozen 199
SAMPSON, Sam. 755
SANDFORD, James 747
SARLEY, Jacob 394
SARLS, L. W. 199
SAUNDERS, Britain 244
SAWYER, Enoch 244
SAXBY, ___ 30
  George 24,29
SCHAW, ___ 52,57,109
  Robert 119,171
SCHEMERHORN, John W. 199
SCHENCK, John 199
SCHOONMAKER, Cornelius C. 199
SCHUYLER, Peter 199
  Philip 152,385
SCOLLAY, William 490
SCOTT, John 244
  William 334,595
SCU R, Henry 199
SCULL, ___ 795
SEAVER, Ebenezer 490
SELLERS, John 243
SENF, ___ 510
SESSIONS, Isaac 314
SEVIER, ___ 235,410
  John 346
SEWALL, Thomas 243
SHAPLEY, Benjamin 645
SHARPE, Edward 243
  John 244
  William 243
SHAW, ___ 419

SHAW (Cont.)
  Sam. 600
SHEPHERD, ___ 765
SHEPPERD, William 244
SHERIFFS
  BENNING, Arthur 98
  CAINE, Christopher 49
    John 181
  JOHNSTON, Thomas 334
  KENAN, Felix 81,154
  LEONARD, Thomas 752
  LEONAREL, Thomas 656
  WILLIAMS, Lewis 46
  WRIGHT, ___ 174
    Thomas 216,503,723
SHERMAN, Roger 356
SHERROD, Thomas 244
SHERWIN, Gilbert 565
SHIPPEN, William 490
  William, Jr. 490
SHUBRICK, ___ 403
SHUTER, John 476,579,587,
  604, 701
SILBY, H. 747
SIMONS, James 472
SIMONT, Edward 243
SIMPSON, Charles 519,751
  Elizabeth 519,751
  James 290,696,743
  John 250,600,636
  Samuel 122
SIMS, Isaac 768
SIMSON, J___ 123
  Jean 379
SINGLETON, Richard 244
SITCREAVES, John 330
SITGREAVES, J. 160
  John 305,520
SKINNER, John 244,311,321,755
  Joshua 244
  William 244
SLADE, Jeremiah 755
  William 244
SLOAN, John 244
SLOCUM, ___ 600
  Samuel 660
SMEETON, William 675
  Wm. 460
SMITH, ___ 81,179,440,510,
  592,606,709,747,772
  Benjamin 200,244,377,652,
    705,708,728,787
  Francis 636
  Jane 222
  Jeremiah 319

SMITH (Cont.)
  John 199
  John Christian 365
  John Nicholas 81
  Melancton 199
  Moses 636
  Neil 747
  Robert 243
  Samuel 243,747
  Thomas 81,180
  William 213,356,463
SNELL, William 768
SOLTER, William 129
SORONG (see STRONG), ab 356
SOUTHERLAND, William 154
SOUTHWICK, George 164
SPAIGHT, R. D. 514
  Richard D. 244,444
SPALDING, ___ 609
  James 208
SPAULDING, Philip 184,275,
  390,530,628,676
SPEIGHT, Joseph 150
SPENCER, Samuel 244
SPENDLOVE, Jeanett 463
SPICER, John 244
SPRAGUE, Stephen 463
SPRINGS, ___ 712
  Sedgick 411
  Sedgwick 768
  Sudgwick 677
SPROUT, James 155
SPRUIL Simson 244
ST. CLAIR, Auther 273
STACEY, Robert 180
STALLIONS, Hugh 798
STANDLEY, Jonathan 768
STANWOOD, Lemuel 600
  Samuel 463
STARK, George 243
  Isaac 243
STAUNTON, Augustine 402
STEED, Jesse 334
STEEL, William 95
STEELE, ___ 384
  John 244,361
  William 364
STEELY, William 431
STEPHENS, Edward 771
  James 192
  William 406
STEUART, A. 20
  Andrew 1
STEVENS, ___ 411
  Philip 367

STEWARD, Thomas 280
STEWART, ___ 186,287,716
  Dougal 243
  Duncan 463
  James 244,428
  John 136,142
  Joseph 244
  Thomas 244
  William 251
STIGREAVES (SITGREAVES)
  John 244
STILES, ___ 434
STIPNEY, John 595
STIRK, Samuel 406
STODDER, Benjamin 761
STOKES, Thomas 747
  William 244
STONE, ___ 671
STOREY, ___ 781
STORM, John 736
STORY, George 480
STRAING, Henry 199
STRINGER, William 81
STRODEVICK, Samuel 243
STRONG, Caleb 341,349,
  448
STROTHER, ___ 727
STROUD, ___ 226
STRUDWICK, ___ 636
  H. F. 600
  Samuel 6,64,463
  William 463
STUART, James 79
STUCKEY, Ann 542
STURGES, Jonathan 356
STYRON, Wallis 244
SULL, Peter 636
SULLIVAN, John 166
  Lee 528
SUTHERLAND, ___ 83,125
  John 243
SWAN, ___ 788
  Mildred 788
SWANN, ___ 219
  John 573
  Mildred 636
SWANSON, Wm. 774
SWANWICK, John 490
SWART, Dirck 199
SWARTWOUT, Jacobus 199
SWEENEY, Doyle 453
SWEENY, Morgan 494
SWISSER, Henry 226
TABB, James 747

TANDY, James Napper 499
TANNER, David 244
TARBET, ___ 600
TATE, James 463
TATHAM, William 234,240
TATOM, A. 244
  Absalom 755
  Joseph 768
TAYLOR, ___ 80
  Abraham 463
  George, Jr. 564
  James 600,636,716,745
  John 429
  Joseph 244
  Thomas 755
  William 244
TAZEWELL, Henry 448
TELFAIR, ___ 411
  John 348,599,636,715
TEN BROECK, Abraham 199
TEN EYCK, Abraham 199
THACKER, B. W. 783
THIBOU, Walter 271
THOMAS, ___ 194
  Caleb 400
  George 74
  Nancy 600
THOMPSON, ___ 226,384
  Andrew 108
  Charles 239,328
  Daniel 164
  Dugald 114
  James 455,747
  John 636
  William 232
THOMSON, Andrew 494
  Charles 153,156
  Daniel 278
  Ezra 199
  Israel 199
THORNBOROUGH, ___ 130
THRELSAL, Robert 112
THULLY, John 716
THURBER, ___ 463
THURSTON, James I. 655
  Sam. J. 433
  Samuel I. 674
  William 243
TIAC, John 164
TIFFANY, Bethankful 447
  Recompence 447
TILLET, ___ 26
TILLINGHAST, ___ 435
TILLMAN, Henry 730
TILMAN, Edward 27

TINNING, Charles 243
TIPTON, ___ 346
  John 244
  Joseph 244
TISDALE, ___ 550,610,
  655,674,749
TOMMINGS, James 366
TOMPKINS, ___ 463
TOOMER, ___ 307,352
  A. 524
  A. B. 638
  Anthony B. 688,768
  H. 411
  Henry 173,202,303,348,
    359,502,542
TORKLEY, ___ 755
TORRINS, Elizabeth 566
TOWERS, John 759
TOWNSEND, Daniel 164
  Samuel 107
  Solomon 107
TRAVERS, Patrick 143
TREADWELL, John 356
  Thomas 199
TRUMBULL, Benjamin 601
  John 696
  Jonathan 448
TRYON, William 38,68
TUBBS, Dan. 600
TUBE, ___ 493,537
TUCKER, ___ 84,316
  Thomas T. 457
  Thomas Tudor 356
TUMAN, David 600,636
TURNER, Amey 463
  George 636
  John 81
  Wm. 768
TUTON, William 768
TWINING, Nathaniel 220
TYLER, ___ 662
  John 230
TYSON, Thomas 244
URQUHART, Henry 307,502,
  600,602,768
USSERY, Thomas 244
VAN HORNE, Abraham 199
VAN NESS, Peter 199
VAN SCHAICK, Peter 199
VAN VECHTEN, A. 199
VANCE, ___ 451,518,533,
  598,615,669,791
  John 243
  Samuel 205,276,720,791
VANDEVOORT, Peter 199

VAUGHAN, ___ 706
VAUGHN, James 244
VEEDER, Volkert 199
VERICK, Richard 270
VERNON, A. Z. 455
VESTAL, William 244
VICKARS, Mary 691
  Thomas 691
VICKEARS, Mary 515
  Thomas 515
VICKERS, ___ 600
VINING, John 429,448
VINSON, James 244
VIRGIN, Samuel 463
VOGEL, ___ 438
VORRIER?, ___ 673
VOSBURGH, ___ 621,768
VROOMAN, Peter 199
WADDELL, ___ 111,226
  Edmund 244
  Hugh 226
  John B. 226
WADE, Thomas 244
  William 565
WADSWORTH, ___ 765
  Jeremiah 356
WAID, ___ 99
WAKELEY, G. 10
WALES, Robert 36
WALKER, ___ 325,600
  ohn 56
  Ann 242
  George 589
  James 6,193,347,411,
    525,526,580,636,646,
    722,768
  James, Jr. 768
  John 67,243,411
  Josias 104
  Mary A. 646
  Thomas 255,636
WALL, ___ 686
  Llewellyn L. 697
WALLEY, Thomas 490
WALLIS, Dennis 164
  William 636
WARD, ___ 99,571
  Anthony 40
  Artemus 152
  Charles 244
  Daniel 154
  Henry 27,636
WARDEN, ___ 130
WARNER, John 463,600
WARRINGTON, Henry 747

WASHINGTON, ____ 157,294, 408
  G. 490,564
  George 152,213,418,425
  William 457
WATKINS, William 34
WATSON, J. 747
  William 243,298
WATTERS, Henry 636
  Samuel 40
  W. 170
WEAKELY, George 31
WEAKLEY, Robert 244
WEBB, ____ 26,180
  Jotham 164
  Nathaniel C. 196
  Robert 747
WEIGLE, Philip 428
WELCH, ____ 494
WENTWORTH, J., Jr. 290
WEST, ____ 316
  Thomas 72
WESTLEY, John 19
WETHERILL, Samuel, Jr. 354
WHEATON, ____ 550,610,655, 674,749
  Daniel 674
WHISTON, Joseph 244
WHITE, ____ 500
  Benajah 736
  James 53,129
  Joseph 755
  Timothy 516
  William 81
WHITEMAN, Nicholas John 180
WHITEMORE, ____ 463
WHITESIDE, James 244
WHITFIELD, Willis 600,636
WHITTY, E. 244
WILCOX, John 18,118,170
WILKIE, Malcolm 325
WILKINGS, ____ 732
  Mar. R. 260,274,348
  Robert 388
WILKINS, John 100
WILKINSON, ____ 795
  Elizabeth 463
  William 115,636
WILLIAMS, ____ 180,787
  Benjamin 243,244,600,636, 747
  Edward 244
  Jacob 158,243
  John 747
  John P. 403

WILLIAMS (Cont.)
  John Pugh 244,247
  Lewis 35,46
  Philip 733
  Richard 161,196
  Robert 244
  Samuel 158
WILLIAMSON, Hugh 386
  Robert 122
WILLING, ____ 80
WILLIS, Henry 664
  John 244,636
WILLKINGS, ____ 768
  John 636
  M. R. 616
WILLSON, Jonathan 164
  Wm. 163
  Zach. 163
WILSON, ____ 772
  George 478
  James 244,384
  Lewis F. 243
  Richard 110
  Samuel 671
  Sweny 591
  Sylvanus 671
  Zachias 244
WIMBLE, James 371
  William 45,371
WINCHESTER, Harvey 768
  James 244
WINGATE, ____ 747
  William 463,600
WINNE, John 199
WINSHIP, Jason 164
  Thomas 164
WINTER, Nathaniel 319
WINTHROP, John 662
WISNER, Henry, Sr. 199
WISS, Peter 484
WOLCOTT, Erastus 356,396
WOLF, ____ 179
WOMACK, John 244
WOOD, ____ 787
  Henry 768
  John 199
  Zebedee 244
WOODBURY, Zachaiah 376
WOODHOUSE, James 465
WOODHULL, Jesse 199
WOODMAN, Constant 600
WOODROW, ____ 137
WOODS, ____ 747
  Benjamin 520
WOODWARD, ____ 252

WOODWARD (Cont.)
  Abisha 463
  George 122
WOOTTEN, William 244
WRIGHT, ____ 174,428, 639
  J. G. 790
  James 792
  John 494
  Jos. G. 582,732
  Joseph G. 690
  Joshua G. 725,726
  Thomas 216,503,723
  Thos. 597
WYER, Hugh 462
WYMAN, Jabez 164
  Nathaniel 164
WYNES, Thomas 244
WYNKOOP, Dirck 199
WYNNS, Tho. 755
WYNS, George 244
YANCEY, Thornton 244
YATES, Christopher P. 199
  Daniel 244
  Robert 199,385
YOUNG, Alexander 442
  Alexr. 461
  Henry 732
  Norley 589
  Peter 716
YOUNGER, ____ 325
YUNDT, ____ 759
ZWISTER, James 576

LOCATION INDEX

BARS
  Charleston 507
  St. Augustine 664
BEACHES
  Long Bay 527
  Tube's 493,537
BLUFF, Bald Head 453
BOROUGH, Reading 478
BRANCHES
  Alegator 787
  Beaver Dam, of Limestone 494
  Long 716
  Rattle-Snake 200
  Ridge's 382
  Waggon 671
  Wild Cat 226
  William's, Richard 161
BRIDGES
  Rock-Fish 716
  Toomer's 352
CAPES
  Delaware, of 366
  Fear 54,80,101,137,174, 453,710,774
  Hatteras 197
  Henry 727
  Roman 727
CITIES
  Baltimore 213,252,342,375, 405,430,480,629,642,760, 761,772,777
  Boston 127,133,144,184, 245,256,300,310,355,384, 397,437,454,490,558,614, 662,793,800
  Charleston 180,183,196,204, 266,319,345,357,364,366, 384,398,407,436,457,461, 472,507,510,529,555,559, 642,659,664,774,777,796
  Marietta 300,318
  Middletown 318
  New-York 9,22,26-28,151, 176,178,179,182-184,187, 197,199,249,254,263,267,

CITIES (Cont.)
  New-York (Cont.) 269,271 284,294,341,366,375,384, 386,394,395,405,427,434, 435,445,447,451,462,539, 576,591,604,621,641,680, 695,718,743,748,765,777, 779
  Philadelphia 2,8,25,52,80, 96,118,152,155,156,165, 170,176,243,278,284,292, 310,341,405,410,428,438, 456,464,465,471,478,479, 490,499,500,522,596,678, 681,744,746,760,771,779
  Raleigh 514,782
  Richmond 408,424,713,795
  Savannah 159,208,266,406, 664,779,800
  Washington 589
COLONIES
  Connecticut 27,153
  Maryland 153
  Massachusetts-Bay 27,140
  New Jersey 27,153
  New-York 27
  Pennsylvania 27,153
  Rhode Island 27,153
  South Carolina 27,153
  Virginia 153
COUNTIES
  Albany (N.Y.) 199
  Anson 95,100,226,736,747
  Beaufort 747
  Bertie 755
  Bladen 5,18,51,79,111,129, 137,150,158,173,174,221, 296,298,323,503,540,551, 562,593,597,656,671,710, 711,736,747
  Brunswick 119,181,253,288, 403,433,452,493,494,528, 537,552,553,571,583,592, 646,736,747,752,797
  Burke 346
  Camden 755

COUNTIES (Cont.)
  Caroline (Va.) 745
  Carteret 244
  Caswell 754
  Chatham 129,226,309, 634,747,754
  Chesterfield (Va.) 254
  Chowan (see Cowhan) 103,755
  Columbia (N.Y.) 199
  Cowhan 244
  Craven 129,147,730, 736
  Craven (S.C.) 81
  Cumberland 118,129,203, 226,296,334,391,546, 736,747
  Currituck 755
  Dobbs 81,129
  Duplin 21,81,99,103, 106,129,154,161,201, 494,528,566,611,657, 716,723,724,736,792
  Dutchess (N.Y.) 199
  Edgcombe 755
  Essex (Mass.) 418
  Franklin 755
  Franklin (Ga.) 554
  Gates 244,755
  Glasgow 736
  Granville 755
  Guilford 95
  Halifax 747
  Halifax (Va.) 254
  Hertford 755
  Hyde 747
  Johnston 736,747
  Jones 736,747
  Kent (Pa.) 25,27
  King's (N.Y.) 199
  Lenoir 736
  Lincoln 273
  Martin 755
  Mecklenburg 95,163
  Mercklenburg 755
  Middlesex (Mass.) 418

COUNTIES (Cont.)
  Montgomery (N.Y.) 199
  Moore 671,736
  Morris (N.Y.) 434
  Nash 747
  Nelson (Ky.) 194
  Newcastle (Pa.) 25,27
  New-Hanover 12,77,82,98,
    129,141,148,247,463,494,
    503,597,600,611,635,636,
    643,685,730,736,738,763,
    775
  New-York (N.Y.) 182,199
  Northampton 81,334,747
  Onslow 35,46,100,129,334,
    724,736,747
  Ontario (N.Y.) 765
  Orange 244
  Orange (N.Y.) 199
  Pasquotank 755
  Perquimans 755
  Pitt 755
  Queen's (N.Y.) 199
  Randolph 334
  Richmond 736,747
  Richmond (N.Y.) 199
  Robeson 671,736,747
  Rowan 95,226,747
  Sampson 201,736,747
  Stokes 755
  Suffolk (N.Y.) 199
  Sullivan (Va.?) 424
  Surry 95
  Sussex (N.J.) 572
  Sussex (Pa.) 25,27
  Tyrrel 244,747
  Ulster (N.Y.) 199
  Wake 747
  Warren 755
  Wayne 243,736
  West-Chester (N.Y.) 199,
    395
COUNTRY, Western 405,766
COURT HOUSE, Bladen 4,60
CREEKS
  Bear 226,671
  Blunt's 309
  Cat 226
  Cedar 671
  Crane 226
  Cross 671
  Duncan's 382
  Dunn's 137
  Fishing 77
  French 455

CREEKS (Cont.)
  German 424
  Harrison's 63,611,769
  Hood's 728
  Jones's 226,382
  Lean's 226
  Livingston 200,494,706
  Long 77,573
  Lynche's 226
  Muddy 724
  Neffy's 504
  Nessy's 504
  Prince George's 111
  Richardson's 226
  Rock-Fish 7,716
  Stewart's 716
  Thompson's 226
  Thomsons 81
  Town 55,403,526,646
  Turkey 597
  Vaughan 706
  Wood's 787
CRICK, Lick 382
DISTRICTS
  Beaufort (S.C.) 407
  Fayette-Ville 402,735
  Hillsborough 170
  Kentucky 239
  Mero 474
  Newbern 337,339
  New Hanover 525
  North Carolina 520,682,737
  Orangeburg (S.C.) 407
  Salisbury 361
  Southwark 490
  Virginia 713
  Wilmington 206,207,541,
    542,624
DUTCH BUFFALO 226
EAST FLORIDA 664
FERRIES
  Blocker's 671
  Brunswick 17
  Clark's 634
  Moore's 671
  Murray's 72
FORD, Chocta 280
FORTS
  Chisel 279
  Johnson 24,29,30
  Johnston 110,141,733
  Schuyler 270
  Washington 554
HAMPTON ROAD 409
HARBOUR, Eastern Branch 589

HAYMOUNT 671
HILLS
  Constitution 411
  Gallows 440
  Rock 567
HOLE, Five Fathom 651,
  781
INLETS
  Cabbage 722
  New 651
  Occacock 639
  Shalotte 493,537
ISLANDS
  Battery 651
  Cape Fear 453
  Edisto 559
  St. Simon 208
LAKE, Waccamaw 597
LANDING, Dutch 716
MARSHES
  Brown 671
  Great 671
  North-East 723
  White 221,540
NECKS
  Caulkin's 433
  Waccamaw 101
NEW-ENGLAND 264,316
NORTH-WEST 174,200,201,
  383,562,703,728
PATHS
  Catabaw 226
  Kentucke 424
  Waxhaw 226
PLANTATIONS
  Appleby 200
  Bellefont 200
  Belville 583
  Blue Banks 200
  Cat Fish lands 200
  Garden of Eden 625
  Golden Grove 106
  Grovely 526
  Hermitage 470,485,509,
    561,635,669,712,716
  Hillton 785
  Marsh-Castle 323
  Mount Pleasant 174
  Mount Vernon 213,780
  Old Court House, The
    611
  Perlemberg 551
  Pleasant Oaks 332
  Poplar Grove 423
  Providence 16,153

PLANTATIONS (Cont.)
  Smithfield 200
  Tweed Side 379
POINTS
  Glo'ster 25
  Maultsly's 200
  Rockey 106,109,117,119, 694
  Rocky 502
PORTS
  New Orleans 696
  Wilmington 520,651,777
PROVINCES
  Jerseys 80
  Massachusetts-Bay 127,144, 152,153,165
  New-Hampshire 153
  New-York 152
  Pennsylvania 80
RIVERS
  Black 200,494
  Broad 81,545
  Cape-Fear 79,82,119,332, 379,453,494,502,534, 597,671,716,721,722
  Catawba 510
  Claret 671
  Cumberland 424
  Deep 671
  Delaware 25,27
  Edisto 384,559
  Ehoree 382
  Flint 166
  Genesee 765
  Green 545
  Haw 634
  Little 288,332,624
  Lookwart's Folly 797
  Neuse 81
  New 35,46,99
  North-East? 16
  North-East 716,723
  Northwest 7,503,551,593, 710,787
  Ohio 300
  Pedee 226
  Pee Dee 382
  Potomac 589
  Roanoak 81
  Sandusky 424
  Shallot 433
  South 4
  Stone's 671
  Tenassee 280
ROADS

ROADS (Cont.)
  Great 716
  Newbern 738,769
  North-east 738
  North-West 200,787
ROCK FISH 611
SALT LICK, Big Bone 405
SOUND 88,99,109,169,174,190, 289,423,506,633,670,764
  Top-Sail 177,611
STATES (see Colonies,Provinces)
  Carolina 80
  Connecticut 182,187,188, 196,255,349,356,396,418, 601,696,765
  Delaware 290,324,349, 429,649
  Franklin 235,346
  Georgia 142,159,166,203, 270,290,346,364,429,696
  Jersey 429
  Kentucky 194,229,671,692
  Maryland 25,72,176,290, 349,589,696,792,800
  Massachusetts 182,194,290, 316,341,349,357,418,765
  New-Hampshire 214,290,349, 779
  New Jersey 8,25,290,349
  New-York 199,246,290,363
  North Carolina 72,80,82, 100,170,228,244,290,330, 332,339,346,361,364,402, 436,453,458,493,510,517, 537,541,542,565,621,637, 671,682,727,730,747,750, 755,782,789,800
  Pennsylvania 25,290,349, 354,458,478,696,794
  Rhode-Island 182,265,290, 366
  South Carolina 24,29,43, 72,81,93,101,140,166, 290,356,384,403,429,458, 466
  Tennessee 671,692
  Vermont 429
  Virginia 72,81,152,189, 209,252,290,324,349,429, 456,595,671,745
STONE, Lime 716
SWAMPS
  Cowshole 716
  Cypress creek 716
  Flat 671

SWAMPS (Cont.)
  Goshen 716
  Maxwell's 716
  Roads 161
  Waggamaw 540
TERRITORY, Western 273
TOWNS
  Acton 164
  Albany 152,363,385
  Alexandria 245,759, 766,780
  Amboy 26
  Augusta 346,554
  Beaufort 507
  Bedford 164,197
  Belvedere 642,705,708
  Belvidere 200,510
  Beverly 164
  Bloomingdale 386
  Bridgwater 355
  Brookline 164
  Brunswick 13,17,38,49, 56,99,105,129,172
  Cambridge 157,164
  Campbellton 129
  Carlisle 478
  Charles City 230
  Charlestown 24,29,135, 140,142,164
  Charlotte 95,163
  Clarendon 729,734
  Concord 140,164,214
  Cross-Creek 18,21,62, 83,99,118,125,131
  Cussewago 455
  Danvers 164,255
  Danville 229
  Debroit 23
  Dorchester 135
  Edenton 103,637,682 723,755
  Elizabeth 711
  Elizabeth-Town 362
  Erie 478
  Exeter 212
  Fayette-Ville 173,197, 201,223,236,283,298, 302,309,312,314,321, 322,334,378,379,384, 391,402,634
  Fayetteville 561,671, 735,736,753,754,775
  Framingham 164
  Franklin 478
  Fredericksburgh 272,745

TOWNS (Cont.)
  George-Town 101,245
  Halifax 747,789
  Hampshire 765
  Hartford 255,418,765
  Hillsborough 68,81,141,
    148,228,235,244,634,671,
    755
  Holstein 279
  Kaskaskias 795
  Knoxville 473,474
  Lancaster 794
  Lansingburgh 765
  Lexington 140,164
  Long-Hill 434
  Lumberton 736
  Lynn 164
  Medford 164
  Menotomy 164
  Morris Town 434
  Muskingum 273
  Nantucket 435
  Natchez 795
  Newark 572
  Newbern 21,68,86,87,129,
    136,149,160,197,422,
    432,514,668,682,727,
    730,736,770
  Newbury Port 595
  New-castle on Delaware
    25
  New-Haven 516
  New-London 196,317
  New Orleans 474
  Newport 291,366
  New-River 46
  Newton 572
  Norfolk 328,342,629,773
  Petersburg 254,279,358,
    425,713,746
  Phillip's Manor 395
  Pittsburg 455
  Pittsburgh 478
  Portland 316
  Portsmouth 779
  Poughkeepsie 182,272
  Providence 195,265,373
  Rocky Mount 510
  Salem 164,255,264,316
  Salisbury 95,226,384,747
  Santee 545
  Smithville 528,578,705,
    757
  South Washington 657,770,798
  Springfield 255

TOWNS (Cont.)
  St. Augustine 159,208,664
  Studbury 164
  Sturbridge 194
  Swannanoe 364
  Tarborough 637
  Warren 478
  Washington 660,794,800
  Waterford 478
  Watertown 146,255
  Westfield 255
  Woburn 164
TRACT, Welch 98
TREES
  Big 765
  Dram 651
UNIVERSITIES
  North Carolina, of 444,
    494,514,624
  Pennsylvania, of 465
VALLEY, Power's 671

www.ingramcontent.com/pod-product-compliance
Lightning Source LLC
Chambersburg PA
CBHW042353070526
44585CB00028B/2909